NEW MEDIA LITERACIES AND PARTICIPATORY POPULAR CULTURE ACROSS BORDERS

WITHDRAWAL

How do students' online literacy practices intersect with online popular culture? In this book scholars from a range of countries including Australia, Lebanon, Nepal, Qatar, South Africa, Turkey, and the United States illustrate and analyze how literacy practices that are mediated through and influenced by popular culture create both opportunities and tensions for secondary and university students. The authors examine issues of theory, identity, and pedagogy as they address participatory popular culture sites such as fan forums, video, blogs, social networking sites, anime, memes, and comics and graphic novels.

New Media Literacies and Participatory Popular Culture Across Borders

- uniquely brings together scholarship about online literacy practices and the growing body of work on participatory popular culture
- pushes forward scholarship about literacy and identity in cross-cultural situations
- advances important conversations about issues of global flows and local responses to popular culture
- addresses ways in which students' out-of-class literacy practices online can be connected to classroom pedagogies

With its focus on transnational new media and online technologies and how they are shaping negotiations of language and culture, its international focus, and its roster of international authors, this volume makes distinctive contributions to an emerging field of study.

Bronwyn T. Williams is Professor of English, University of Louisville, USA.

Amy A. Zenger is Associate Professor of English, American University of Beirut, Lebanon.

NEW MEDIA LITERACIES AND PARTICIPATORY POPULAR CULTURE ACROSS BORDERS

Edited by
Bronwyn T. Williams
University of Louisville

Amy A. Zenger
American University of Beirut

Routledge
Taylor & Francis Group
NEW YORK AND LONDON

First published 2012
by Routledge
711 Third Avenue, New York, NY 10017

Simultaneously published in the UK
by Routledge
2 Park Square, Milton Park, Abingdon, Oxon OX14 4RN

Routledge is an imprint of the Taylor & Francis Group, an informa business

© 2012 Taylor & Francis

Library of Congress Cataloging in Publication Data
New media literacies and participatory popular culture across borders / edited by Bronwyn Williams, Amy A. Zenger.
p. cm.
Includes bibliographical references and index.
1. Literacy--Social aspects. 2. Media literacy. 3. Online social networks. 4. Popular culture and globalization. I. Williams, Bronwyn. II. Zenger, Amy A.
LC149.N49 2012
302.2'244--dc23
2011048709

ISBN: 978-0-415-89767-9 (hbk)
ISBN: 978-0-415-89768-6 (pbk)
ISBN: 978-0-203-80374-5 (ebk)

Typeset in Bembo
by Integra Software Services Pvt. Ltd, Pondicherry, India

Printed and bound in the United States of America by
Walsworth Publishing Company, Marceline, MO.

For Mary and Steve and their limitless encouragement, insights, and patience.

CONTENTS

PREFACE

If you ask young people how they determine their popular culture preferences, they often attribute them to matters of individual taste. Pushed a bit further they acknowledge the influence of friends and their community—if someone recommends a movie or video game or song to them they are likely to give it a try. Twenty years ago the community in which a young person exchanged recommendations about popular culture would have largely been comprised of the people she knew face to face. Today, however, such conversations about popular culture could just as easily have come from someone in another country as someone in the same neighborhood. For an increasing number of young people around the world, the experience of popular culture is an online, participatory experience that engages with texts and people from across diverse cultures. Such experiences challenge young people to negotiate issues of language, rhetoric, and culture in order to understand each other as well as to create and understand movies, videos, websites, songs, and other texts they find in front of them every day on their computer screens.

At the same time they are encountering different cultures and texts online, young people are taking advantage of the opportunities provided to them by new media to participate in the composition and interpretation of popular culture. When a young person sits down to a computer to watch a music video remix of a movie scene on YouTube, for example, he can not only watch the video, but also read comments from other audience members that may help him interpret the video, as well as add his voice to the conversation. And, if he feels so inspired, he can create his own video, upload it, and see what other people think. The participatory opportunities provided by new media have shifted the conception of who creates popular culture and how it is consumed. Young people at their computers now engage with popular culture texts with the expectation that they can interact with them and respond to them, even if they do not always do so. They also expect that getting more information about a band or television program is as easy as opening up a new web search page.

For literacy educators and researchers, what is particularly noteworthy about all of this engagement with participatory popular culture across borders is that it very often has young people involved in reading and writing, in multiple contexts and with multiple media. Whether it is posting a comment on a fan forum or sharing video clips on a social media site, the online conversations about popular culture require people to compose and interpret texts. Regardless of our individual feelings about online communication, if we want to understand the literacy practices of young people—and many older people as well—we must seriously investigate what they are learning when they spend much more time reading and writing online than they do in the classroom. What's more, we have to examine how, since so much of that reading and writing takes place both about and *with* popular culture, the content and rhetoric of popular culture is shaping literacy practices around the world.

In *New Media Literacies and Participatory Popular Culture Across Borders* we explore how students' online literacy practices intersect with online popular culture. The book draws together chapters from literacy and popular culture scholars from a variety of countries including Australia, Lebanon, Nepal, Qatar, South Africa, Turkey, and the United States, to illustrate and analyze how literacy practices that are mediated through and influenced by popular culture create both opportunities and tensions for secondary and university students. The chapters in the book cover issues of theory, identity, and pedagogy as they address participatory popular culture sites such as fan forums, video, blogs, social networking sites, anime, memes, and comics and graphic novels.

Among the central issues addressed in the book are the ways students draw from international popular culture when creating their own texts. In addition, the contributors examine how students' multimodal literacy practices with online popular culture are changing their conceptions of texts and of rhetorical concepts such as audience and authorship; the ways in which issues of politics, power, and resistance influence such literacy practices; and how issues of identity (gender, social class, ethnicity, sexual orientation) connect to these online literacy practices.

Though there is a considerable amount of scholarship about online literacy practices and a growing body of work on participatory popular culture, this book brings those two areas together in ways that we hope make a significant contribution to an emerging field of study. In particular, the chapters in the book explore how the convergence of popular culture and online literacy practices shape the ways in which identities are constructed and interpreted. Even more important is the international lens this project brings to questions of popular culture and online reading and writing. We hope the book contributes to the important conversations taking place about issues of global flows and local responses to popular culture.

In order to get a sense of the variety of responses to popular culture through online literacy practices taking place across cultures, we realized early on that this project would work best as an edited collection. There has been important research about young people and online literacy practices, some including issues of cross-cultural contact. What we want to add to those conversations is a perspective on the complexity of these responses in a variety of cultures. By engaging with different instances, in different cultural contexts, yet within the same book, we can highlight the scope of literacy practices and connections and conflicts taking place in multiple cultural settings and with multiple media. Toward that end, this book not only contains chapters from a number of different locations on the globe, but also reflects a number of different popular culture media, from television and comics, to video games and social networking sites. This book, then, allows us to consider how these social practices look when we see them in conversation.

In an attempt to draw from as many perspectives as possible, we distributed the call for papers for this volume on email lists and to scholars from six continents and have received chapters addressing a set of diverse and varied projects that challenged our thinking as we read them individually and collectively. Reading such varied research from around the world can help us understand how people use local contexts to read and respond to trans-cultural texts and offer possibilities for how the use of popular culture across cultures could be used in the classroom to talk about issues of literacy, global communication, and power.

Overview

The book is divided into two sections. Part I, *New Media Literacies Across Cultures*, focuses on the effects that crossing cultural boundaries has on literacy practices. The chapters in this section examine what happens to texts, and to our uses of such texts, when they are distributed online and then read and responded to in cultures different to their own. As the authors in this section point out, the cross-cultural contact that takes places through these online texts is often an exciting and fertile environment for exploration and negotiation of cultural differences. Yet, these chapters also make clear that the cross-cultural contact in online spaces is not always a place of happy multicultural synthesis. Negotiations of differences of language and culture are often incomplete or frustrated. The chapters in this section illustrate how such cross-cultural contact is often mediated through popular culture and how young people make use of it outside the classroom. Finally, these chapters also remind us that new media is not restricted to print as a means of communication, and that the ways in which texts are composed and interpreted through multiple modes is an essential part of popular culture and online communication.

Part II, *Constructing Identity in an Online, Cross-Cultural World*, focuses on how people around the world use popular culture as semiotic, rhetorical, and cultural resources for constructing and reading identity online. Popular culture, which is seemingly ubiquitous, as well as often regarded as available for use by individual audience members, provides people with a set of resources they can draw on to make common cultural connections with others. The rhetorical displays of identity online are often shaped by the forms and genres of popular culture. Yet, as the chapters in this section demonstrate, when popular culture content and forms cross cultural borders, they are often remade or rethought in ways quite different from their original conception. What's more, as people in different parts of the world make use of popular culture in their local contexts to express their distinctive conceptions of identity, such practices not only help us rethink the assumptions of the original texts, but allow us new ways of thinking about identity perception and performance in a world of increasing cross-cultural contact. Individual chapter summaries can be found in the Introduction.

This book brings together our mutual interests in a number of ways. We have both long had an interest in understanding more about how the literacy practices that students engage in outside of school influence how we can work with them in the literacy classroom. And, as our previous collaboration showed, we also share an interest in the intersections between popular culture and literacy practices. This book has allowed us to explore another of our ongoing interests in terms of how cross-cultural contact and communication influences, and is influenced by, reading and writing.

Just as popular culture itself, and its role in our lives and the lives of our students, is neither simply good nor bad, so the changes in cross-cultural contact brought by participatory popular culture and new media are neither inherently positive nor negative: they challenge us to think carefully about what students are learning through their contemporary literacy practices, about everything from their sense of control of texts, and their understanding of literacy and power, to their perceptions of language, rhetoric, and culture.

ACKNOWLEDGEMENTS

An edited collection is, by nature, a venture realized by the work of many hands. First, then, we would like to thank the intelligent, thoughtful, and patient contributors who have made this book an exciting and enriching project from the beginning

We would also like to thank Naomi Silverman from Routledge for her support and guidance in this project. Her questions as we shaped the proposal helped us think through and improve the book in a number of substantive ways. We would also like to thank Julie Ganz and Kevin Henderson for their help throughout the editorial process, Dan Harding for his thoughtful copy editing, and Christine Romesburg for compiling the Index. We also have several people we would like to thank individually.

Amy: My first expression of appreciation goes to Bronwyn, who conceived of this project and has been a great inspiration and friend throughout the process of putting the collection together. I would also like to thank the organizers of the Watson Conference 2011 in Louisville, particularly Min-Zhan Lu, for the opportunity to attend, and to all of the participants for making the meeting so exceptionally exciting. I am fortunate to have colleagues in Beirut and other places who have contributed to my thinking and been good friends: Lina Choueiri, Rula Baalbaki, Ulrike Pölzl, William Degenaro, Carol Haviland, Joan Mullin, Tiane Donohue, Cinthia Gannett, Natasha Frank, Nicole Khoury, Lisa Arnold, and many others. I particularly appreciate the good nature and enthusiasm of students who have engaged in this research. I am beholden to the members of my family, who have continued to support, love, and feed me, even after I became "an English teacher." Stephen Link, my constant companion in life, has embraced this project, and done a great deal to make it happen. In his unwavering presence I have a true home, and I am grateful for this good fortune.

Bronwyn: It has been such a pleasure to work on a project again with Amy, my dear friend and collaborator, who always shows me the way to new ideas and insights and makes the work of everyone around her better and more thoughtful. I am grateful for your intelligence and patience with me. As always, it has been great fun.

There are also many colleagues and friends, both here in Louisville and in other places, who have helped me think through the issues involved in this book. Dan Keller, as always, has been an invaluable critic and collaborator in matters of popular culture and literacy. I'm also grateful for the support, questions, and ideas from Sandra Abrams, Julia Davies, Myrrh Domingo, Bruce Horner, Michele Knobel, Karen Kopelson, Colin Lankshear, Min-Zhan Lu, Kate Pahl, and Brian Street. In addition, I have had the benefit of working with many smart and thoughtful graduate students here at the University of Louisville, many of whom have offered useful insights to the concerns of this book, including Nancy Bou Ayash, Lisa Arnold, Ashly Bender, Laura Detmering, Matt Dowell, Tika Lamsal, Eric Leake, Brice Nordquist, Shyam Sharma, John Vance, and Caroline Wilkinson.

At home, my sons, Rhys and Griffith, (and our "third son," Alec) have provided me with provocative and smart conversation, great links and popular culture recommendations, and much needed laughter. You three are invaluable to my work and my sanity. And finally, but never least, I thank Mary for her encouragement, intellectual vision, and willingness to be my fellow world traveler through our lives together.

1

INTRODUCTION

Popular Culture and Literacy in a Networked World

Bronwyn T. Williams and Amy A. Zenger

A student from Brazil uses a soundtrack of techno music from the U.S. and images including Darth Vader, Dr. Evil, and Peter Pan to create a video she posts online. Another video from Lebanon mixes personal photos and images from Japanese manga with a U.S. hip hop soundtrack. On a fan forum for the movie *Harry Potter and the Deathly Hallows, Part One,* the young people discussing the movie gather from around the world, including New Zealand, Japan, Argentina, Spain, Britain, and the U.S. Meanwhile, on FanFiction.net the authors of fan fiction also come from many countries, including, Jordan, Finland, Tanzania, and Korea. And students from India to Australia to Lebanon have Facebook pages that include lists of their favorite music and movies, as well as clips from videos and links to other popular culture webpages.

These are just a few of the exciting and disruptive, but certainly significant, shifts in literacy practices and popular culture brought about by digital technologies. As one recent study of young people in the U.S. found, in a typical day 8- to 18-year-olds spent more than seven and a half hours using some form of media, from television and computers to music, with almost half of that time spent using a computer and with the amount of computer use increasing substantially among adolescents (Kaiser Family Foundation, 2010). Digital technologies have created opportunities for individuals to create, distribute, and read multimodal texts with ease and enthusiasm. These new media and online technologies have not only changed literacy practices (Alvermann, 2010; Brooke, 2009; Lankshear & Knobel, 2008) and popular culture (Bruns, 2008; Buckingham & Willett, 2006; Jenkins, 2006), but have also allowed digital texts to cross borders with increasing speed and have brought languages, cultures, and texts into contact as never before.

New media technologies have created a participatory popular culture in which audience members do much more than interpret the movies, television programs, video games, and music produced by large corporations. Digital technologies allow individuals to sample and remix popular culture content, write back to popular culture producers, and connect with fellow fans from around the corner and around the world. Personal webspaces such as Facebook are filled with popular culture images, links, and video as ways of performing identities rather than expository, written personal statements. Individuals sample and remix music and video to create their own films that they post on YouTube. Any new movie, video game, or recording becomes the subject of page after page of written reviews, analysis, and discussion. Fan fiction and fan film creators use the characters from existing pop culture narratives to create their own stories. Not only is popular culture changing how people are reading and writing, such shifts in reading and writing online are changing popular culture. Whether as subject matter, discourse, or rhetorical patterns, popular culture often shapes the content and form of current online reading and writing. It is important that we understand not just how online technologies have changed literacy and popular culture practices, but why popular culture dominates the online literacy practices of our students.

Although popular culture has crossed international borders for some time, digital technologies have both increased the access people have to popular culture from around the world and put them in contact with audience members in other countries. The literacy practices shaped by popular culture online are also influenced by the ways in which popular culture images, ideas, and references are read across borders. As students from around the world read and write with popular culture, their literacy practices raise important questions about the interplay of rhetoric, power, technology, and global capitalism. Students who are already reading popular culture texts from other countries, or communicate with online friends across borders, are developing ideas about literacy and culture that are significantly different than those of previous generations.

In *New Media Literacies and Participatory Popular Culture Across Borders* we explore how students' online literacy practices intersect with online popular culture. The book draws on literacy and popular culture scholars from Australia, Lebanon, Nepal, Qatar, South Africa, Turkey, and the United States, to illustrate and analyze how literacy practices that are mediated through and influenced by popular culture create both opportunities and tensions for secondary and university students. The chapters in the book cover issues of theory, identity, and pedagogy as they address participatory popular culture sites such as fan forums, video, blogs, social networking sites, anime, memes, and comics and graphic novels. There are two central focuses to this collection. First, the authors explore the ways in which new media and online technologies are shaped by, and influence, the connections and tensions between transnational popular culture and local cultural practices. Participatory popular culture raises new questions about the interplay between the mass popular culture and local audience members. This collection will explore the role of new media in the economic and cultural debates about "globalization" and how those are complicated by the local uses of popular culture texts. Technologies that allow an individual to not only access popular culture texts from around the world in an instant, but also share, comment on, appropriate, and remix those same texts alter the way the individual perceives popular culture, and alter his or her sense of agency in regard to the texts. New media technologies have changed the relationship between mass popular culture text and individual users, and they engage individuals in new ways of negotiating language and culture.

Those negotiations of language and culture define the second focus of the collection: the influence of participatory popular culture on the literacy practices of young people. Through cross-cultural participatory popular culture, young people are engaging with and responding to global audiences in ways and to an extent simply not available to previous generations. Though we should, of course, be wary of being naïvely celebratory in our approach to studying these practices, there is no denying that many young people are in contact with texts and people around the world through the lenses of popular culture: popular culture provides the rhetorical, linguistic, and semiotic building blocks through which they engage in cross-cultural discourse. They encounter these texts on a global stage, deal with issues of difference and unfamiliarity, and then rebuild them in local contexts. While their practices and ideas are certainly shaped by the popular culture content that corporations produce and distribute around the world, it is also the case that young people are appropriating and reusing these same texts to perform identities and make meaning in their own lives.

The chapters in this book, then, analyze how people interpret, create, and distribute popular culture texts across cultures, and how they think about the role of culture in defining the nature of texts, the negotiations of language use, the employment of rhetoric, and the construction and performance of identity. Individual chapters offer many different perspectives about local responses to these global forces from scholars working in a wide range of international contexts. How do young people access transnational texts online, but then respond and rework them according to their local contexts and concerns about identity (gender, social class, ethnicity, sexual orientation)? How do these online practices influence their approaches to reading and writing, both with print as well as with images, sound, and video? Such research offers obvious possibilities for conceiving of how the use of popular culture across cultures could be used in the classroom to talk about issues of literacy, cross-cultural communication, identity, and power. Some chapters include discussions of the innovative ways in which instructors around the world connect participatory popular culture with classroom pedagogy, particularly the ways in which students' out-of-class literacy practices online can be connected to the literacy classroom.

The collection itself also reflects the diverse opportunities and practices within participatory popular culture. As the contributors sent us their chapters, we found that their conceptions of participatory popular culture and literacy often challenged us to expand and rethink our own. What you will not find in this book is a lock-step set of definitions or scholarly approaches to this subject matter. The contributors represent not only a number of different countries, but also several different academic fields and approaches to research and scholarship. We encouraged these authors to demonstrate how their scholarly backgrounds and local cultural contexts led them to conceive of the issues involved with participatory popular culture across borders. The result is a book that ranges widely on this subject, but around every corner provides new and provocative ways of thinking about how people in different cultures work with and respond to the affordances of new media and popular culture. The effect is a book with intriguing juxtapositions, unusual connections, and often unexpected tensions and insights, all drawn together by the idea that literacy as a social practice is being changed by participatory popular culture in a transnational world.

In order to have a sense of the focus of this book, it is useful to review, briefly, the three threads of scholarship concerning new media that we are drawing together with this project: Participatory Popular Culture, Literacy and Writing, and Global and Local Contact.

New Media and Participatory Popular Culture

Much has been written in recent years about the effect of digital technologies on popular culture. In a little more than a decade and half, the way people around the world engage with popular culture has changed dramatically. For most of the twentieth century popular culture was a mass-produced phenomenon that people could consume and interpret, but not easily respond to or change. The advent of digital media and online technologies, however, has radically changed the paradigm of popular culture production and consumption. Perhaps one of the best-known critiques of the changes brought to popular culture by digital media, and one that certainly influences our work in this book, is Henry Jenkins' (2006) theorizing of this participatory space as a "convergence culture" in which individuals privilege having the ability to participate in a variety of ways with popular culture, including sampling and remixing their own texts, discussing texts with other fans, and responding to producers of mass popular culture texts. In addition, he points out that convergence culture allows individuals to move quickly and easily from one media platform or mode to another while engaged with popular culture. So, for example, a student sitting at a computer can now open multiple programs and move between web pages, video games, music, video clips from movies, and, yes, even printed text. Such movement in Jenkins' eyes, however, marks more than mere technological innovations. Instead, he argues, "convergence occurs within the brains of individual consumers and through their social interactions with others" (p. 3). Understanding convergence culture as a social practice is vital if we hope to gain insights into how and why young people engage in participatory popular culture. For the student in the example above is very likely not simply "watching" or "listening" to popular culture in passive isolation, in the stereotype often invoked by critics of popular culture. Instead, she is just as likely to be reading comments about the videos she is watching, gaining ideas about how to advance in her video game from fan forums, or sampling popular culture content to reuse on her social networking site to perform her identity and make social connections with her friends.

The example above is indicative of the conclusion of much of the research about the online practices of young people (Burgess & Green, 2009; Ito, 2010; Kaiser Family Foundation, 2010), that it is often directly or indirectly connected with participatory popular culture. Popular culture, then, has clearly become something that is not only read and written *about*, but that is also written *with*. Digital technologies have made popular culture content available as a semiotic and rhetorical resource for composing, not just a text to consume. Given the time young people spend engaged with participatory popular culture, it is small surprise to see the rhetorical and discursive influence of popular culture in their new media literacy practices, whether in print, sound, or video. For young people, participatory popular culture texts are regarded as available for interpretation, but also for critique, appropriation, response, and reuse. A growing emphasis on speed, visuals, and combining multiple modes of communication on any given text means that individuals now have the same concerns and capabilities that have been available to popular culture producers for decades. As the authors in this book make clear, young people from around the world are making use of the participatory elements of contemporary popular culture and, in turn, their deep and extensive engagement with popular culture is having a profound effect on how they interpret and compose with digital technologies.

New Media and Literacy and Writing

At the same time that much has been written about the ways in which digital technologies have changed the perception and engagement with popular culture, there has been a great deal of attention paid to the ways in which new media are changing the conceptions and practices of reading and writing. Developments in digital technologies have focused the attention of scholars on the role of technology in literacy practices in ways that had not been as explicit in the long period dominated by print as a medium. New technologies make it all but impossible to discuss literacy practices without also confronting the complexity of interpreting and composing texts that have been created by new media and online technologies. Even in the circumstances where print is the dominant form of communication, the reality is that it is just as likely to be composed, distributed, and displayed in digitized form on a computer. Indeed, every word of this introduction will have been written on a computer and sent back and forth electronically between the two authors who work in universities on the other side of the world from each other. At the same time, in cultures around the world, computer technology, and the ability to compose with and read texts on computers, is considered part of the essential core of sophisticated literacy practices.

Exploring the ways in which digital media shape literacy practices has been part of the focus of New Literacy Studies on literacy as a socially constructed and defined set of activities. With the general acceptance that literacy is social practice, not a set of a-contextual skills, comes the necessity of understanding how such a practice intersects with the uses of technology for writing and reading. For example, new media creates opportunities for collaboration, interactivity, copying and recomposing, and publishing and distributing with a much greater ease than print on paper technologies of the past, and Cope and Kalantzis (2010) argue that new media have changed the "social relations of meaning making" (p. 89). As new media allow audiences the capacity to become users, and not just consumers, the division of labor between creator and audience member has changed. For Cope and Kalantzis, this means that "knowledge and authority are more contingent, provisional, and conditional-based relationships of 'could' rather than 'should.' This is what we mean by a 'shift in the balance of agency,' from a society of command and compliance to a society of reflexive co-construction" (p. 89). New media, then, have not only changed the nature of the social practices of literacy, but have also made the social aspects of literacy practices more visible, explicit, and open for examination.

The collaborative and interactive opportunities offered by new technologies emphasize the social contexts of literacy with an immediacy and power far different than in the era of the printed page. A blog provides an explicit interaction between writer and reader quite different than writing in a print journal, for example. Such interactive activities have raised important questions about the nature of reading and how it can become a more immediately and explicit dialogic activity. Other new media forms, such as wikis, also emphasize collaboration and dialogue, as well as the instability of the texts being created. Wikis and discussion forums also draw on what Jenkins terms "collective intelligence" in which knowledge is created and shared by individuals contributing their knowledge and comments around an issue of common interest. Such collaborative spaces also require attention to questions of genre and audience. A young person contributing to an online fan forum must know more than simply how to read and write. Misunderstanding the social contexts and power dynamics of the forum, which can vary widely from one online group to the next, can make it difficult to negotiate the rhetorical situation and communicate with others.

Literacy scholars have also realized that digital technologies raise important issues about the composing and distributing of texts in ways that have not been as fully in play since the invention of the printing press (Welch, 1999). Not only are individuals now faced with many choices in terms of the modes and media they use to communicate information, but digital technology also makes it possible to post the texts online so that they might be read by countless readers across the world. People are able to publish and distribute the information as quickly as it is finished and in multiple places, though they then face the possibility that others may respond to, adapt, or change the original text almost as quickly as it is posted.

The ability of individuals to more easily create and distribute their own texts means that the literacy practices that exist in different domains of life can come increasingly into contact. In terms of the focus of this book, it means that a person sitting in South Africa can post a video or a piece of fan fiction that can be instantly read and commented on by someone in Japan. The interaction among these different cultural positions is exciting, or sometimes contentious, as the context in which the original text was composed is less clear to the reader who can access it so quickly.

At the same time that New Literacy Studies has illuminated questions of literacy as a social practice, scholars in rhetoric and composition, and literacy education have explored questions of the effect of digital media on writing pedagogy in terms of concepts such as writing processes, student collaboration, and multimodality (Alexander, 2006; Davies & Merchant 2009; Johnson-Eilola, 2005; Selfe, 1999). The research into the ways that digital technologies have changed literacy practices has taken many different directions. As with studies of literacy practices outside the classroom, the scholarship on new media in the writing classroom has demonstrated that new technologies facilitate teaching such concepts as revision, peer review, and critical reading (Cooper, 1998; Anson, 1999; Yancey 2004). Other scholars have focused on the growing capacity within new media to create texts that combine print, images, video, and sound (Burn, 2009; Keller, 2007; Stein, 2008; Wysocki, 2004). The role of printed words online, once the dominant form of online communication, has changed as the power of computers and software have changed. These new capabilities raise increasingly complex and exciting questions about the most rhetorically effective ways to communicate. New media offer many options in composing a text, including the ability to compose with images, graphics, and video, each with its own affordances and limitations. When individuals compose with and read multimodal texts, it requires a different approach to making meaning than the traditional print literacy emphasis on linearity. Now it is possible to compose a text on a computer that emphasizes the juxtaposition of elements in space, and works associatively rather than linearly (Kress, 2003). In terms of cross-cultural communication, the ability to compose with images, music, and video, also means that communication is no longer limited to language, so that a text composed with a combination of words, images, and sound, may still be largely comprehensible across linguistic borders.

Finally, new media have challenged traditional ideas of authorship and the stability of texts by allowing for the easy copying and recomposing of texts. Virtually any text available online is also one that might be available for copying and reworking into a new version of the existing text, or a reworked text altogether. The question of sampling and reuse of texts in cross-cultural contexts is the focus of the next chapter.

The conversations about new media and literacy studies often intersect with continuing research on literacy and popular culture. In recent years, the scholarship on literacy and popular culture has argued that students read popular culture texts more critically than conventional wisdom assumes and that their reading and writing, both in and out of school, draws from the genres and discourses of popular culture (Alvermann, Moon, & Hagood, 1999; Dyson, 1997; Faulkner, 2003; Williams, 2002). Over the last decade, this research, including this book, has followed popular culture into the digital world to study the intersections of popular culture and literacy with new media. What we see now, though, is young people participating in popular culture online and interpreting and composing texts in widely varied and fascinating ways (Black, 2008; Thomas, 2007; Vasudevan & Hill, 2007; Williams, 2009). If we hope to understand how people make meaning from texts in a digital world, then we need to follow them to the participatory popular culture texts with which they compose and interpret on a daily basis.

New Media and Global and Local Contact

The third area of scholarship that influences the focus of this book is the work that has been done in cultural and literacy studies on the movement of culture and texts, including popular culture, across cultural borders. The questions of "globalization," from the use of the term itself to the relationships of economics, power, and culture between transnational flows of information and capital and local responses and practices, have been the focus of much discussion, in terms of new media, literacy practices, and popular culture.

We, and the other authors in this collection, resist a simplistic, binary conception of global–local relations. We do not regard "global," cross-cultural forces as inherently good, evidence of a "flat" world where access and opportunity are equal, yet we also don't regard those same economic and cultural forces as necessary harbingers of the destruction of "authentic" local culture. What is more interesting to us in this project is the interaction of the global and the local. The questions that motivate the authors in this book relate to how young people in cultures around the world not only interpret, but also create, in response to popular culture that moves so easily across national borders. There is no doubt that new technologies and economic relationships have allowed for a global, capitalist connection of economies. An important part of these new, transnational economic relationships are the new communication technologies and media that allow for the fast and large-scale movement of information from one part of the world to another. Such rapid flows of information, of which popular culture is a central part, wield substantial cultural power and no doubt influence the lives of the people they touch, regardless of their location. At the same time, however, there is more than enough evidence that transnational popular culture is not a totalizing force that overwhelms the local. If anything, new participatory technologies have revealed the degree to which individuals make use of popular culture texts in ways that make sense to them in their local contexts (a fuller exploration of the connections between current theories of the global and local and their connection to participatory popular culture takes place in Chapter 2). Understanding the ongoing negotiations between popular culture and the local allows us to conceive of such global phenomena as "multi-centred or 'nodal.' Rather than remaining with established polarities of north/south or centre/periphery, we can conceive of different places being centres of different types of 'globalities.'" (de Block & Buckingham, 2007, p. 7).

The question of space and place and the connections between our embodied experiences and our online practices is one implicit in many of these chapters. The way in which participatory popular culture works as a mediating element in online, cross-cultural spaces is, perhaps, one of the most fascinating, and even hopeful, ways the practices described in this book work out in people's lives.

On popular culture fan sites it is easy to find people posting who come from a range of different cultural and linguistic backgrounds. Though they may be writing in English (or, more to the point, in Englishes) there is a not a single set of usages that govern the conversation. Instead, usage and rhetorical style varies from the participants and they often engage in a back-and-forth of negotiations over words or usage or genre until a meaning is found that satisfies all sides. It is intriguing to observe such negotiations and the patience and generosity—rather than judgment or exclusion—that participants usually show each other.

Suresh Canagarajah (2011), in his research on linguistics and world Englishes, theorizes a "translocal space" as a more useful conception of where negotiations of language occur than the idea of a geographic "place." He perceives place as a static, bounded concept that does not offer the same vision of space as an environment where things happen—interactions, negotiations, meaning making. It is interesting to overlap this theorizing of space with Gee's (2004) ideas of online "affinity spaces" where people gather online, drawn by their interests in common popular culture texts more than their conceptions of home identities. If we think about the way online and cross-cultural affinity spaces are also translocal spaces of language and rhetorical contact and negotiation, it raises interesting questions of how the popular culture texts help mediate and facilitate these negotiations of language and meaning. Not only do the popular culture texts draw individuals together online, and across cultures, but they offer both a common cultural and linguistic touchstone for the participants. The popular culture text provides common content, rhetorical structures, and language that participants use as a resource and catalyst for their communication.

Overview

The chapters in Part I, *New Media Literacies Across Cultures*, explore the effects of popular culture texts as they cross cultures. The contributors examine the recursive relationship between local culture and transnational popular culture.

In Chapter 2, "The World on Your Screen: New Media, Remix, and the Politics of Cross-Cultural Contact," Bronwyn Williams further develops the theoretical framework presented in Chapter 1. This framework is necessary for the book's focus on the role popular culture plays in debates about global and local constructions of culture and considers how the interactive, online media of convergence culture changes the interplay between the mass popular culture and local audience members. He looks at both the history of the relationship between mass popular culture and the material dimensions of globalization before examining how the literacy practices of textual poaching and remixing across cultural borders have developed and flourished with the spread of new media.

In Chapter 3, "Constructing 'Local Context' in Beirut: Students' Literacy Practices Outside of Class," Amy A. Zenger takes a case study approach to study university students' use of popular culture and new media outside of class in Lebanon. The study focuses on two videos that draw on images, text, and music found online to design texts intended to achieve their specific purposes. One video was circulated online to students to promote a strike on campus; the second was composed privately and never published online. As instances of participatory popular culture, these two texts are considered in relation to questions about what it means for a text to be "local" in a globalized and networked world.

Cheng-Wen Huang and Arlene Archer, in Chapter 4, "Uncovering the Multimodal Literacy Practices in Reading Manga and the Implications for Pedagogy," focus on a different aspect of what happens when popular culture crosses borders online. Their study of how online Japanese manga are represented and read in South Africa focuses specifically on issues of translation and visual interpretations of the comics. They study two different English translations of the manga, *Naruto*—one an official version and one distributed by fans—and analyze how changes in layout and text differ between the two versions. In this way they demonstrate the influences of social and cultural practices on text composition and how popular culture texts challenge us to rethink concepts of modes and genres as we help students to discuss and critique texts across cultures.

In Chapter 5, "Adolescent Literacy Practices in Online Social Spaces," Jessica Schreyer explores issues of genre, audience, and popular culture in an online game. She argues that, while engaging in such games may not, in itself, help students to a better understanding of transnational cultural contact, the games do provide students with an important entry point for exploration and conversation. By bringing together theories of literacy and cross-cultural contact with an analysis of a specific online game, she provides a framework and example for how to connect students' use of online social gaming, as well as the literacy practices surrounding this gaming, to discussions of literacy and transnational relations.

Chapter 6, "The 'Popular' Turkish Academy," focuses on the implications of the disconnect between young people engaged in a world of rapidly developing online participatory popular culture and a traditional, print-based conception of learning that still dominates the university culture in Turkey. Tüge T. Gülsen shows how young people in Turkey are influenced by popular culture that crosses and re-crosses borders, both online and off, from a young age. Yet, when they enter the university they encounter a system that remains committed to privileging print-based literacy and excluding any connection with students' out-of-class learning experiences with popular culture. She proposes a different approach, aimed at addressing this gap between the popular culture literacy practices of students' lives and academic learning.

In Chapter 7, "Digital Worlds and Shifting Borders: Popular Culture, Perception, and Pedagogy," three authors offer different examples of how students in the U.S. use new media to rethink and reach beyond their physical location. Sandra Schamroth Abrams, Hannah R. Gerber, and Melissa L. Burgess study the out-of-classroom literacy practices facilitated by computer games and multi-user virtual environments. Their research reveals the complexity of such practices for the young people involved in them and contrasts it with traditional text-based assumptions of literacy the participants face in school. They argue for a reconceiving of the writing classroom that includes digital games and environments as important and relevant literacy practices.

Chapter 8, the final chapter in Part I, examines how speed and remixing shape textual practices of writing and reading online. Lynn C. Lewis, in "The Participatory Meme Chronotope: Fixity of Space/Rapture of Time," uses popular online memes as a way to explore how participation and speed are valued and reproduced online. In her examination of popular memes such as the Star Wars Kid, Numa Numa Dance, and Snakes on a Plane, she argues that certain texts point to a particular emphasis on speed that requires us to rethink how time and space work in online texts. Understanding the importance and uses of speed and remixing online has implications for how we think about issues of texts, identity, and ethics when we read and write with new media and popular culture.

Constructing Identity in an Online, Cross-Cultural World

Part II, *Constructing Identity in an Online, Cross-Cultural World*, examines how popular culture is employed by people in different cultural contexts as a semiotic, rhetorical, and cultural resource for constructing and reading identity online.

In Chapter 9, "Faceless Facebook: Female Qatari Users Choosing Wisely," Mohanalakshmi Rajakumar shows how something as standardized and ubiquitous as the Facebook template is adapted to local cultural traditions and concepts of identity. She illustrates how Qatari women create online identities that negotiate between the public expectations of online social networking sites and local cultural expectations of gender, class, and ethnicity. The women in this research have complex and thoughtful responses to the creation of their online identities, making their way between the expectations of family and community and a desire to participate in online environments.

The creation of fan communities, and how those communities respond to the identities of characters in television programs, is the focus of Chapter 10, "Russell T Davies, 'Nine Hysterical Women,' and the Death of Ianto Jones." Laurie Cubbison examines how digital technologies facilitated and mediated a conflict between the producers of a television program and audience members from a variety of countries. When a favorite character of many fans was killed off in an episode, fan members took to social networking sites to debate, discuss, and voice their displeasure. Cubbison uses Roland Barthes' distinction between the work and the text—the commodity and the conceptual field—in order to explore how the relationship between producer and fan has not only changed in the digital age, but also how it spreads across cultural borders to join fans together in reaching particular readings of popular texts.

In Chapter 11, "Leapfrogging in the Global Periphery: Popular Literacy Practices of Nepalese Youth Online," Ghanashyam Sharma and Bal Krishna Sharma interview a range of Nepalese young people—both those still living in Nepal and those who have moved abroad—to explore how increasing access to global popular culture and literacy practices has enabled these young people to challenge traditional hierarchies of knowledge and access to literacy. They argue that the experiences of Nepalese youth with new media often runs counter to conventional constructions of center–margin conflicts between the "global" and the "local." Instead they illustrate how the participants in this research draw together transnational popular culture and traditional local culture in a mix of literacy practices that both create community as well as allow them to escape constraints of traditional power structures.

In Chapter 12, "Queering the Text: Online Literacy Practices, Identities, and Popular Culture," Mark Vicars applies a queer lens to participatory cultural practices. He approaches Queering as a deconstructive disruptive way of knowing that has the potential to be transgressive and subversive. And the act of Queering, as a critical hermeneutical approach, is productive for textualizing identity as something that gets done in multiple locations and that can be a source of knowledge in communities, practices, and social relations. Blending the critical tools of cultural literacy, critical literacy, and Multiple Literacies Theory to trace participatory cultural practices' ever increasing protean quality, shape-shifting excesses, self-reflexivity, and performativity, he considers how literacies as texts are produced, online and off, and consumed by gay male communities of practice.

Karen Hellekson, in Chapter 13, "Creating a Fandom via YouTube: *Verbotene Liebe* and Fansubbing," examines how fans across cultures have remixed a German soap opera to focus on the narrative of a gay couple on the show. She discusses how these fans, by using new media, find public and private online spaces that allow them to participate in the reading and writing of popular culture online. They draw on the source material, remix and repurpose it, distribute it, and discuss it—all online and across cultures. Hellekson shows how the modified, English-language fan-subtitled (fansubbed) cut versions posted on YouTube, both created a new audience for the new narrative that expanded the soap's audience and engaged in an alternative textual productivity centered around homosexuality, an alternative sexuality, to create a queer space as a form of advocacy.

In Chapter 14, "Virtual Places in the Physical World: Geographies of Literacy and (National) Identity," Rick Carpenter explores the implications of thinking about "space" in terms of new media and popular culture. He juxtaposes ideas of physical and online space to discuss how engagement in these spaces influences how people negotiate difference. He points out how individuals in online, transnational spaces often figure out how to read and respond to the embodied materiality of texts that come originally from quite different geographic and social spaces. He argues that though online, popular culture texts remain culturally and geographically situated, within the material-metaphoric territory of the nation-state, and mean that while cross-cultural contact and negotiation happen online culture is never absent or transcended.

Summing Up

The authors in this book explore how mass popular culture texts are consumed, resisted, or adapted by individuals in their local lives in varied and unpredictable ways. For us, in this book, what is important is charting the ways in which the interactions of global flows of popular culture lead to the interpretation, response, and creation of texts online. It is the convergence of these issues of trans-cultural popular culture and students' literacy practices that intrigued us and prompted this research project.

References

Alexander, J. (2006). *Digital youth: Emerging literacies on the World Wide Web*. Cresskill, NJ: Hampton Press.

Alvermann, D. E. (Ed.). (2010). *Adolescents' online literacies: Connecting classrooms, digital media, and popular culture*. London: Peter Lang.

Alvermann, D. E., Moon, J. S., & Hagood, M. C. (1999). *Popular culture in the classroom: Teaching and researching critical media literacy*. Chicago, IL: National Reading Conference.

Anson, C. M. (1999). Distant voices: Teaching writing in a culture of technology. *College English, 61*(3), 261–280.

Black, R. W. (2008). *Adolescents and online fan fiction*. London: Peter Lang.

Brooke, C. G. (2009). *Lingua fracta: Towards a rhetoric of new media*. Cresskill, NJ: Hampton Press.

Bruns, A. (2008). *Blogs, Wikipedia, Second Life, and beyond*. London: Peter Lang.

Buckingham, D., & Willett, R. (2006). *Digital generations: Children, young people, and new media*. Mahwah, NJ: Lawrence Erlbaum Associates, Publishers.

Burgess, J., & Green, J. (2009). *YouTube: Online video and participatory culture*. Cambridge: Polity Press.

Burn, A. (2009). *Making new media: Creative production and digital literacies*. London: Peter Lang.

Canagarajah, S. (2011). Codemeshing in academic writing: Identifying teachable strategies of translanguaging. *The Modern Language Journal, 95*(3), 401–417.

Cooper, M. (1998). Postmodern pedagogy in electronic conversations. In C. L. Selfe & G. E. Hawisher (Eds.), *Passions, pedagogies, and 21st century technologies* (pp. 140–160). Logan, UT: Utah State University Press.

Cope, B., & Kalantzis, M. (Eds.). (2000). *Multiliteracies: Literacy learning and the design of social futures*. London: Routledge.

Cope, B., & Kalantzis, M. (2010). New media, new learning. In D. R. Cole & D. L. Pullen (Eds.), *Multiliteracies in motion: Current theory and practice* (pp. 87–104). London: Routledge.

Davies, J., & Merchant, G. (2009). *Web 2.0 for schools: Learning and social participation.* New York: Peter Lang.

de Block, L., & Buckingham, D. (2007). *Global children, global media: Migration, media, and childhood.* New York: Palgrave Macmillan.

Dyson, A. H. (1997). *Writing superheroes: Contemporary childhood, popular culture, and classroom literacy.* New York: Teachers College Press.

Faulkner, J. (2003). "Like you have a bubble inside of you that just wants to pop": Popular culture, pleasure and the English classroom. *English Teaching: Practice and Critique, 2*(2), 47–56.

Gee, J. P. (2004). *Situated language and learning: A critique of traditional schooling.* London: Routledge.

Ito, M., et al. (2010). *Hanging out, messing around, and geeking out: Kids living and learning with new media.* Cambridge, MA: MIT Press.

Jenkins, H. (2006). *Convergence culture: Where old and new media collide.* New York: New York University Press.

Johnson-Eilola, J. (2005). *Datacloud: Toward a new theory of online work.* Cresskill, NJ: Hampton Press.

Kaiser Family Foundation. (2010). Generation M2: Media in the lives of 8- to 18-year-olds. Washington, DC: Kaiser Family Foundation.

Keller, D. (2007). Thinking rhetorically. In C. L. Selfe (Ed.), *Multimodal composition: Resources for teachers* (pp. 49–63). Cresskill, NJ: Hampton Press.

Kress, G. (2003). *Literacy in the new media age.* London: Routledge.

Lankshear, C., & Knobel, M. (Eds.). (2008). *Digital literacies: Concepts, policies, and practices.* London: Peter Lang.

Selfe, C. L. (1999). Technology and literacy: A story about the perils of not paying attention. *College Composition and Communication, 50*(3).

Stein, P. (2008). Multimodal instructional practices. In J. Coiro, M. Knobel, C. Lankshear & D. J. Leu (Eds.), *Handbook of research on new literacies* (pp. 871–898). New York: Peter Lang.

Thomas, A. (2007). *Youth online: Identity and literacy in the digital age.* New York: Peter Lang.

Vasudevan, L., & Hill, M. (2007). *Media, learning, and sites of possibility.* New York: Peter Lang.

Welch, K. (1999). *Electric rhetoric: Classical rhetoric, oralism, and a new literacy.* Cambridge, MA: The MIT Press.

Williams, B. T. (2002). *Tuned in: Television and the teaching of writing.* Portsmouth, NH: Boynton/Cook.

Williams, B. T. (2009). *Shimmering literacies: Popular culture and reading and writing online.* London: Peter Lang.

Wysocki, A. (2004). Opening new media to writing: Openings and justifications. In A. Wysocki (Ed.), *Writing new media: Theory and applications for expanding the teaching of composition.* Logan, UT: Utah State University Press.

Yancey, K. B. (2004). Made not only in words: Composition in a new key. *College Composition and Communication, 56*(2).

PART I

New Media Literacies Across Cultures

2

THE WORLD ON YOUR SCREEN

New Media, Remix, and the Politics of Cross-Cultural Contact

Bronwyn T. Williams

Popular culture has been "global" for a long time. In the broad and sometimes contradictory range of issues covered by the term "globalization," few are as visible and pervasive in the daily lives of people around the world as popular culture. While one adolescent in South Africa wears an Eric Cartman t-shirt, another in the U.S. watches hours of the Japanese anime series, *Gurren Lagen*. While the phrase "Rambo politics" has become a pejorative term in political discourse from France to Ireland to Canada, protests take place from Greece to India to South Korea over a Hollywood film such as *The Da Vinci Code*. I've discussed *World of Warcraft* with students in Beijing and browsed video shops in Beirut stocked with films produced from the U.S. to Europe to Lebanon. And, when I recently checked into a hotel in Indiana, I found, in addition to the U.S. television channels, four channels of Bollywood movies and South Asian news and sports, and two channels of Spanish-language programming. It is almost impossible to open one's eyes without encountering examples of globally circulating popular culture.

From music to movies to television, popular culture moves across national borders with a speed and an ease that, while commonplace in our contemporary world, is still sometimes quite astonishing. The advent of the Internet has only increased the breathtaking pace at which popular culture texts circulate through cultures in every hemisphere. The growth of global economic systems and technologies has been accompanied by the expansion and rapid communication of popular culture around the world and across cultures. This trans-cultural popular culture has influenced communication and discourse at all levels.

In many ways the engines that drive mass popular culture across borders and around the globe are the ones that drive the economic and cultural forces that are often lumped together under the label of "globalization." The growth of multi-national corporations, the rapid movement of economic capital, and advanced technologies of communication and transportation have facilitated the expansion of mass popular culture in the same way they have facilitated the expansion of global financial and manufacturing systems. Indeed, as the means of technology transfer have become more sophisticated, mass popular culture, with its ability to be transmitted cheaply over long distances, has been particularly well suited for the kind of global distribution and profit model that defines capitalist market globalization. New media technologies have been a part of this expansion and today popular culture crosses borders with increasing ease, bringing languages, cultures, and texts into contact as never before.

At the same time that new media and online technologies have enabled the cross-cultural movement of mass popular culture, they have also changed the relationship between popular culture producer and audience member. As new media technologies have allowed individuals to respond to producers, or interact with other audience members, or even sample, remix, and distribute their own popular culture-based content, the relationship between the global and the local has shifted significantly. Local, individual voices are now present in the mix of popular culture online, and connect with other voices and ideas across cultural and political borders. While in the Indiana hotel I could have, while watching Bollywood films in my room, found an online forum about the films and had my own conversation about them with other audience members from around the world, enriching and extending my reading of the texts on the television and on my computer. Had I done so I would have communicated largely through print, as much of the communication in participatory popular culture still happens through alphabetic literacy. Yet new media are also making it possible for individuals to create and communicate through multimodal media such as video and images that had, in the past, been the province of mass popular culture producers. The changes new media are creating in literacy practices and popular culture are indeed global in scope and the cross-cultural nature of these practices is both significant and important to understand as we consider the current state of reading, writing, and popular culture.

In this chapter I discuss the important role popular culture plays in debates about global and local constructions of culture and consider how the interactive, online media of convergence culture change the interplay between mass popular culture and local audience members. I will first briefly trace the relationship between mass popular culture and the economic and material mechanisms of global capital and information flow. Then I will discuss how, in terms of the circulation and interpretation of popular culture, global/local, producer/audience, center/periphery relationships are not simple or one dimensional, but contain overlapping and sometimes contradictory dynamics. I will follow this by addressing how the literacy practices of textual poaching and remixing across cultural borders have developed and flourished with the spread of new media. Finally I argue that, as economic globalization and new media have transformed transnational contact and relationships, understanding the connections between literacy and participatory popular culture has important implications for how literacy scholars think about language, literacy, rhetoric, identity, and pedagogy in an increasingly mobile and cross-cultural world.

Mass Popular Culture and Global Imperialism

Although "globalization" is a slippery term that has been used to describe a variety of different political, economic, and cultural phenomena, some aspects of the practices and forces that regularly fall into conversations about globalization are particularly relevant to an understanding of contemporary popular culture. A definition of "globalization" that is relevant here, and that I will start from, is that it describes the "global integration of economies, rapid media and information flow facilitated by new communication technologies, international migration of labor, the rise of transnational and panregional organizations, and resultant cultural transformations challenging traditional social structures" (Lam, 2006, p. 214). Of particular interest for this book is the articulation between cultural transformation and global economic integration: in a "globalized" world, the material and cultural relationships created and sustained by transnational economic relationships have been, and continue to be, central to the creation and distribution of popular culture.

When modern, industrial societies developed, the creation and consumption of popular culture shifted. As industrial methods of production and distribution competed with and often replaced traditional cultural practices of local participation in music or dance or crafts, mass popular culture developed in the industrialized world, first with printing and subsequently with electronic media such as radio, television, and movies. The industrial model of mass popular culture is defined by the large amounts of capital necessary for producing and distributing content. Labor, with specifically defined jobs, such as sound engineers or camera operators, produce the work, rather than individual artists. Large corporate organizations are necessary to reproduce and distribute the content, by producing films or recordings, and building theatres or television broadcasting stations. The role of the audience is to consume the content, but not to alter it, as few would have the material means to do so. During the last century, this model of mass popular culture was compatible with transnational corporate economic relations, in which industrial societies mass produced goods then sent them to countries that did not have the same production capabilities, so could only consume the goods. Mass popular culture was particularly well suited for this model, in that the capital required to produce the content in film or music was substantial, while the capital required to consume it, such as film projectors or record players, was much smaller.

Today, the material forces that shaped mass popular culture in the industrial era continue in many ways, even as film, music, and television production has changed in response to global economies and technological developments. Although new technologies have greatly reduced the capital necessary to produce popular culture content, it is still the case that U.S. movie studios, for example, are essentially alone in their ability to finance and stage technically complex blockbuster films, such as *Avatar*, or even films that began as texts outside the U.S., such the Harry Potter series, and distribute them on a global level. These material forces lead many to argue that mass popular culture largely remains entrenched in the West, particularly in the U.S., and reflects the ideologies and conceptions of identity rooted in U.S. culture, which are then adopted by consumers, particularly youth, in less affluent countries (Logue & McCarthy, 2007; Shome & Hegde, 2002; Suarez-Orozco & Qin-Hilliard, 2004). The adoption of Western popular culture in less affluent nations is regarded as challenging and undermining local cultural practices and values. The criticism, both academic and political, of the global reach and influence of Western corporate popular culture, sometimes disrupts easy distinctions between left and right as proponents of workers' rights or indigenous cultures can find themselves aligned with conservative, pro-nationalist forces (Lukose, 2008).

The role of the U.S. in producing and distributing mass popular culture in a global context continues to be one of the most contentious issues in debates about the production and reception of popular culture. There is no disputing that the U.S. popular culture industry is a powerful global economic force. It has "exploded the pace" at which images, information, and identities are available and often empowering to people around the world, while simultaneously reinforcing "the gross inequalities that remain unchanged in the contemporary world" (McCarthy et al., 2003, p. 455). Even countries with substantial popular culture industries of their own find they are influenced by U.S popular culture forms. The introduction of MTV in India, for example, had an effect on the look and style of Bollywood movies (Dissanayake, 2006). This is not to argue that U.S. popular culture is consumed uncritically around the world, only that its distribution and production are influential and controversial. An acknowledgement of this influence came in 2005 when the General Conference of UNESCO adopted by an overwhelming majority the Convention on the Protection of the Diversity of Cultural Contents and Artistic Expressions, a measure advocated by its authors in France and Canada as a direct response to the power and influence of U.S. popular culture. The U.S. was one of only two countries to vote against the proposal. U.S. popular culture icons resonate as symbols of larger issues of U.S. economic, military, and cultural imperialism and have frequently served as the focal points of protests against U.S. policies, as has happened, for example, at McDonald's restaurants from France to China. On the other hand, some have argued that the spread of U.S. popular culture, while connected to the economic and political power of the U.S., also reflects the ability and willingness of U.S. popular culture producers to adapt and repackage content and ideas from other cultures, both for domestic consumption and to appeal to audiences across national borders (Olson, 1999).

Resisting and Adapting Popular Culture

Even in the context of mass popular culture, however, the transnational relationships between industrial popular culture producers and audiences in other cultures have never been simple or one sided. Popular culture scholars have long made the argument that the relationship between producer, text, and audience is a complex mixture of acceptance and resistance (Fiske, 1996; Hall, 1974; Morley, 1992; Morse, 1998). On the one hand, popular culture texts have a powerful and pervasive influence on cultural conceptions of identity and ideology, and yet it is also the case that audience members—individually and collectively—can and do resist some popular culture texts or adapt them into the local contexts of their lives.

The same mixture of acceptance, resistance, and adaptation takes place when popular culture texts cross borders. The workings of globalization, in regards to popular culture, are not homogenous or smooth, but are instead marked by connections and gaps, understanding and confusion, acting both in concert with local culture and in opposition to the same culture: "The conditions and contradictions of, and within, the nation intersect with the global and vice-versa in strategic and unequal ways, and never with any guarantees regarding the 'outcome' of such intersections" (Shome & Hegde, 2002, p. 174). In research into the responses of young people in Europe to Disney films—another potent symbol of the reach and influence of U.S. popular culture—the participants in countries such as Britain and Denmark tended to not read the films as specifically American, and sometimes even ascribed the qualities of positive characters to represent the local culture (de Block & Buckingham, 2007). Even adults who were also asked for their responses to Disney films often displayed ambivalent or contradictory attitudes, critical of Disney as a corporation but finding pleasure in the films they watched with their children. "It may be that the symbolic importance of Disney as a bearer of U.S. capitalist values tends to provoke a principled critical discourse, even where that discourse might not actually reflect how individuals respond to the films themselves" (de Block & Buckingham 2007, p. 83). The complexity of such responses means that it is possible, at a given moment, to see mass popular culture as either an inexorable hegemonic cultural force, or as a text that is being resisted or adapted for individual uses in local contexts. It also means that it is impossible to read either of those moments as a complete and comprehensive reading of the relationship between the global and local in popular culture.

We can't know, just on an initial consideration, what is happening rhetorically or culturally when a boy in South Africa wears a *South Park* t-shirt. Is he a fan of the show, or is it just a shirt he was given? Is wearing it declaring an affiliation with other fans of the show or affirming the attitudes of the show, or is it, in his mind, just a funny-looking cartoon? Is his wearing of this particular shirt an acceptance of U.S. cultural ideology, or is he wearing the shirt as an ironic statement about power and authority? And what will others in his community who see the shirt make of it? If this was not complex enough, our consideration of this display of transnational popular culture is immediately complicated by questions of the age, ethnicity, and class status of the boy. Other studies of youth and global popular culture reveal, for example, ambivalence about popular culture among youth in less affluent countries, who may resent government policies and powerful economic forces that make it the predominant popular culture available, yet also be fans of the movies, music, or television (Lukose, 2008). They also reveal generational tensions between older people who want to maintain local cultural traditions, and young people who envision themselves as part of a transnational youth culture that is less rigid than that of the local culture (Koh, 2008). What de Block and Buckingham (2007) remind us, in their work with young people and global popular culture, is equally applicable to adolescents and adults:

> The notion of cultural imperialism does to some extent describe what is taking place here, at least at an economic level; but it fails to account for the diversity and complexity of how children use and interpret cultural texts. However, there are reasons to be cautious about the postmodern emphasis on hybridity and fragmentation: access to global markets is not equally open to all, and consumers are clearly not free to choose their cultural identities from an infinite range of global possibilities.
>
> *(p. 89)*

Considerations of global popular culture become further complicated when we remember that the mass popular culture that circulates across borders does not come exclusively from the U.S. or even the West, as seen in the popularity in recent years of *Pokemon* and manga from Japan, martial arts films from China and Hong Kong, and Bollywood films from India, to name just a few examples. The physical movement of people across borders today, particularly in urban areas, creates spaces in which diverse cultures—including their popular culture texts—live side by side and come into contact on a daily basis. Popular culture producers, in turn, represent these urban landscapes with a variety of cultural influences, so that to some extent "to represent Bombay is to partially represent Los Angeles" (Dissanayake, 2006, p. 35). Recognizing that the popular culture producers have realized that there is money to be made in representing the more complex cultural settings of our contemporary world, however, can also lead to a somewhat simplistic celebration of a "stylish hybridity, or an influx of performative representations of hyphenated persons and cultural (mis) translations occupying spaces in mainstream media" (Giardina, 2008, p. 74). Such representations, for example in films such as *Slumdog Millionaire* or *Bend it Like Beckham*, can offer false reassurances that popular culture producers, in responding to market demand, will address questions of transnational contact and culture in movies that end happily, but don't address fundamental questions of power and inequality. In any consideration of popular culture across borders, then, it is essential to remember the complicated and varying mix of global reach and local use, of access and economic power, of acceptance, resistance, and adaptation.

If there is no simple binary relationship between global mass popular culture and local responses to the texts, it is more helpful to think of what is happening as overlapping sets of phenomena and forces that vary in importance and impact depending on the time, place, and culture. Arjun Appadurai (1996) argues that the phenomena that get lumped together in the easy center–margin binary of the global and the local are actually ideas, forces, and ideology that reflect a global cultural economy that is disjunctive, fluid, and overlapping. The production and consumption across borders are better thought of as cross-cultural flows that travel in both directions through the interaction of various "scapes": "ethnoscapes, mediascapes, technoscapes, finanscapes, and ideoscapes" (p. 33). These "scapes" according to Appadurai, like landscapes, appear different and present different opportunities and obstacles depending on where you're standing. "They are deeply perspectival constructs, inflected by historical, linguistic, and political situatedness of different sorts of actors: nation-states, multinationals, diasporic communities, as well as subnational groupings and movements (whether religious, political or economic), and even face-to-face groups, such as villages, neighborhoods, and families" (p. 33). The advent of new media and online technologies has only heightened and complicated the "imagined worlds" that result from the engagement with these different scapes through the transnational flow of information and the social imagination. Such imagined worlds cannot be clearly defined as either empowering or oppressive, but instead create spaces of contestation. Just as we should be wary of simplistic celebrations of the new "flat" world in which global economic and cultural forces empower people across the planet—indeed, the world only looks flat to those standing on one hilltop looking across to other hilltops (Hudson, 2010)—we should also question a romanticizing of the local as a site of mythic or natural culture without flaws. Instead it is important to always be looking for ways in which the local and global interact and feed each other (Dissanayake, 2006), Again, this is not to argue that power does not remain important in issues of popular culture, technology, and literacy, or that mass popular culture is without influence on issues of identity and rhetoric. Still, the interpretation and appropriation of mass popular culture texts by youth literacy demonstrates that they are "also playing the role of active cultural workers, reshaping and recontextualizing global materials in the particular communities and local settings" (Lam, 2006, p. 223).

Popular Culture as a Textual Resource

The appropriation and reuse of popular culture content for individual and local purposes provides a useful example of the complex ways in which new technologies both distribute popular culture content beyond borders, and also have complicated notions of literacy, interpretation, and the agency of individuals in responding to these texts. The idea that readers appropriate texts for their own uses is not new, and certainly not new to how individuals engage with popular culture.

As Michel de Certeau (1984) pointed out, "everyday life invents itself by poaching in countless ways on the property of others" (p. xii). Engaging with texts, then, is not simply a matter of interpretation, but is just as often an act of appropriating pieces of the texts and using those pieces to create new texts that serve our interests. Such appropriation can range from something as simple as quoting a line from a song as part of a conversation to putting a poster for a movie on a bedroom wall. In both actions, the people involved may be able to trace the image or line to the original text, but also understand the new meaning, whether ironic or sincere, it takes on in the new context. The literacy practices involved in such appropriations and reuses are common in all creative forms and are certainly not a new activity, as anyone quoting the Bible or Shakespeare knows. Popular culture has long provided particularly inviting material for textual poaching because it is perceived as culturally insubstantial and yet widespread so that popular culture references are more likely to be understood by others.

In the context of transnational distribution and readings or popular culture content, audience members have also long appropriated and used poachings from texts in their own lives. I've sat in English pubs listening to people sing U.S. country songs or listened to a university student in China quote lines from a Hollywood movie, in both cases to express ideas distinctive to their own contexts. Until very recently, however, the ability to appropriate and reuse pieces of any text was limited by the realities of production and cultural power. The creation and distribution of mass popular culture, in particular, could only happen if you had the material means to make a movie, recording, or television program. For most people who went to a movie or read a book or watched a television program, the extent to which they could communicate what they were appropriating and reusing from the text was limited to the people with whom they could speak directly. Only the most committed fans, such as those who founded fan clubs or wrote and distributed fan fiction, would compose substantial and complex new texts that would satisfy their own individual and social needs.

Now, however, new media technologies have altered what it means for individual audience members to engage in textual poaching. Jenkins' (2006) idea of "convergence culture," where participation through multiple modes and multiple media is not only possible but expected by many, makes sampling and remixing easy and attractive to everyday audience members, not just the most dedicated fans. The level and amount of participation ranges from those who simply link to an online video from a social networking page, to those who rip clips from DVDs and edit them into new video remixes that they then post on sites such as YouTube or Vimeo. Regardless of the level of commitment or technological expertise, what is important to note from the perspective of literacy practices is the way in which the participatory possibilities of convergence culture reinforce the reality that, more than ever, we must regard popular culture content as "texts" that people read and write about, and write with. Whether it is a television program or movie or computer game or song, the audience not only is not a passive audience, but is actively remaking and remarking on those texts with other audience members, very often across borders and cultures. Students from around the world, as noted in the introduction to this volume, are often heavily involved with participatory popular culture and regard these texts as available for interpretation, as well as critique, appropriation, response, and reuse. The new texts created by audience members involve print, but also new media resources including images, sound, and video.

In other recent research I have conducted (2008, 2009) observing and interviewing first-year university students, I noticed that their social networking pages defined their identities through, among other things, substantial samplings and references of popular culture texts. They regarded any website they visited as offering the opportunity for sampling and reusing the material for their social networking pages. Sometimes the students searched for specific images or music to add to a page, but just as often composed their pages from what they happened to come across that they found provocative or entertaining or would represent some part of their identity. Like de Certeau's textual poachers, they were textual hunter-gatherers, always reading with an eye toward what could be taken and reused for themselves. They then reassemble these disparate pieces of popular culture texts into collages of identity "according to their own blueprints, salvaging bits and pieces of the found material in making sense of their own social experience" (Jenkins, 1992, p. 26). What we see when we look at the social networking pages of students from different countries are similar moves of sampling and reuse, but employed in different contexts and read in potentially very different ways.

Remixing and Rethinking Culture and Politics

In the context of global or transnational participatory popular culture, the ability to sample, remix, and distribute new texts raises several intriguing implications and questions. First, participatory popular culture provides an obvious opportunity for far ranging and more democratic contact across cultures. The remix and distribution of mass popular culture content happens not only within a local context, but back to the industrial nations, such as the U.S., that produced the texts. The local uses of popular culture, facilitated by technologies that make it possible for individuals to distribute texts directly across cultural borders, are more available now in communications that flow in almost every direction around the world. Visiting a fan forum on popular music, for example, may put a person in conversation with others from several continents. Such contact makes issues of culture and language always present and in negotiation, whether explicitly or implicitly. People involved in reading and writing transnational popular culture also make connections—and often consciously seek contact—across cultures that broaden their sense of culture and identity. Jenkins (2004) uses the term "pop cosmopolitanism" to describe this form of grassroots cross-cultural consciousness and ability to negotiate online transnational spaces. The practices that Jenkins describes include, for example, the way that Japanese manga are not only read across cultures but also sampled and remixed in fan fiction and music videos across those same cultures, which in turn influences the producers of manga. As Jenkins notes, these contacts moves in multiple directions:

> Much as teens in the developing world use American popular culture to express generational differences or to articulate fantasies of social, political, and cultural transformation, younger Americans are distinguishing them- selves from their parents' culture through their consumptions of Japanese anime and manga, Bollywood films and bhangara, and Hong Kong action movies.
>
> *(p. 117)*

Jenkins acknowledges that this conception of pop cosmopolitanism does not necessarily constitute an explicitly political consciousness that critiques the power relationships in transnational popular culture, yet he also argues that the participants creating and reading all of these texts encounter a broader range of cultural experiences and perspectives that encourage "new forms of global consciousness and cultural competency" (p. 117).

Although Jenkins' caution in ascribing political consciousness to all the activities that take place in what he defines as "pop cosmopolitanism" is well founded, participatory popular culture has also provided a space for the critique of mass popular culture. Among the discussions on multiple fan forums there are often direct and vigorous discussions about the political implications of both the produc- tion and distribution of popular culture texts. Discussions about the film *Avatar*, for example, have included discussions regarding how the film is read politically, from environmental polemic, to critique of corporate capitalism, to orientalist romanti- cized portrayals of postcolonial subjects. Such conversations can include, within a single discussion, participants from dozens of countries. Often the critique operates through parody, such as the multiple fan parodies of films and television created and posted on YouTube and other sites or written as fan fiction. Again, using *Avatar* as an example, there are numerous fan-created parodies of the film on sites such as YouTube, some of which are simple mockings of the film's conventions while others are more specific satires of the film's politics, while still others use clips from the film to criticize events such as the Deepwater Horizon oil spill in the Gulf of Mexico. Participatory popular culture allows for the contested meanings of a popular culture text to become an open and shared conversation. The other explicit political role that participatory popular culture enables is the creation of community through the common text of popular culture. Nadine Dolby (2007) notes how the online conversations and websites spurred by the television program *Big Brother Africa* engaged audience members from multiple countries in political and social issues that reached beyond the program. The conversations that began with the program eventually "ranged from the trivialities of on-screen romances, to discussions of premarital sex, AIDS, the role of women in African societies, and the innumerable shared challenges of many African countries" (p. 469). Online technologies allow fans to use popular culture texts as catalysts for the exploration of political ideas, and sometimes common interests define new cross-cultural communities.

It is this capacity for creating transnational spaces that is perhaps the most important and intriguing issue raised by participatory popular culture. James Gee (2004) has noted that online communities have facilitated the growth of "affinity spaces" where individuals are brought together not by identity or location but by their shared interests in popular culture or other common interests. As Gee has pointed out, online technologies have created virtual affinity spaces for an almost inconceivably wide range of interests. The transnational flows of capital and culture that contribute to global economic systems, as well as global popular culture, create the desire for affinity spaces that bring people from all corners of the world together around popular culture. The combination of affinity spaces and the flow of capital also challenges the political and linguistic boundaries of the nation-states in which people live their embodied lives and, through new media, create new symbolic spaces (Kramer, 2006) for individuals to meet, converse, create, and find community. A group playing or discussing an online game, for example, is not there primarily to find out about embodied identities or material homes, but to engage through the popular culture content first. The "social imagination" that Appadurai theorizes is demonstrated in such virtual online affinity spaces through transnational daily contact and communication. Yet, it is also true that while the affinity spaces draw people in by common interests in popular culture, communication requires negotiations of language and culture. The affinity spaces may have begun and been organized around popular culture, but the rest of culture, politics, and identity necessarily seeps into the spaces and leaks out into the embodied lives of the participants. The result is that participants have to think about and adjust to cultural differences and respond to others in ways that are sensitive to and thoughtful about issues of cultural power and subject positions (Bury, 2005; Williams, 2009). These negotiated communications do happen and provide opportunities for cross-cultural contact and understanding that none of us could have imagined fifteen years ago. Students report meeting people in other countries through popular culture affinity spaces such as fan forums or fan fiction that they soon consider friends and often then communicate with outside of the fan space (Williams, 2009).

One example of how all of these things happen is through hip hop. Although hip hop is acknowledged as an African American popular music form, like many forms of popular culture it had roots in a number of different cultures, from west Africa, to the West Indies, to Irish and Scots folk music (Hess, 2007). What's more, hip hop as it developed in the U.S. marked an important moment in the use of electronic media to facilitate the new music as MCs and DJs scratched and sampled tracks from existing rock or funk to provide the backdrop for their raps. Hip hop culture, then, valued sampling and remixing—explicit textual poaching—well before the growth of digital media. During the last decade, however, new media have allowed for even more robust and creative approaches to sampling and remixing to take place within hip hop. What has changed in hip hop as a result of new media affordances, as with so much of popular culture, is the growth of participatory, cross-cultural contact. Individuals are now not only able to create and distribute songs more easily than before, but they have opportunities to access and draw from a global range of music, lyrics, and cultural influences in their work.

In Turkey, for example, young people engage in a participatory hip hop community with young diasporic Turks in Germany, as a way of both facilitating their work, and avoiding potential government censorship (de Block & Rydin, 2006). In London, Filipino youth use literacy practices online in several ways in their hip hop projects. They record and distribute raps and videos online, drawing not only on music from the U.S. and the Philippines but on clothing and dance moves as well. Just as interesting are the online writing communities they have developed with other groups of Filipino youth in the Philippines and other countries. These groups of young people write, read, and respond to writing—done in a mix of Tagalog and English—using the forms of hip hop to facilitate their creative writing and reading (Domingo, 2011). And, during the recent uprisings in Tunisia and Egypt, hip hop supporting political dissent was created, sampled, and distributed online. All these examples illustrate how an existing popular culture form has been transformed into a participatory set of practices. Even as the mass popular culture forms shape the reading and writing taking place by individuals, digital media have changed the relationship of the audience to the popular culture in terms of both what they can appropriate as well as how they communicate and negotiate with others in the same online affinity spaces. Cross-cultural, participatory popular culture is changing ideas about collaboration, text, and audience on a daily basis.

This is not to say that such affinity spaces are neutral, always happy, or uncontested. Even with the changes and opportunities created by new media, the questions of popular culture, power, and cultural hegemony remain. Mass popular culture continues to be a powerful cultural force shaping concepts of identity and culture. Mass popular culture still requires large amounts of capital and labor and distribution networks that are grounded in modernist conceptions of economics and, corporate, industrial methods. In addition, the transnational participation in popular culture does not mean that issues of essentializing and exploiting the Other are not present in industrialized nations. As Jenkins (2004) notes: "The pop cosmopolitan walks a thin line between dilettantism and connoisseurship, between orientalist fantasies and desire to honestly connect and understand an alien culture, between assertion of mastery and surrender to cultural difference" (p. 127). Just as there are connections made and conversations negotiated across cultures in online affinity spaces, there are also moments of miscomprehension, cultural stereotyping, and insult and anger. Convergence culture does not offer a smooth technological path to a happy, liberal conception of multiculturalism, but instead provides spaces where the struggle toward communication may be at times difficult, chaotic, and tense, but also possible and encouraging.

Traveling Far Through Popular Culture

For literacy scholars and teachers, it is important to remember that literacy practices are at the center of the development of participatory popular culture (Alvermann, 2010; Black, 2008; Burn, 2009; Thomas, 2007; Williams, 2009; Williams & Zenger, this volume). Whether through words, images, or video, new media are changing literacy practices (Cope & Kalantzis, 2010; Davies & Merchant, 2009; Knobel & Lankshear, 2007; Kress, 2003; Selfe & Hawisher, 2004) and changing the ways that writers and readers think about texts, audiences, and language (Canagarajah, 2002; Pennycook, 2010; Stein, 2007). As students bring their abilities to read popular culture texts critically and rhetorically to online settings, they are also learning how to compose with new media in no small part from the popular culture genres and discourses they engage with on a daily basis.

New media and online technologies have led us to the moment where it is easier than ever not only for mass popular culture to cross borders, but for participatory popular culture, for audience-produced materials, to cross them as well. Although the levels of access people have to online technologies, and the quality of their online connections and software, vary widely—though the increasing power of smart phones may be changing those situations—it is still the case that, for many people around the world, the experience of popular culture is fundamentally more participatory and involves more complex literacy practices than ever before.

There are several implications to consider, then, for literacy practices across cultures. First, understanding how students—and others as well—interact with and think about both cross-cultural contact as well as new media technologies requires understanding how they engage with participatory popular culture online. Their encounters with language and culture are often going to be filtered and shaped by the rhetorics and discourses of popular culture. In part this means they will draw from the popular culture with which we have been familiar, such as film or television, because new media reproduce the rhetorical conventions of older media (Manovich, 2001; Stephens, 1998). Familiar rhetorical and narrative structures of popular culture are shaping the discourses and rhetoric of participatory popular culture across borders. Yet there are also the rhetorical approaches sponsored by new media and online technologies that require us to think about how students respond to new discursive situations such as fan forums, online video, or social networking sites. In all instances it is vital to attend to central rhetorical concerns of audience, genre, textuality, authorship, and style. The advent of new media technologies, however, means that students are engaging with multiliteracies on a daily basis and that much of this online engagement with video, image, sound, gesture, and print happens through their engagement with participatory popular culture and usually after they leave the classroom.

Finally, and most important for the focus in this book, is that through cross-cultural participatory popular culture, young people are engaging with and responding to a global audience in ways simply not available to previous generations. Though I am a little wary of getting carried away with phrases such as "world kids" (Luke & Carrington, 2002) or "digital natives" (Prensky, 2001), there is no denying that many young people are in contact with texts and people around the world through the lenses of popular culture. Popular culture provides the rhetorical, linguistic, and semiotic building blocks through which they engage in cross-cultural discourse. They encounter these texts on a global stage, deal with issues of difference and unfamiliarity, and then rebuild them in local contexts. Wan Shun Eva Lam (2006) argues that, while these practices and ideas are certainly shaped by the kinds of popular culture content corporations produce and distribute around the world:

> what we also see is that young people are using these corporate-sponsored materials in conjunction with their local and cross-cultural experiences to create new forms of communities and creative practices. Here developing knowledge, defining oneself, and producing symbolic goods and materials takes place through active engagement with heterogeneous cultural sources and multilayered identifications.
>
> *(p. 223)*

To observe young people interpreting, creating, and distributing popular culture texts across cultures raises questions of how they are thinking about the role of culture in defining the nature of texts, the negotiations of language use, the employment of rhetoric, and the construction and performance of identity. Such questions have implications for our research and our pedagogy, as the other chapters in this book make clear in a variety of places and with various approaches.

The long-standing issues of global mass popular culture, and local resistance and appropriation, are growing both more complicated and more exciting every day. Just as popular culture and its role in our lives and the lives of our students is neither simply good nor bad, so the changes in cross-cultural contact brought by participatory popular culture and new media challenge us to think carefully about what students are learning through their contemporary literacy practices about everything from their sense of control of texts, their understanding of literacy and power, and their perceptions of language, rhetoric, and culture. Students today are often traveling far without leaving home and we should be along on their journeys.

References

Alvermann, D. E. (Ed.). (2010). *Adolescents' online literacies: Connecting classrooms, digital media, and popular culture*. London: Peter Lang.

Appadurai, A. (1996). *Modernity at large: Cultural dimensions of globalization*. Minneapolis, MN: University of Minnesota Press.

Black, R. W. (2008). *Adolescents and online fan fiction*. London: Peter Lang.

Burn, A. (2009). *Making new media: Creative production and digital literacies*. London: Peter Lang.

Bury, R. (2005). *Cyberspaces of their own: Female fandoms online*. New York: Peter Lang.

Canagarajah, A. S. (2002). *A geopolitics of academic writing*. Pittsburgh, PA: University of Pittsburgh Press.

Cope, B., & Kalantzis, M. (2010). New media, new learning. In D. R. Cole & D. L. Pullen (Eds.), *Multiliteracies in motion: Current theory and practice* (pp. 87–104). London: Routledge.

Davies, J., & Merchant, G. (2009). *Web 2.0 for schools: Learning and social participation*. New York: Peter Lang.

de Block, L., & Buckingham, D. (2007). *Global children, global media: Migration, media, and childhood*. New York: Palgrave Macmillan.

de Block, L., & Rydin, I. (2006). Digital rapping in media productions: Intercultural communication through youth culture. In D. Buckingham & R. Willett (Eds.), *Digital generations: Children, young people, and new media* (pp. 295–312). Mahwah, NJ: Lawrence Erlbaum.

de Certeau, M. (1984). *The practice of everyday life* (S. Rendall, Trans.). Berkeley, CA: University of California Press.

Dissanayake, W. (2006). Globalization and the experience of culture: The resilience of nationhood. In N. Gentz & S. Kramer (Eds.), *Globalization, cultural identities, and media representations* (pp. 25–44). Albany, NY: State University of New York Press.

Dolby, N. (2007). The new global citizens: Public life and popular culture in Africa. In C. McCarthy, A. S. Durham, L. C. Engel, A. A. Filmer, M. D. Giardina, & M. A. Malagreca (Eds.), *Globalizing cultural studies: Ethnographic interventions in theory, method, and policy* (pp. 459–478). New York: Peter Lang.

Domingo, M. (2011). Migratory practices in e-learning and e-communities research. In R. Andrews, R. & C. Haythornwaite, *E-Learning: Theory and practice*. London and New York: Sage.

Fiske, J. (1996). *Media matters: Everyday culture and political change*. Minneapolis, MN: University of Minnesota Press.

Gee, J. P. (2004). *Situated language and learning: A critique of traditional schooling*. London: Routledge.

Giardina, M. D. (2008). Consuming difference: Stylish hybridity, diasporic identity, and the politics of youth culture. In N. Dolby & F. Rizvi (Eds.), *Youth moves: Identities and education in global perspective* (pp. 69–84). New York: Routledge.

Hall, S. (1974). The television discourse—encoding and decoding. *Education and Culture*, *25*, 8–14.

Hess, M. (2007). *Is hip hop dead? The past, present, and future of America's most wanted music*. New York: Greenwood.

Hudson, J. B. (2010, August). *State of the College address*. Speech presented at the University of Louisville. Louisville, KY.

Jenkins, H. (1992). *Textual poachers: Television fans and participatory culture*. London: Routledge.

Jenkins, H. (2004). Pop cosmopolitanism: Mapping cultural flows in an age of media convergence. In M. M. Suarez-Orozco & D. B. Qin-Hilliard (Eds.), *Globalization: Culture and education in the new millennium* (pp. 114–140). Berkeley, CA: University of California Press.

Jenkins, H. (2006). *Convergence culture: Where old and new media collide*. New York: New York University Press.

Knobel, M., & Lankshear, C. (Eds.). (2007). *A new literacies sampler*. New York: Peter Lang.

Koh, A. (2008). Disciplining "generation m": The paradox of creating a "local" national identity in an era of "global" flows. In N. Dolby & F. Rizvi (Eds.), *Youth moves: Identities and education in global perspective* (pp. 193–206). New York: Routledge.

Kramer, S. (2006). Transcultural narrations of the local: Taiwanese cinema between utopia and heterotopia. In S. Kramer & N. Vittinghoff (Eds.), *Globalization and media studies: Cultural identity and media representations* (pp. 45–48). Albany, NY: State University of New York Press.

Kress, G. (2003). *Literacy in the new media age.* London: Routledge.

Lam, W. S. E. (2006). Culture and learning in the context of globalization: Research directions. *Review of Research in Education, 30,* 213–237.

Logue, J., & McCarthy, C. (2007). Shooting the elephant: Antagonistic identities, neo-Marxist nostalgia, and the remorselessly vanishing pasts. In C. McCarthy, A. S. Durham, L. C. Engel, A. A. Filmer, M. D. Giardina, & M. A. Malagreca (Eds.), *Globalizing cultural studies: Ethnographic interventions in theory, method, and policy* (pp. 3–22). New York: Peter Lang.

Luke, A., & Carrington, V. (2002). Globalisation, literacy, curriculum practice. In R. Fisher, M. Lewis, & G. Brooks (Eds.), *Raising standards in literacy.* London: Routledge.

Lukose, R. (2008). The children of liberalization: Youth agency and globalization in India. In N. Dolby & F. Rizvi (Eds.), *Youth moves: Identities and education in global perspective* (pp. 133–150). New York: Routledge.

Manovich, L. (2001). *The language of new media.* Cambridge, MA: MIT Press.

McCarthy, C., Giardina, M. D., Harewood, S. J., & Park, J.-K. (2003). Contesting culture: Identity and curriculum dilemmas in the age of globalization, postcolonialism, and multiplicity. *Harvard Educational Review, 73*(3), 449–465.

Morley, D. (1992). *Television, audiences, and cultural studies.* London: Routledge.

Morse, M. (1998). *Virtualities: Television, media art, and cyberculture.* Bloomington, IN: Indiana University Press.

Olson, S. R. (1999). *Hollywood planet.* New York: Lawrence Erlbaum.

Pennycook, A. (2010). *Language as a local practice.* London: Routledge.

Prensky, M. (2001). Digital natives, digital immigrants. *On the Horizon, 9*(5), 1–6.

Selfe, C. L., & Hawisher, G. E. (2004). *Literate lives in the information age: Narratives on literacy from the United States.* Mahwah, NJ: Lawrence Erlbaum Associates.

Shome, R., & Hedge, R. (2002). Critical communication and the challenge of globalization. *Critical Studies in Mass Communication, 19*(2), 172–189.

Stein, P. (2007). *Multimodal pedagogies in diverse classrooms.* London: Routledge.

Stephens, M. (1998). *The rise of the image, the fall of the word.* Oxford: Oxford University Press.

Suarez-Orozco, M. M., & Qin-Hilliard, D. B. (2004). Globalization: Culture and education in the new millennium. In M. M. Suarez-Orozco & D. B. Qin-Hilliard (Eds.), *Globalization: Culture and education in the new millennium* (pp. 1–37). Berkeley, CA: University of California Press.

Thomas, A. (2007). *Youth online: Identity and literacy in the digital age.* New York: Peter Lang.

Williams, B. T. (2008). "What South Park character are you?": Popular culture, literacy, and online performances of identity. *Computers and Composition, 25*(1), 24–39.

Williams, B. T. (2009). *Shimmering literacies: Popular culture and reading and writing online.* London: Peter Lang.

3

CONSTRUCTING "LOCAL CONTEXT" IN BEIRUT

Students' Literacy Practices Outside of Class

Amy A. Zenger

"Literacy is situated," writes Taylor (2000), reiterating assertions by many other theorists who have worked to represent reading and writing as complex social practices, inextricable from their uses in specific times and places (Barton, Hamilton, & Ivanic, 2000; Gee, 1996; Scribner, 1984; Street, 1984). In stressing the situated nature of literacy, social theories counter traditional conceptions that see literacy as a discrete set of skills residing in individual, cognitive abilities. Taking it as given that "literacy is situated," theorists have been challenged in the past few decades to comprehend how current technological and social changes play out in terms of literacies: economic globalization, digital communication, and world-wide migration all have consequences for how we read and compose texts (Kress, 2003; Lankshear & Knobel, 2007; New London Group, 1996). When the space of composing is virtual space, and texts and images flow easily across borders; when individuals and groups of people move with ease from one part of the globe to another; and when personal identities are becoming more and more layered and complex, defining the "situatedness" of reading and writing becomes a complicated question.

Features of literacies emerging today have been characterized in a number of different ways. Thinking broadly about the means we use to make meaning, Kress (2003) notes that the dominance of alphabetic writing is giving way to the use of images, and the medium of the book and the page is gradually being eclipsed by the medium of the screen. Digital technologies foster differences in the kinds of texts that are composed, since they make it much simpler than before to retrieve and to distribute texts of all kinds, and much easier to sample and remix alphabetic texts, music, sounds, and images. While new media have opened up new technical possibilities, they are also leading to the formation and the privileging of new sets of values, sensibilities, and perspectives among readers and writers, according to

Lankshear & Knobel (2007). They describe a distinctive ethos identified with new literacy practices: "The more a literacy privileges participation over publishing, distributed expertise over centralized expertise, ... collaboration over individuated authorship, ... relationship over information broadcast and so on, the more we should regard it as a 'new literacy'" (p. 21). Together, these characteristics and practices of new literacies represent a profound shift in the nature of reading and writing.

To a great extent, new literacy practices are mediated by popular culture, which often shapes the content and form of online reading and writing (Williams, 2009). Popular culture fans go online to read and write comments about films and television shows; compose their own fan films and fan fiction; and perform personal identities in online social media through the "language" of popular culture references (Williams, 2009). In this chapter, I consider the use of new literacies within the context of Lebanon. This study is grounded in two video texts I encountered in the course of my work at the American University of Beirut. I chose the videos because they have been composed using new media, and also because they both use images appropriated from popular culture. Just as important, I was interested in them because of the ways in which they intersected the domain of academia; while both were composed outside of the university, they were introduced strategically to accomplish goals within the educational setting. These two videos disclose the permeable boundaries of academic settings. If traditional classrooms and academic environments do not overtly reflect new literacy practices, these practices, and the rhetorical and authorial values that accompany them, are already implicitly present in the experiences and knowledge that students bring with them.

The large issues shaping our world today have immediate effects in Beirut and Lebanon, inside and outside of the university. Migration touches the country deeply, in that the number of Lebanese residing outside of Lebanon far exceeds the number of those who live inside its borders. Lebanon is also host to large migrant populations, especially domestic workers and manual laborers such as construction workers and farm laborers. While the nation encompasses several distinct cultural groups, multilingualism is the norm among the Lebanese, not only as a result of their political and social history but also by national educational policy, which decrees that all schoolchildren learn formal Arabic, French, and English.

The student population of the American University of Beirut uniquely reflects that diverse population of Lebanon and the wider Middle East. Throughout the more than 150 years of its existence, the institution has been recognized as a space where differences coexist in a region otherwise fraught with socio-cultural and political tensions. Mobile phones, social media, and general Internet use are virtually ubiquitous on campus. While all students must be able to use new media, to some extent, if they are to succeed in their courses, informal surveys of students in my classes suggest that they enter the university with a wide range of familiarity and experience in this area. At one end of the spectrum I find avid gamers, bloggers, social media devotees, and inveterate popular culture consumers. But circumstances ranging from socio-economic challenges, to political unrest, to parental or governmental surveillance inhibit others from having engaged with global popular culture or the Internet to any great extent. Satellite television and legal and pirated versions of films and television shows make current popular culture from around the world widely available in Beirut.

The Student Protest Video

One of the texts examined in this study was posted anonymously on YouTube in the hours leading up to May 19, 2010 when, anticipating the announcement of changes in university tuition and financial aid policies, students at the university called for a strike. During the three days that the strike lasted, normal activity at the university was out of the question for administrators, faculty, and students. Protest rallies and marches filled the common spaces across the campus, and strikers barricaded buildings to prevent classes from taking place as usual. As disagreements arose within the ranks of the protesters, and the administration decided to postpone changes in the tuition policy, the strike ended.

The video makes an urgent appeal to students, inviting them to participate in the protests. The link to the video on YouTube circulated via Facebook. In the video, text and images are juxtaposed in a slide show set to a vivid, pounding soundtrack. The initial slide reproduces the official University Student Faculty Committee black-and-white strike poster, which features a raised, clenched fist, and details the times and places of the first rally (see "Note" on accessing images discussed in this essay). The textual elements in the video offer stark arguments against the planned tuition changes. In one slide, figures are presented to compare the cost of university tuition with the median per capita income in Lebanon, and to contrast this with the tuition/per capita income ratio for an expensive university in the United States. Another slide quotes Martin Luther King, Jr.: "Our lives begin to end the moment we become silent about the things that matter."

Arguments in the video are supported most strongly, however, through the use of images, predominantly stills clipped from *300*, a 2006 Hollywood action film directed by Zack Snyder. Heavily enhanced by computer-generated effects, the film visually acknowledges the 1998 comic book that provided its inspiration. The movie narrates the story of the Battle of Thermopylae, which took place in 480 BCE. In the film version of this event, a troop of 300 Spartans, commanded by the Spartan king, Leonidas, hold off a Persian army of 100,000, allowing the Greek city-states the time they needed to build up their defenses against the invaders. The film glorifies the supposed austerity, democratic values, and military virtues displayed by the Spartan warriors as they are drawn at each turn inexorably towards their deaths. The invading Persians, by contrast, while wealthy, numerous, and powerful, are represented as decadent, effete, and locked passively into a hierarchical social structure.

Though parts of *300* are set in Sparta, far from the battlefield, the student protest video draws on the Hollywood film representation of the battle between the

Greeks and the Persians as a shorthand way to characterize the conflict between students and administrators. In the protest video, images identified with the students' position show the Spartan fighters in the midst of battle. The earthy tones and graphic simplicity of these images underline the harshness of the battle scenes. The ferocity of the film action is reflected in one online comment, which admiringly describes the long, slow motion fight segments as a "ballet of blood done so nicely" (CrassActionHero). One iconic shot in the video shows Leonidas (Gerard Butler) in medium close-up, with his sword raised and his face distorted by a fierce shout. Arrows pierce his bare chest, and in the dim field behind lie the chaotic bodies of his fallen troops. Other images in the video feature the Greek phalanx, with shields raised and spears bristling.

If images of the Spartan warriors clearly stand in for the student protesters, another set of images from *300*—images of Xerxes, the Persian commander and king—refer to the opposition: the university administration. Unlike the Greek soldiers, who dress simply and functionally for fighting, Xerxes (Rodrigo Santoro) appears surrounded by the material symbols of his wealth and power. He is dressed in chains of gold, and his body is oiled, pierced, and ornamented lavishly. Images in which Xerxes is depicted are composed symmetrically and statically, suggesting the inertness of his power, an impression that is reinforced by the subservient attitudes of his minions towards him. A scattering of other illustrations clipped from the web graphically support the video's arguments by implying administrative waste and excess—for example, a photograph of piles of currency, and a roll of toilet paper made of dollar bills.

On one level, throughout the events related to the strike, literacy practices themselves come to define the two positions on the question of the tuition policy. The student protest, which materialized virtually overnight, was organized to a great extent through new media—Facebook, YouTube, mobile phones. Other videos, besides the one studied here, were posted on YouTube to support the strike and to document events through interviews and raw footage, while local bloggers debated the questions raised by these events. Administrators and faculty members, in the meantime, took up the questions in town-hall-style meetings with the various stakeholders, and presented the case in favor of tuition changes through PowerPoint slide presentations, and closely reasoned and spelled out arguments, circulated in memos attached to emails. Differences in terms of "mindsets" that characterize "mere" literacies versus "new" literacies, as categorized by Lankshear and Knobel (2007), map over onto the differences that arise over the impending tuition hike.

For the composer of the protest video, the images from *300* provided a persuasive and readily available narrative that could be tapped quickly for the fast-edited call to protest. The decision to turn to these images points to the fund of knowledge of popular culture that the composer could call upon, and also suggests confidence in the assumption that other students would be familiar, if not with *300* in the original, at least with the genre conventions it shares. For the identifications implied in the video to work, students would need to be able to "read" the Greeks as the passionate underdogs, and to "read" Xerxes as omnipotent, but decadent. It seems ironic—a reversal of logic—for students in Lebanon to identify with characters who represent the West, while alienating themselves from the characters associated with the East. In this instance, identification with the narrative itself, and with the circumstances of the characters, trumps identification with characters along ethnic or cultural lines, a phenomenon that has been observed by media scholars (Gitlin, 2001; Medved, 2002).

Although the protest video draws upon images produced in the West, and all of the text and materials are written in English, it would be a mistake to overlook the local nature of the concerns of the video maker and the student protesters. The poster for the strike includes a quote from the words of Daniel Bliss, who founded the university in 1866: "The college is for all conditions and classes of men." Some of the strikers identified their protest with earlier student movements on the same campus, and they posted a photograph of a protest in 1971 on their Facebook page, an image scanned from *A Campus at War* (Rabah, 2009), a history of the American University of Beirut in the mid-twentieth century. Other supporting documents include a scanned section of text from the same book, and a typed account of events that paralyzed the campus in 1974, not long before the outbreak of the Lebanese civil war.

FIGURE 3.1 "Speakers' Corner," American University of Beirut, spring 1971. Students are staging a strike against increases in tuition. Courtesy of the Department of Archives and Special Collections, University Libraries, American University of Beirut.

In an analysis of "the local" Appadurai (1996) has argued that locality must be understood not as something that is simply *there*, but as a carefully constructed and tended communal project designed to maintain a common felt experience. Spaces are turned into places through myriad, repeated practices and rituals performed by members of the community. Adapting Appadurai's understanding to this analysis of the student protest video allows us to see it as a literacy performance that appropriates globally available sources, and uses them to *locate* the student population both in relation to a geographical region and in relation to the students of the same university in history—"AUBites." One commenter has suggested that drawing upon a film of Hollywood origins, rather than suggesting a vulnerability to foreign influence, might indicate a decision to choose a means of expression that is free of any associations with sectarian or political affiliations inside of Lebanon (N. Bou Ayash, personal communication, February 2011). From this perspective, it might be the global status of the film and its images that affords them their usefulness within this local context, allowing them to appeal to a student population that crosses many different and often conflicting ethnic, religious, and linguistic boundaries.

"My Love"

A second video came to my attention in the context of a required course on Advanced Academic English, for which I was the instructor. One student in the course had uploaded a wispy drawing of a barefoot girl as her profile image on the online course management system, rather than using a photograph of herself, as most of the other students had done. When I asked her about this picture, she told me that it was a character from anime, something that she liked; she had made a video using similar images, and would be happy to show it to me.

Her video is primarily composed of images showing SasuSaku—the couple formed by Sasuke Uchiha and Sakura Haruno, two characters in the Japanese manga *Naruto*, an ongoing series drawn by Masashi Kishimoto and first published in 1999. (Interestingly, the *Naruto* manga is also studied in the context of South Africa by researchers Arlene Archer and Cheng-Wen Huang in Chapter 4, evidence of the circulation of these popular culture artifacts throughout the world.) The *Naruto* series has been animated for film and television, and an English animated version was created for television distribution in the United States. These two characters are fighters, each with special attributes of their own. Sakura is in love with Sasuke, but he is focused on his mission, and does not always reciprocate in kind. The romantic relationship between these two characters has attracted a specialized fan following.

The student's video shares generic qualities of anime music videos, works composed by fans who download pictures from the Internet and create videos with a musical soundtrack. The artistic qualities of the images vary considerably, since some are actually replicated from the original source, while others are drawn in pencil or painted in watercolor by fans, who share their images on fan sites and social media groups devoted to SasuSaku. Unlike typical anime music videos, however, the focus of this student's video is not the anime narrative or characters, but on her own relationship with her boyfriend. Interspersed with the images of SasuSaku are photographs they have taken of each other. Lankshear and Knobel (2007) have observed that rather than being motivated by a desire to communicate information, new media literacies are often called upon to create relationships, a feature that is a strong characteristic of this video.

"Superman," a song by the Los Angeles hip hop artist Brown Boy, provides the soundtrack for the video, and is the common thread that links all of the images together. Text, when it appears on the screen, reiterates more often than not the lyrics of "Superman," in English and in Spanish. At times the lyrics are superimposed on the images. At other times, the text is more personal, and the language is addressed to the writer's boyfriend. In these instances, the words are written in English or in colloquial Lebanese Arabic, using the letters of the Latin alphabet (sometimes referred to as SMS Arabic, because the letters are used for text messaging when the keypad does not have Arabic characters). In the video, the private expressions written in Arabic are idioms expressing love and infatuation.

The video suggested insights into the student's critical academic work, and her academic essays, likewise, suggested a critical edge to the video that would not have otherwise been evident to me. In one academic essay submitted for the course she writes: "This country [Lebanon] is open to the west therefore it has acquired many characteristics of the western culture and life style. The media has played a big role in spreading a wrong, exaggerated and a bad picture about this country which affected women in a big way." She argues that Arab stereotypes of Lebanese women place a heavy burden on them to constrain their behavior, while Lebanese men do not need to worry about similar constraints. Considered in light of this essay, the video can be seen not only as a young woman's love letter to a boyfriend; it also suggests a critical engagement with the representations that others have made of her in the stereotypes she perceives of Lebanese women. It is notable that the images of SasuSaku show the two characters together, embracing, some-times in explicitly erotic scenes, while the photographs of the video maker and her boyfriend always show them separately. In this respect, the anime images can be seen as expressing elements of personal experience that might not be viable for to the video maker to present in the personal photographs.

While popular culture is understood in the United States and other Western countries within a framework that valorizes it as "low" in relation to "high" culture, the designer of this video commented that she sees popular culture as productions "that are interesting for others—not only for one country" (personal communication). Films, television shows, and music originating in Japan or the West belong to this "universal" category, to be distinguished from "old" "Lebanese" or traditional Arab music and other cultural expressions, even those productions that media scholars would identify as Arab popular culture. Her comment suggests interesting shades of difference in the uses she might make of popular culture and the uses a young person in the United States might favor. While the young Lebanese woman's engagement with *Naruto* does seem to share a generational urge among the youth to differentiate themselves from the tastes of older people, she does not really fit the description of a "pop cosmopolitan" either—as the term is used by Jenkins (2004) to define a population of young Americans who are entranced with Japanese manga and anime and who pursue a knowledge of these productions and of Japanese culture, in part as a way to "escape the confines" of local American culture. Based on her own account, her engagement is more opportunistic than purposeful: "I used to watch anime until the satellite guy removed the channel," she commented. In the diverse cultural landscape of Beirut, available television channels ordinarily include French, Armenian, American, Turkish, and Kurdish television programming, in addition to the many channels of Arab media talk shows, news, and entertainment. It is possible that the variety of cultural products, and the variety of experiences available to members of Lebanese society through migration and travel might preclude a similar urge to pop cosmopolitanism from developing here.

As corporate-produced popular culture has become ever more global, fears, understandably, have focused on its potential for domination and the corrosive effects it could have on local and traditional cultures, artistic expressions, and traditions. A stenciled graffiti on a wall near my apartment in Beirut is inspired by this concern: the Disney castle with its overarching rainbow is painted in gray; written in place of the Walt Disney name is "War makes coffins and castles." Jenkins (2004), however, questions classic theories of media imperialism, which "ascribed almost no agency to the receiving culture" and assumed, with very little basis in actual observations, that corporate-produced mass entertainment had corrosive effects on local traditions and cultures (p. 118). The actual picture, Jenkins argues, is much more complicated. Flows of media and images are in fact not one-directional, but multidirectional, and meanings ascribed to images may be "unpredictable and contradictory" (p. 115). As he observes, individuals make "different investments ... in ... cultural materials depending on their own personal backgrounds and intellectual interests" (p. 133).

Finally, the anime music video is instructive in the ease with which it shifts expression between different languages and registers in English, Spanish, and colloquial Arabic. This student speaks colloquial Arabic at home, was educated in a French-language medium school, and studied formal Arabic and academic English throughout her school years. In the university, an English-language teaching and learning environment, virtually all of the work she is expected to produce must follow the conventions of monolingual academic English writing. In the music video on the other hand (a private expression not constrained by the monolingual expectations of academic work), the text is multilingual in response both to the song and to the private meanings she wants to convey. For students like the composer of this video whose identities are layered and multilingual, conventional language teaching, which focuses on inculcating "native-like" abilities and stresses monolingual linguistic achievements, can no longer be considered to address learning needs effectively (Canagarajah & Jerskey, 2009). The New London Group argued in 1996 that the diversity of languages and cultures today makes traditional language pedagogies increasingly difficult to rationalize or to maintain. In the modern era, nation-states have sought to foster a common national identity by privileging one culture and enforcing uniform language standards (New London Group, 1996).

As a composition instructor, I was impressed by the effectiveness and sense of authority evident in the student's anime music video. A sense of personal motivation and investment clearly informed work on the video, qualities that were much less evident in her work for the academic writing course. The student informed me that she had taught herself to use a software program to create the video, and had completed the project in one long sitting, staying up late into the night. "There is a big difference between in school and out of school," she said. "From six to five, I'm one person. When it's over, I'm another person. I just come here to pass the course." Nevertheless, participating in this research project and offering the video she had composed outside of class for me to view indicate that the stark difference she describes between the "two people" she experiences is not irrevocable. Indeed, these actions prove to be yet another way in which this student is using literacy to engage in and affect her environment.

Conclusion

While advocating for social conceptions of literacies, Gee (2000) has called for an expanded view of *context* in these theories, to make room for more interaction between composers and the contexts in which they are working. Gee argues that the contexts in which literacy events take place are too often imagined in a way that is overly static. "Situations (contexts) do not just exist," he writes. "Situations are rarely static or uniform, they are actively created, sustained, negotiated, resisted, and transformed moment-by-moment through ongoing work" (p. 190). By insisting on the dynamism of the context, Gee advocates for a more active conception of composers, for taking into account the person who is speaking or writing as "an actor engaged in an effort to achieve purposes or goals" (p. 190). Gee's thinking is useful for representing the two makers of the videos that have been the object of study in this essay, not as persons who possess (or do not possess) linguistic and genre skills measured according to certain standards; nor as persons learning to succeed within a particular discourse community; but rather as persons who are using the means available to them to design these texts as a way of achieving their desired social aims.

Social theorists and theorists of literacy in the age of new media have suggested for some time now that pedagogies must shift in response to new social, economic, and technological landscapes. Perhaps the most forceful argument for change is still "A pedagogy of multiliteracies: Designing social futures" (New London Group, 1996), an essay that calls for framing students as designers—persons who make use of resources available to them to design new meanings. While the New London theorists see teachers, too, as designers of learning contexts, academic settings are known for being "inherently conservative" (Gardner, 2004). Studying students' actual literacy practices, inside or outside the classroom, however, points to the facts that new literacies have already emerged in response to social and economic changes happening on a global scale, and that our students are often already adept users of new media. In light of this, transforming approaches to literacy teaching and learning can begin by observing and listening to the work students engage in when they are not in class.

Notes

Images discussed in this chapter are readily available online.
The official poster published for the student strike at the American University of Beirut in May 2010 can be seen in "The AUB problem breakdown," a post on *Gino's Blog* at: http://ginosblog.com/2010/05/16/the-aub-problem-breakdown/
Scenes and images from *300* can be seen on the Internet Movie Database (IMDb): http://www.imdb.com/
Specific images discussed in reference to the student protest video can be found at the following locations:
King Leonidas: http://www.imdb.com/media/rm2604568320/tt0416449
Xerxes: http://www.imdb.com/media/rm2470350592/ch0002515
Numerous representative images of SasuSaku can be found through Google Images and on the many SasuSaku fan sites, such as "SasuSaku" on *fanpop* at: http://www.fanpop.com/spots/sasusaku
For one example of an anime music video of SasuSaku see "Shattered (SasuSaku)"—viewed by more than half a million viewers—on YouTube at: http://www.youtube.com/watch?v=S3LSgXOr20g

References

Appadurai, A. (1996). *Modernity at large: Cultural dimensions of globalization*. Minneapolis, MN: University of Minnesota Press.
Barton, D., Hamilton, M., & Ivanic, R. (2000). *Situated literacies: Reading and writing in context*. London: Routledge.
Canagarajah, S., & Jerskey, M. (2009). Meeting the needs of advanced multilingual writers. In R. Beard, D. Myhill, J. Riley, & M. Nystrand (Eds.), *The SAGE handbook of writing development*. Los Angeles: SAGE Publications.
CrassActionHero. (2007, March 31). Forget the Naysayers, 300 Delivers! Message posted to Reviews & Ratings for 300 on Internet Movie Database. Retrieved from http://www.imdb.com/title/tt0416449/reviews
Gardner, H. (2004). How education changes: Considerations of history, science, and values. In M. M. Suarez-Orozco, & D. B. Qin-Hilliard (Eds.), *Globalization, culture, and education in the new millennium*. Berkeley, CA: University of California Press and Ross Institute. 235–258.
Gee, J. P. (1996). *Social linguistics and literacies*. London: Taylor and Francis.
Gee, J. P. (2000). The new literacy studies: From "socially situated" to the work of the social. In D. Barton, M. Hamilton, & R. Ivanic (Eds.), *Situated literacies: Reading and writing in context*. London: Routledge

Gitlin, T. (2001). Under the sign of Mickey Mouse & Co. In N. Frank, N. Khoury, & A. Zenger (Eds.), *When silence speaks*. London: Pearson Custom Publishing. 155–163.

Jenkins, H. (2004). Pop cosmopolitanism: Mapping cultural flows in an age of media convergence. In M. M. Suarez-Orozco, & D. B. Qin-Hilliard, (Eds.), *Globalization, culture, and education in the new millennium*. Berkeley, CA: University of California Press and Ross Institute. 114–140.

Kress, G. (2003). *Literacy in the new media age*. London: Routledge.

Lankshear, C., & Knobel, M. (Eds.). (2007). Sampling the "the new" in new literacies. In *A new literacies sampler*. New York: Peter Lang. 1–24.

Medved, M. (2002). That's entertainment? Hollywood's contribution to anti-Americanism abroad. *National Interest*. Summer. Retrieved from http://nationalinterest.org/article/thats-entertainment-370

New London Group. (1996). A pedagogy of multiliteracies: Designing social futures. *Harvard Educational Review, 66*(1), 60–92. Retrieved from http://her.hepg.org/content/17370n67v22j160u/?p=d56e28a2ebd143948065473bdfeb7276&pi=5

Rabah, M. G. (2009). *A campus at war: Student politics at the American University of Beirut, 1967–1975*. Beirut: Dar Nelson.

Scribner, S. (1984). Literacy in three metaphors. *American Journal of Education, 93*(21), 6–21. Retrieved from http://www.jstor.org/stable/1085087

Street, B. (1984). *Literacy in theory and practice*. Cambridge: Cambridge University Press.

Taylor, D. (2000). Introduction. In D. Barton, M. Hamilton, & R. Ivanic, (Eds.), *Situated literacies: Reading and writing in context*. London: Routledge.

Thomas, A. (2007) *Youth online: Identity and literacy in the digital age*. New York: Peter Lang.

Williams, B. T. (2009). *Shimmering literacies. Popular culture and reading and writing online*. New York: Peter Lang.

4

UNCOVERING THE MULTIMODAL LITERACY PRACTICES IN READING MANGA AND THE IMPLICATIONS FOR PEDAGOGY

Cheng-Wen Huang and Arlene Archer

In the past, certain educators have tended to view popular culture texts as lacking content and not appropriate for academic use. Today, however, literacy researchers are validating these texts, arguing that popular culture texts can provide access for literacy development (Gee, 2003; Rubinstein-Ávila & Schwartz, 2006). We became interested in analyzing manga after noticing its increasing popularity in South Africa, particularly among university students. Manga refers to comics emanating from Japan, which have swept across international borders. The art form has inspired manga-style comics in the West such as "la nouvelle manga" in France and "Amerimanga" in the United States. Conventions employed in manga are distinctly different from that of Western comics. Although its origins are said to date back to the seventh century (Rubinstein-Ávila & Schwartz, 2006; Ito, 2005), modern manga is noted to have emerged in the 1950s along with the flourishing film industry (Kinsella, 2000). Manga's popularity worldwide has come to the attention of teachers and researchers alike with some educators taking advantage of its popularity and validating the text for classroom use (Alvermann & Heron, 2001).

Reading comics involves a set of literacy practices that is very different to reading novels. It involves being able to make sense of semiotic resources which have not been taught through regular schooling. This means that meanings are less standardized and they can be lost to those who are not accustomed to the reading culture of comics. For the Western audience this is perhaps more so with manga, since much of the manga world is constructed around the culture from which it emerges.

Due to the strong cultural nuances in manga, the South African students in our first year film and media class viewed it as explicitly Japanese although some of them pointed out that the storytelling techniques are no longer confined to manga alone. In most cases, they viewed reading manga as requiring different approaches and a "different mind-set." The greatest difference and obstacle noted was the reading path as they found it easy to forget the right to left reading path in manga. When this happens, it causes confusion and hinders the narrative flow. In addition to this, there are cultural nuances that require negotiation. The students pointed out storytelling devices and the manner in which the story unravels as different to Western comics. Because of these differences, some of them regard reading manga as requiring more imagination and input from the reader. The majority of the students point to anime as the text which enabled them to better understand the different storytelling techniques employed in manga. They start out watching anime, Japanese animation, based on manga. Because animes are produced long after the manga, the students turn to the original source in order to keep up to date with the storyline. Besides this, anime also has the tendency to stray from the original as it waits for the manga to fill out the story. Since anime is based on manga, the students suggest this eases the transition from motion picture to paper and enables them to visualize the action, sounds, and plots in manga successfully.

Manga and Semiotic Resources

Our theoretical approach to looking at the literacy practices involved in reading manga is a multimodal social semiotic one. According to this view, texts and literacy practices are socially situated and as students read across cultures they come to develop new notions of literacy. It recognizes that different modes have different meaning-making potentials. "Modes" describe semiotic resources that are culturally and socially shaped for representation and communication, for example, language, image, and gesture (Kress, 2003). In a social semiotics approach, all modes are seen as possessing particular meaning-making potentials. As Kress (2000, p. 157) writes:

semiotic modes have different potentials, so that they afford different kinds of possibilities of human expression and engagement with the world, and through this differential engagement with the world they facilitate differential possibilities of development: bodily, cognitively, affectively.

This approach assumes that texts are composed of a combination of representational resources which are produced in particular cultural, social, and historical contexts.

The analysis focuses on the literacy practices involved in reading manga through the analysis of one particular text, *Naruto*, by Masashi Kishimoto. We chose it for analysis primarily because of its current popularity. Our analysis focuses on two different English translations of this text. The one edition is the officially translated version authorized for publication distributed by *Viz Media*. In this edition various aspects of the text, such as layout and sound effects, have been changed to accommodate the Western audience. The other edition is a fan-translated version, often considered an unauthorized scan of the original. They are usually available for free online and can be found soon after the latest releases in Japan. Manga enthusiasts generally prefer the fan translations since much of the text is kept as close to the original as possible. Layout, names, and sound effects are generally unaltered and translations kept as close to the original as possible. Through a close examination of the two English translations, this chapter will highlight the influences of social and cultural practices on text composition. We first look at how layout can affect our interpretation of text through an analysis of the two translations. Second, we look at how reading paths are influenced by the reading practices of a culture and how this in turn affects the way in which texts are composed. The aim is to contribute towards an understanding of students' literacy practices as they read across cultures. We examine the various meaning-making affordances of modes and the pedagogical potentials of using hybrid popular culture texts such as manga in the classroom.

Layout as Meaning-Making

Layout is an important semiotic resource in visual narratives. Figure 4.1 presents the prologue to the narrative in the fan-translated version. The original version in Japanese is on the left, and the fan-translated version is on the right. It is evident that other than the translation from Japanese to English, everything else is left unaltered.

FIGURE 4.1 The original *Naruto* and the fan English translated version (Kishimoto, 1999, p. 4).

At first glance the page, with its strange yet distinctively foreign symbols, may appear different to the Western eye. On closer examination, however, it is possible to observe features typical of Western literary practices. For one, punctuation marks such as the colon and exclamation marks are not common features of traditional Japanese writing, neither is the left to right reading path. The general layout of the page, the chapter title above and the content of the narrative below, can be said to be based on the Western style layout of novels. The practice of starting a chapter with a number and a title is also a feature of Western novels. While the page layout features certain aspects of Western literary practices, it is clear that they have been used here in a very different way.

In the fan version of *Naruto*, the narrative begins with the chapter title "Uzumaki Naruto!!" Uzumaki Naruto is the name of the main protagonist in the story and the chapter title indicates that the first episode is centered on him. The heading of this chapter title is more decorative than most. The paw icon on the left and the double exclamation mark on the right function as visual representations of Naruto's character. The paw icon serves as a visual symbol for Uzumaki Naruto as he literally has a demon fox sealed within him. Naruto's hyperactive personality is reflected in the double exclamation mark which suggests extreme emotion and energy. In this manner, the chapter title presents Naruto as the focus of the story as well as providing a summary of his character.

In language-based narratives, chapter titles are usually separated from the body of the narrative through white space. In this case, it is separated from the narrative by a frame. This frame clearly makes a distinction between the world outside the narrative and the world inside it. According to Baldry and Thibault (2006), frames provide a "metacomment on the depicted world of the picture" and specify "how the things inside the frame are to be taken" (p. 10). In this case, the frame indicates that the reader is crossing into the world of fiction.

Inside the frame, the center/margin composition of the text draws the reader's attention to the various shapes, lines, and symbols at the center of the page. The image evokes a sense of an ancient and mysterious world. The orderliness of the pattern suggests design rather than chance. The written text unlocks some of this code. There are no frames binding the words to a specific speaker, suggesting the voice of an omniscient narrator. According to this narrator, there was once a demon fox that had nine tails. Ninjas (Shinobi) were called upon to overpower this destructive demon fox. In the end, the fox was captured and sealed but the ninja who achieved this lost his life. Reading the narrative in relation to the image, the symbols come to take on particular meanings. There are exactly nine swirls with their tails all directed towards the center circle. This suggests that the symbol at the center is of importance. The nine swirls can be said to represent the nine tails of the demon fox and the central circle, the demon fox himself. The central circle is boxed in by a thick frame and this in turn is boxed in by other frames. Two of the lines that function as the outermost frames are connected to another circle at the bottom of the page. This circular form appears to hold the frames in place.

At the center of this circle is a Chinese word meaning tolerance, a symbol commonly associated with ninjas. The image can be understood as the seal binding the demon fox in its container.

Although the written text is essential in unlocking the meaning of this image, it forms an integral part of the image. The image is more dominant as a result of its size in comparison to the written text and, importantly, its position at the center of the page. Kress and van Leeuwen (1996) point out that while central composition is less common in the West, this organizational principle is employed frequently in the East. They attribute this to "the greater emphasis on hierarchy, harmony and continuity in Confucian thinking" (Kress & van Leeuwen, 1996, p. 206). The central positioning of the image establishes the mood of the narrative at the outset. The swirls and symbols evoke the sense of an ancient culture, a level of fantasy and mystery. They take on specific meanings as they are read in conjunction with the written text. Spread out on four corners as if to anchor the page, the written mode pins down the meaning to the otherwise abstract image. The role of the image is to arouse the reader's curiosity and the written text is meant to satisfy it.

In the English edition of *Naruto* (Figure 4.2), the layout has been altered which results in a very different reading experience. The chapter title is omitted here and the prologue leaps straight into the narrative world. A possible reason for this is that the title would be seen as redundant since it is stated again in the page after. This translated text is situated in a Western context, and it is perhaps more of a Western practice to discourage redundancy. Kress and van Leeuwen (1996) mention that in contrast to the center/margin composition of texts in the East, Western compositions tend to polarize elements. This is certainly the case here. In this version, the written text is positioned at the top and bottom of the page, encouraging the reader to read from top to bottom. However, in changing the reading path, the value previously attributed to the image is altered. The image is no longer the central element, even though it is still positioned at the center of the page.

A number of compositional techniques have been used to guide the reader to the written text first. The written text is boxed in frames and superimposed over the visual image. This contrasts with the Japanese edition where the writing is framed by the pattern. The visual image is also printed in a lighter shade compared to the written text. It appears as if its function is to serve as "wallpaper," a decorative element to the narrative. This is reinforced by the fact that the written text is in a bold font and runs across the pattern.

By directing the reader's attention to the written text first, the narrative begins with facts. The reader is told there was once a destructive fox spirit who caused great suffering to the people. Ninjas were called upon to subdue this fox and one ninja was eventually able to imprison its soul. The idea of imprisonment is visually supported by the image at the center. After this break in the narration, the narrator continues to inform the reader of the ninja's identity and how he died. A visual symbol for ninja follows the verbal narration. The composition here places the

FIGURE 4.2   The official English edition of *Naruto* (Kishimoto, 2007, p. 4).

written text as the principle element and the image plays a supportive function. This not only removes the mystery from the visual image but it establishes a strong sense of hierarchy. The written text is presented as the facts of the story, and so affords the narrator a strong authorial voice. In contrast, the narrator's voice is less authoritative in the Japanese edition as a result of its position at the corners of the page. By foregrounding this enigmatic and encoded image, the reader's curiosity is aroused.

The reading tempo is another element that is changed through the altered layout of the English edition. By placing the written text on all four corners of the page, the reader is required to follow the narration from corner to corner. In doing so, pauses are embedded in the narration which establishes tempo. In this case, the rhythm in the narrative is created through the use of space. In the English edition (Figure 4.2), the pace of the narrative is established through framing. Frames can connect or disconnect elements of a text (Kress & van Leeuwen, 1996). By boxing sentences in frames, the flow in the narration is disrupted and visual pauses are established.

In comparing these two editions of *Naruto*, it is clear that textual composition plays an important role in establishing the mood of the text and affects the overall reading experience of a narrative. The composition in the Japanese version evokes a sense of mystery while the English edition conveys a sense of authority. It is evident that layout is not a given but socially situated, and that cultural practices play an important role in the composition of a text (Jewitt & Oyama, 2001). On the whole, it emerges that center/margin composition creates a sense of balance and harmony while top/bottom composition evokes hierarchy.

Sequential Frames as a Resource in Visual Narratives

Sequential frames in manga and comic art in general create a flow in the narrative by segmenting one moment in a narrative followed by another. This creates the illusion of the passing of time and the notion of cause and effect. Grounded in Halliday's (1978) metafunctional theory, Matthiessen (2007) proposes that sequences of images may be developed through "projection" and "expansion." "Projection" develops a sequence of images through words usually in the form of direct or indirect speech. "Expansion," on the other hand, extends the narrative through an image. Another meaning-making potential of the frame is its ability to evoke a sense of duration in time through manipulation of the size or the borders of the frame. A frame protruding off the edges is often able to convey a sense of timelessness, while a small frame suggests an instant in time. The length of time conveyed establishes a certain pacing or tempo within the narrative.

The sequence of images in Figure 4.3 follows the prologue. They function as orientation, introducing the audience to the time, place, people, and their role in the narrative. Frame 1 of Figure 4.3 is a wide shot which broadly introduces the reader to the larger setting of the narrative. From this image we can deduce that the story takes place in a village. The electricity wires linked from pole to pole suggest that it is set in modern times, yet the buildings ascribe to the ancient architecture of the East. This sense of the orient is supported by the Chinese character situated at the center of the page. The character means "fire" and it is a symbol that readers will come to recognize as having importance as the narrative progresses.

FIGURE 4.3 Orientation, establishing the setting (Kishimoto, 2007, p. 9).

The reader's attention is guided to the facial engravings and the building with the fire symbol by a number of compositional resources. First, these elements are positioned at the center of the page, emphasized by the shading on the margins. The different shades of black and grey provide depth to the image as well as direct the eye to the center due to the color contrast. The color also provides a sense of realism as it evokes the concept of "light" and "shadow." The roof ridges of the building on the right create a vector, a horizontal line, which guides the reader's attention to the building at the center.

While the compositional resources in Frame 1 guide the reader's attention to the center of the page, it is the representational resources at the center which arouse the reader's curiosity. Even from a distance, it is evident that something is amiss with the facial engravings. The faces appear to have blood pouring out of their eyes and noses; there are spirals on the cheeks. On closer examination, it is possible to make out some writing on one of the faces. This peculiarity cues the reader for some form of explanation and the next frame provides the answer through an "elaboration" of the image; that is, through magnifying the image. By magnifying the image so that the represented elements are seen in greater detail, it becomes evident that these marks are the result of vandalism. The culprit, a boy, is still laughing deviously at the scene of the crime.

Both Frames 1 and 2 in Figure 4.3 employ a framing technique commonly referred to as "bleeds." According to McCloud (1994), bleeds establish "the mood or a sense of place for whole scenes through their lingering timeless presence" (p. 103). The "timeless presence" is created by the frame that goes off the border, evoking a notion of a time without end. This feeling of timelessness is felt more strongly in Frame 1 than in Frame 2 because of the space proportion afforded to Frame 1. In contrast, the presence of time is vividly felt on the next page where smaller and tighter frames evoke a sense of time passing.

As the reader turns the page, the narrative shifts to another scene where the characters in the story are introduced (Figure 4.4). We are told that the boy from the previous page is in fact our protagonist, Naruto. He is a mischievous boy who often causes trouble for the villagers. We are also introduced to other main characters in the narrative, Lord Hokage, the chief of the village, and Iruka, Naruto's teacher.

Transitions expand an image through a temporal or spatial shift. McCloud (1994) refers to this type of image development as "scene-to-scene" transition. This type of transition creates a considerable lapse in time and space and consequently weakens the flow of the narrative (Lim, 2007). In this case, the transition occurs at the same time as the turning of the page. When a page is turned, there is also a lapse in time and the reader's attention is likely to escape the narrative momentarily. It is therefore appropriate that the scene change coincides with the page turning. By incorporating this aspect into the composition of the text, it turns the act into a transitional element. The turning of the page thus becomes part of the reading experience.

FIGURE 4.4 Orientation, establishing the characters and their situation (Kishimoto, 2007, pp. 10–11).

From Page to Screen: Reading Manga Online

For Western audiences, "scanlations" (translated scans of the original manga, made available online) are far more accessible and feasible than manga in the traditional book form. "Scanlations" are done by fans or anyone interested in translating and editing manga. The practice is coordinated through the Internet and translators can come from all over the world. Omanga, Mangaproject, and Mangascreener are a few examples of organized "scanlation" groups. These groups provide websites for readers to read manga online or to download cost free soon after the originals are released. Online mangas are therefore likely to attract more readers than manga in book form. The shift from book to screen, however, greatly alters the reading experience.

In order to navigate manga in its online form, one must make extensive use of either the mouse or the keyboard. To view the next page, a click of a button or a tap of the keyboard is necessary. Even in countries with fast Internet connections, the limitations of HTML means that there will always be a short yet noticeable delay as the page loads. This impedes the flow of the narrative somewhat. Online, only one page can be "turned" at a time. This means that the narrative is read as a single page narrative instead of a double page narrative as in the book form. Once again, this reduces the narrative flow and the story may also appear fragmented. In addition, the online environment does not offer an inherent indexing system. This means that it is up to the website designers to decide how best to index each page. Unless the reader wishes to read the manga in one sitting, returning to the last viewed page can be problematic. This also becomes a problem when one wishes to recap or check previous parts of the story. Without the ability to adequately "bookmark" online renditions of manga much frustration can ensue, particularly with the longer chapters in certain series.

In addition, the reading of the narrative is affected by the shift from book to screen. The screen cannot provide a full view of a page thus making it impossible to hold the complete image in one's eye. A single page narrative is therefore read as fragments. By contrast, the book provides the reader with a complete image of a narrative thus allowing the reader to become more engrossed in the story, as if from a first person perspective. The screen obscures the view, placing the reader at a distance, as if viewing the narrative through a narrow window.

Manga, by and large, is currently produced and distributed with only the book form in mind with a few notable exceptions. The narrative flow, the design of the page and the images are all designed with this medium in mind. While online mangas are more feasible, accessible, and perhaps even more convenient given the enhanced search capabilities of the Internet, book form manga is still the better choice in terms of providing a reading experience closer to the one envisaged by the authors.

Reading Direction and Meaning-Making

One of the most notable differences in reading practices between manga and Western comics is the change in reading direction. While Western comics are read from left to right, manga is read from right to left. The official English edition notifies the reader of this change in directionality with a sign on the top right hand side of the page. This sign also serves as a reminder that the text emerges from a culture different to the West and therefore requires a different set of literacy practices.

The change in reading direction has an effect on the overall composition of the text. As mentioned earlier, textual composition in the West tends to be polarized into top and bottom or left and right, while in the East center/margin compositions are more common (Kress & van Leeuwen, 1996). This seems to apply to the placement of speech bubbles in comics too. In Western comics, speech bubbles tend to be placed on the top while the image is at the bottom. This positioning is said to reflect the tendency in the West of favoring language over image since the top signifies the ideal position and is often read first. In manga, speech bubbles are generally placed on either side of the image, following the right to left reading path. This layout establishes a sense of balance between language and image, speech, and action.

Not only does the reading direction affect the placement of the speech bubbles but it also determines the positions of represented participants. This is clearly evident in Figure 4.4, Frames 8 and 9. The ninja is taking in a deep breath in Frame 8. His position on the left side of the page is crucial for the smooth transition between frames. As mentioned earlier, projection develops a sequence of images through dialogue whether it is in the form of direct or indirect speech. The move from Frame 8 to 9 is an example of projection through direct speech. In Frame 8, the sound "SHF" along with the ninja's body posture suggests that he is taking in a very deep breath. Frame 9 carries this action forward as his words burst through the speech frame. His body posture in Frame 8 serves as a catalyst for the pan to the next frame. In Frame 9, the intensity and volume of the ninja's voice are expressed in the jagged speech frame. This corresponds with his big body movement. Despite the frames dividing the two images, the ninja's position, the speech bubble following directly after the ninja, and the positions of the represented participants, allow a continuous flow in the reading of the narrative.

Since the reading path influences the positioning of represented participants, this also means that the reading path establishes the meanings attributed to positions on a page. According to Kress and van Leeuwen (1996), Western texts tend to position the given, the familiar, on the left side of the page while the new and the unfamiliar is placed on the right. Since one tends to move from the familiar to the unfamiliar, it makes sense to have the represented participants which are the given on the left and the new on the right. In manga, the reading direction is reversed and the given/new theory appears to reverse too following the reading path. For example, in Frame 8, the old man dressed in a gown known as Lord Hokage has already been introduced to the reader earlier on, and is placed on the right. The ninja, on the other hand, is the new character, and is placed on the left. This demonstrates that information value is deeply rooted in the reading practices of a culture.

Socio-cultural Influences on Manga as Genre

Manga is a comic genre but we have shown how some conventions employed in manga are distinctively different from that of Western comics. The influence of social and cultural practices on the conventions of a genre emerges as an important factor for the differences. Luke (1996) points out that "many educational descriptions of 'how texts work' tend to separate analytically ideology from function" (p. 318). In other words, while students are taught the codes and conventions of a genre, they are not shown how the rules function as social strategies for instilling ideologies. Viewing genre as a social practice situated in the context of situation and context of culture foregrounds the social constructedness of texts and genres.

We have already mentioned the right-to-left reading direction in Japanese texts as a key difference between Western comics and manga. Another difference is the greater use of interpersonally-oriented resources in manga. McCloud (1994, 2006) has noted that compared to Western comics, in manga there is a higher level of engagement, or reader participation, and a greater emphasis is placed on pacing out the narrative to create a sense of "being there." The difference in the narrative approach can be attributed in part to the influence of film on manga but also to the social and cultural context of Japan. Unlike Western comics, which have origins in print and caricature drawings (Sabin, 1996), manga draws its inspiration from film. The semiotic resources in manga, therefore, often mimic that of film conventions, for example, point of view, camera distance, and angle. These resources provide the reader with a level of engagement similar to that found in film.

Another reason for the high level of participation in manga is due to the social and cultural context of Japan. In his comparative analysis of Japanese and English recipes, Martinec (2003) discovered that Japanese recipes tend to be "more elaborate in the extent to which they engage the reader/viewer, in the degree of detail with which they represent the portrayed action, and in the explicitness of marking the procedures' stages" (p. 43). According to Martinec (2003), Japan is a country where status differentiation is "finely graded" (p. 61). In a business setting, the client is always treated with respect and every effort is made to satisfy his/her needs. This kind of relationship also extends to the relationship between a producer and a consumer of text. This may explain why considerable effort is made to draw the reader into the narrative in manga where the high level of engagement acknowledges the presence of the reader. Martinec (2003) also notes the degree of empathy in Japanese culture as an additional factor for the high level of engagement. Citing from Lebra (1976), Martinec (2003) writes that "[f]or the Japanese, empathy [omoiyari] ranks high among the virtues considered indispensable for one to be really human, morally mature, and deserving of respect" so a concerted effort is made to accommodate for the other's needs (p. 61). Perhaps this explains the extensive use of resources that highlight interpersonal relations such as close-ups, facial expressions, and other emotionally expressive effects. These resources draw empathy from the reader.

It is thus clear that the social and cultural practices of a society influence the conventions of a genre. This extends to the ways in which modes of communication are employed. The functional specialization of modes derives from their affordances and "by repeated uses in a culture, or by the interested use of the individual sign-maker / designer" (Kress, 2003, p. 46). This means that modes and their specializations are socially oriented and the manner in which they are employed may differ from culture to culture. In the West, logocentrism has resulted in the written mode being well developed as a communicational resource. This means that in Western texts, writing tended to dominate. From Martinec's (2003) research, he found that there was "greater communicative load of the visual mode in Japanese culture as compared with English, and, perhaps generally, Western culture" (p. 65). He attributes this phenomenon to the stronger emphasis on face-to-face relationship in Japan and the nature of the writing system:

> the Japanese writing system, and the pictographic and ideographic characters imported from China (*kanji*) in particular, is certainly a factor in the greater use of images as well.
>
> *(Martinec, 2003, p. 66)*

This indicates that culture plays an important role in the development of modes and their semiotic potentials. As Kress (2003) suggests "[a] culture can work with or against affordances, for reasons that lie with concerns other than representation" (p. 46). In the West, the written mode is privileged at the expense of other modes of meaning because of the belief that it is the "instrument of cultural and scientific progress" (Cope & Kalantzis, 2000, p. 217). According to Kress and van Leeuwen (1996), the written mode is so weighted with the concept of "literacy" that "the move towards a new literacy, based on images and visual design" is "seen as a threat, a sign of the decline of culture" (p. 15). Of course, this struggle between modes of representation is actually a struggle over power and capital (Luke, 1996).

In sum, social and cultural factors play an important role in shaping genre conventions. These include influences on the functional specialization and the functional load in a text. Conventions are social and cultural resources employed by individuals to produce texts for certain purposes. Taking into account social and cultural factors when analyzing a text provides a better understanding of how and why texts work the way they do.

Pedagogical Implications of Exploring Multimodal Literacy Practices

New genres of texts are constantly emerging in a globalized world, where people from various socio-cultural backgrounds are interacting, sharing knowledge, and creating new texts. Texts such as manga are strongly situated in the society in which they emerge, yet they are read by a diverse global audience and constitute international popular culture. Such texts are a reminder of the importance of a metalanguage which can "identify and explain difference between texts, and relate these to the contexts of culture and situation in which they seem to work" (New London Group, 2000, p. 24). We have examined the role layout plays in determining the flow of the narrative, how time is constructed through frames, and the ways in which popular culture texts can reshape our concepts of modes and genres. In this chapter, we have not been able to look at the ways in which manga draws on a range of other semiotic resources, such as angle positions, typography, lines, and shapes. However, what has become clear from our analysis is that different semiotic resources have different meaning-making potentials and each contributes to the narrative in different ways.

In the last decade or so there have been changing perspectives on popular culture and literacy as the pedagogic efficacy of using popular cultural texts in schooling becomes more apparent to educators (Alvermann & Heron, 2001; Norton & Vanderheyden, 2004; Gee, 2003; Rubinstein-Ávila & Schwartz, 2006). Norton and Vanderheyden's (2004) research with second language learners and *Archie* comics, for example, demonstrates how these texts can function to cross cultural and linguistic barriers and allow both second and first language speakers to engage in active class discussions. Popular cultural texts are reflective of ideologies and meaning-making mechanisms of our current society. According to Foucault (1995), "each society has its regime of truth, its 'general politics' of truth: that is, the types of discourse which it accepts and makes function as true" (p. 131). Truth is not a given, but a social construct that exists in time and space.

Texts are always sites of struggle. The struggle for representation and which texts will "count" in academic literacy practices may not have been obvious or challenged in periods of stability but in the current fast-changing and culturally diverse societies, power relations are changing, boundaries between social practices are blurring and overlapping (Kress, 2003; Cope & Kalantzis, 2000; New London Group, 2000). In this changing landscape, it is insufficient to privilege one type of text over another. Accordingly, Kress (2003) suggests that "[a] new theory of text is essential to meet the demands of culturally plural societies in a globalizing world" (p. 120). This should be "an encompassing theory of text" where genres from the aesthetically valued to culturally salient and even the banal should be included in the curriculum (Kress, 2003, p. 120). Since literacy education aims to equip students to survive in a changing world, an encompassing theory of text is in accordance with the needs of current social practices.

In order to survive in the workplace of the twenty-first century, it is no longer adequate to be able to just replicate the rules of genres. As Kress (2003) points out:

> [i]n a world of stability, the competence of reliable reproduction was not just sufficient, but the essence—on the production line as much as at the writing desk. In a world of instability, reproduction is no longer an issue: what is required now is the ability to assess what is needed in this situation now, for these conditions, these purposes, this audience—all of which will be differently configured for the next task.
>
> *(p. 49)*

In other words, what is needed in order to survive in a fast-changing environment is the ability to "design" (Kress, 2003; New London Group, 2000). The assumption is that semiotic resources should be seen as design resources, "designs of meaning," capable of shaping and reshaping to fit the needs of the user. Because manga conventions are comparable to other visual narrative genres such as storyboards, graphic novels, picture books, and two-frame political cartoons, we advocate manga as an effective text to use in presenting the idea of conventions as design resources. This means that the conventions of one visual narrative genre can be used to reflect on the conventions of another in the classroom, even though these are employed differently from genre to genre. The notion of design resources exemplifies the permeability of genre boundaries and the social constructedness of genres.

References

Alvermann, D. E., & Heron, A. H. (2001). Literacy identity work: Playing to learn with popular media. *Journal of Adolescent & Adult literacy, 45*, 118–122.

Baldry, A. P., & Thibault, P. J. (2006). *Multimodal transcription and text analysis. A multimedia toolkit and coursebook.* London and New York: Equinox.

Cope, B., & Kalantzis, M. (2000). *Multiliteracies: Literacy learning and the design of social futures.* London: Routledge.

Foucault, M. (1995). *Power/knowledge: Selected interviews and other writings.* C. Gordon (Ed.). New York: Harverster Wheatsheaf.

Gee, J. P. (2003). *What video games have to teach us about learning and literacy.* Houndmills, Basingstoke: Palgrave Macmillan.

Halliday, M. A. K. (1978). *Language as social semiotic. The social interpretation of language and meaning.* London: Arnold.

Ito, K. (2005). A history of manga in the context of Japanese culture and society. *The Journal of Popular Culture, 38*(3), 456–475.

Jewitt, C., & Oyama, R. (2001). Visual meaning: A social semiotic approach. In T. van Leeuwen & C. Jewitt (Eds.), *The handbook of visual analysis* (pp. 134–156). London: SAGE.

Kishimoto, M. (2007). *Naruto.* Volume 1. San Francisco: VIZ Media.

Kinsella, S. (2000). *Adult manga: Culture and power in contemporary Japanese society.* Richmond, Surrey: Curzon.

Kress, G. (2000). Design and transformation: New theories of meaning. In B. Cope & M. Kalantzis (Eds.), *Multiliteracies: Literacy learning and the design of social futures* (pp. 153–161). London: Routledge.

Kress, G. (2003). *Literacy in the new media age.* London: Routledge.

Kress, G., & van Leeuwen, T. (1996). *Reading images: The grammar of visual design.* London: Routledge.

Lebra, S. T. (1976). *Japanese patterns of behaviour.* Honolulu, HI: University of Hawaii Press.

Lim, V. F. (2007). The visual semantics stratum: Making meaning in sequential images. In T. D. Royce & W. L. Bowcher (Eds.), *New directions in the analysis of multimodal discourse* (pp. 195–214). Mahwah, NJ: Laurence Erlbaum Associates.

Luke, A. (1996). Genres of power? Literacy education and the production of capital. In R. Hasan & G. Williams (Eds.), *Literacy in society* (pp. 308–338). New York: Longman.

Martinec, R. (2003). The social semiotic of text and image in Japanese and English software manuals and other procedures. In T. van Leeuwen & C. Caldas-Coulthard (Eds.), *Critical Social Semiotics (Special Issue), 13*(1), 43–69.

Matthiessen, C. M. I. M. (2007). The multimodal page: A systemic functional exploration. In T. D. Royce & W. L. Bowcher (Eds.), *New directions in the analysis of multimodal discourse* (pp. 1–62). Mahwah, NJ: L. Erlbaum Associates.

McCloud, S. (1994). *Understanding comics: The invisible art.* New York: HarperPerennial.
McCloud, S. (2006). *Making comics: Storytelling secrets of comics, manga and graphic novels.* New York, London, Toronto, Sydney: Harper.
New London Group. (2000). A pedagogy of multiliteracies: Designing social futures. In B. Cope & M. Kalantzis (Eds.), *Multiliteracies: Literacy learning and the design of social futures* (pp. 113–131). London and New York: Routledge.
Norton, B., & Vanderheyden, K. (2004). Comic book culture and second language learners. In B. Norton & K. Toohey (Eds.), *Critical pedagogies and language learning* (pp. 201–222). Cambridge: Cambridge University Press.
Rubinstein-Ávila, E., & Schwartz, A. (2006). Understanding the manga hype: Uncovering the multimodality of comic-book literacies. *Journal of Adolescent & Adult Literacy, 50*(1), 40–49.
Sabin, R. (1996). *Comics, commix and graphic novels.* London: Phaidon.

5
ADOLESCENT LITERACY PRACTICES IN ONLINE SOCIAL SPACES

Jessica Schreyer

With the growing number of adolescents joining online environments, popular culture is increasingly influenced by youth around the globe entering into a common, virtual space. Concurrently, youth are using new literacies online. Transnational online social spaces that embrace popular culture phenomena allow youth from around the world to begin understanding the concept of border crossing. Adolescents shape the discourse conventions in these transnational spaces by participating in online conversations, as well as producing and editing online texts about popular culture. They are creating ever-changing online communities about a common interest, such as comics, games, or books. Online spaces are becoming a primary space where young adults write and communicate with the world. In fact, Black and Steinkuehler (2009) state that "online spaces have become the preferred sites for many adolescents from across the globe to meet, interact, play, and share their thoughts, perspectives, and languages with one another" (p. 271).

Online spaces can lead to the creation of virtual, transnational youth communities. These include social gaming networks, fan fiction pages, blogs, and chat rooms. While involvement in these communities alone will not necessarily enable students to consider what transnationalism means to society, it can provide an entry point for further discussions about how their online connections could be understood in the global context. This chapter offers an alternative approach to understanding transnationalism through discussions of online literacy practices and online youth culture. The essay begins by providing an overview contextualizing transnationalism and online technology. Next, it explores definitions of literacies, including digital literacies. Then, it provides a rationale for why popular culture and literacy practices between youth in various nations should be considered a transnational experience. Finally, I offer pedagogical suggestions to link students' use of online social gaming, as well as the literacy practices surrounding this gaming, to discussions of literacy and transnational relations.

Contextualizing Transnationalism and Online Technology in the Classroom

Vertovec (2009) defines transnationalism as "sustained cross-border relationships, patterns of exchange, affiliations and social formations spanning nation-states" (p. 2). Further, people may be considered transnational when "they have moved bodily across national borders while maintaining and cultivating practices tied—in varying degrees—to their home countries" (Hornberger, 2007, p. 325). In this chapter, however, people are deemed transnational even if they have figuratively, not bodily, crossed these borders.

Although the theory is complex and continually evolving, hints of modern transnationalism can be found in Glissant's 1997 work *Poetics of Relation*. He noted that "Contacts among cultures—one of the givens of modernity—will no longer come across the huge spans of time that have historically allowed meetings and interchanges to be active but almost imperceptibly so" (p. 27). Transnational contacts influence individuals and communities; further, he explained that what "happens elsewhere has immediate repercussions here … today the individual, without having to go anywhere, can be directly touched by things elsewhere" (p. 27). As alluded to by Glissant, Vertovec (2009) described transnationalism as affecting migrants, as well as those who remain in their home nation (p. 15). Vertovec provided a detailed description of transnational practices:

> When referring to sustained linkages and ongoing exchanges among non-state actors based across national borders—businesses, non-government organizations, and individuals sharing the same interests (by way of criteria such as religious beliefs, common cultural and geographic origins)—we can differentiate these as "transnational" practices and groups (referring to their links functioning across nation-states). The collective attributes of such connections, their processes of formation and maintenance, and their wider implications are referred to broadly as "transnationalism."
>
> *(p. 3)*

With the economies of various nations dependent on each other, and communication tools and media enabling people to connect across borders, transnationalism is an increasingly important phenomenon in our lives. Yet, the level and type of participation in transnational activities is dependent on their lifestyles, culture, and access to goods and ideas across borders.

When considering transnationalism, it is important to keep in mind Vertovec's claim that one need not cross physical borders to be involved in transnational events, or to further his claim, to be involved in transnational literacy practices.

Warriner (2007) reaffirmed this idea: "[T]he term 'transnational' can be used productively ... to accurately depict social practices, political processes, and cultural phenomena among individuals who do cross geopolitical borders regularly as well as those who do not" (p. 209). Therefore, while some see transnationalism as only affecting migrants with roots elsewhere, in reality, individuals in cultures with sustained connections to other cultures, including through the media and Internet, may be affected by and involved in transnational events. Warriner continued by noting "that the specific ways that individual people, families and communities engage in transnational processes and practices (including transnational literacy practices) differs according to a large number of factors" (p. 209). These differences do not dilute the significance of transnationalism, but rather demonstrate how crucial it is to examine transnational issues because they affect so many people, both immigrants and non-immigrants alike, in a variety of ways.

An important issue in considering transnationalism, then, is transnational literacy. Transnational discourse may take place between people who are reaching beyond their borders in a virtual environment to communicate with others and engage in common causes and interests. As Dobrin and Weisser (2006) explained, "all of us are members of many different groups, ecosystems, and discourse communities, and the language we use at any given moment can never emerge from one exclusive location or environment" (p. 286). Although students who have lived in one country for their entire lives and who may have had limited or no travel experiences may have difficulty understanding how they may be connected to and enmeshed with citizens of other nations, online technologies provide many opportunities for students to explore these connections. While students may be inundated with news stories and class discussions about global issues, it may be complicated to connect these stories meaningfully with their daily lives. Therefore, discussions about border crossing are often vague and inaccessible to them. However, by pairing students' digital online literacies and popular culture practices with a study of transnational rhetoric, students can gain an understanding of how they are already engaged in border crossing in their daily lives, albeit in transnational social spaces of a virtual world. Transnational social spaces are defined, created, and maintained in a variety of ways. Brittain (2002) described transnational social spaces "as a form of human collectivity where individuals engage in activities and processes (e.g., social exchanges) that link the individuals to multiple localities across boundaries, thus overlapping these boundaries" (p. 15). It stands to reason that these sustained connections may happen online because the Internet allows students to figuratively cross borders and to engage in transnational literacy practices. To some extent, the Internet makes most of us more aware and engaged as transnational subjects.

By giving students the opportunity to engage in transnational dialogues happening online—such as within online social games, blogs, or fan sites—teachers can connect them with literacy practices that are interesting and relevant to their lives. Further, such opportunities introduce students to understandings of how transnationalism is affecting their lives and the world. By incorporating student interests into class discussions, teachers start with what students know, and can help them engage in critical dialogue. This may inspire students to look at how they are crossing borders, or influenced by transnationalism, in other areas of their lives. It may also allow them to consider more meaningful ways to engage with their peers in other countries while they are online.

Students may envision online space as another part of their world, or possibly a world of its own. They may have online friends who they do not "know" in their physical world, and engage in conversations that are out of the realm of their face-to-face discourse. The concept of transnationalism can help students understand the possibility of traveling among these two worlds—the physical and virtual. Hattori and Ching (2008) explained the opportunity inherent in a transnationalist view: "Within a national border, to exist between worlds signifies alienation and exclusion; in contrast, across a global geography, to imagine traveling *among* worlds becomes a space of possibility" (p. 42, emphasis added). The Internet provides so many opportunities to travel among worlds that it is truly a space of possibility. Therefore, transnationalism can help bridge the gap that exists between where people live and the things that shape their lives, whether these are local or global factors, or a combination of both.

McGinnis, Goodstein-Stolzenberg, and Saliani (2007) noted that "technologies and media serve to build transnational social networks and identities, and to enable transnational spaces that center on the flow of goods, ideas, and cultural and material productions" (p. 284). Therefore, transnational social spaces allow individuals to exist within their own nation while also connecting with individuals from other nations. Further, it allows immigrants to remain connected to their nation of origin. Composition and Literacy Studies scholars need to examine how the literacy practices present in online transnational social space are affecting education. Hesford (2006) suggested:

> The global turn necessitates new collaborations and frameworks, broader notions of composing practices, critical literacies that are linked to global citizenship, a reexamination of existing protocols and divisions, and the formation of new critical frameworks in the light of a changing world.
>
> *(p. 796)*

We need to explore these new frameworks of literacy practices, particularly in connecting students' literacies to school literacies. This will make education, and learning new types of literacies, meaningful to students.

New Literacy Studies and the Development of Digital Literacies

In the past, literacy was often conceptualized as the ability to read and write. However, many scholars of literacy have moved beyond these definitions.

New Literacy Studies can be a valuable frame for the understanding that all literacies are bound up with power, identity, and local context. Street (2003) explained that New Literacy Studies "entails the recognition of multiple literacies, varying according to time and space, but also contested in relations of power" (p. 77). Further, literacy "practices are deeply social activities; familiarity with and understanding these practices takes place in specific social contexts, which are overlaid with ideological complexities" (Lea, 2008, p. 230). In addition to recognizing the various social contexts literacies occur within, New Literacy Studies rejects a hierarchical value being assigned to different types of literacies. Rather, Carter (2008) explained, it "necessarily flattens hierarchies among literacies—where one literacy is inherently more significant or valuable than another—as the value of one literacy over another can only be determined by its appropriateness to context" (p. 17). New Literacy Studies scholars believe that "in practice literacy varies from one context to another and from one culture to another and so, therefore, do the effects of the different literacies in different conditions" (Street, 2003, p. 77). When we allow students to value all of their literacies, they can take the first step towards understanding new literacies they will encounter throughout their lives, including academic ones.

Digital literacies emerge from a New Literacy Studies notion that literacy takes on many shapes and forms, including hypertext, multimodal composition, and text messaging. Digital literacies may have some similar qualities to traditional print media, but they also have distinctive properties, particularly in the ability of users to quickly exchange information and to link to other online sources. However, despite their popularity among adolescents, digital literacies are often not valued even by Composition and Literacy teachers. Faigley (2001) noted: "What is overlooked in these pronouncements of the Internet as our salvation or our demise is that significant new practices of literacy have come into existence along with the Internet" (p. 257). With new types of digital literacies and thought processes encouraged in online environments, many young people now "crave *interactivity*—an immediate response to their each and every action. Traditional schooling provides very little of this compared to the rest of their world" (Prensky, 2001, p. 4). Most students are involved in some sort of popular culture literacy practice, whether it includes blogging, Facebook, online gaming, reading fan fiction, or the like. Some lament what online tools are supposedly doing to reading and writing practices of youth; in fact, though, students learn about audience, context, and genre by participating in online text construction. Educators can help students critically examine their textual choices within this literacy environment. In addition, students can learn about crossing boundaries—even though they are digital—to engage in a transnational discourse.

McGinnis, Goodstein-Stolzenberg, and Saliani (2007) stated that transnational digital literacies are "sophisticated literacy practices that allow the youth more freedom in choice of topic, modes and medium, and in their audience" (p. 302). Further, these online social networks "allow for the interacting across borders and boundaries, which can engage youth in more critical inquiries of their own lives, as well as the global context in which their lives are situated" (p. 302). Adolescents participate in popular culture through comics, games, and online activities, which means they are also involved in the consumer culture inherent within much popular culture. However, they also subvert some of the norms of consumerism—including mass consumption of a singular product—by recreating parts of that culture and by lobbying for changes in the product to better suit the needs of the online community. For instance, users in a game may create forums to discuss features they want within a game, and individuals may note that they will quit playing the game until these features are added. Also, users may create "hacks" or add code to a game to create the features they want, even if this is against the user license. Adolescents create these online texts to influence the ideas and opinions of their peers. This online consumption and re-creation of text has transnational components. Lam (2005) explained that a transnational border space of popular culture includes "multiple linguistic and cultural affiliations where the formation of identity reaches beyond the national borders ... and where new subject positions emerge out of cross-cultural exchange and the negotiation of difference" (p. 95). Therefore, when engaging in the online community, students have crossed a border from their physical world to the virtual world.

The Internet is an important tool in communication for youth, and they use it to connect to others around the world. The connections being made on the Internet are changing lives, and it has become difficult for many to imagine living without those connections. Lindgren and Owens (2007) noted that "we increasingly need to use the Internet—arguably one of the primary media of globalization—to understand how every experience of the local is now shaped by global forces, often in ways we cannot see or understand very easily" (p. 209). The authors further question whether individuals can truly locate themselves and their ideals without the help of the Internet. That is a strong statement about its power, and the connections we make on the Web, within our lives.

While an initial result of these online social spaces may be for adolescents to see how they have much in common with individuals from a variety of nations, this could then lead into further discussions about how to bridge differences in order to resolve conflict and create a more peaceful world. Many students are resistant to talking about politics in the composition or literacy classroom, but are eager to discuss their personal interests, whether they be comics, video games, music, film, blogs, or fan fiction sites. This provides an entry point for the discussion of how online literacy and rhetoric can help create transnational connections. Yagelski (2000) reinforced this point, and noted:

> If computers ... are indeed changing how we understand ourselves and reshaping how we interact with each other and our worlds, they nevertheless also reaffirm the deep and never ending needs of readers and writers to construct themselves in ways that enable them to claim some sense of control over their lives.
>
> *(p. 156)*

The sense of finding a place and community, or even nation, within online boundaries is a difficult and complex exploration that there is not room to assess in this chapter. However, I posit that online communities form less around a formal sense of place and more "along lines of shared interests and beliefs ...Virtual communities may even work against the traditional notion of a neighborhood because they provide another alternative to talking with people who live around us" (Faigley, 2001, pp. 258–259). Therefore, while it is possible that online communities could exist at the expense of physical communities, they can also provide opportunities for new literacy practices and for transnational communication, understanding, and exploration of shared areas of interest.

The evolving nature of literacy is making many educators consider how to incorporate the expertise students have in online areas of communication—such as online social networking—with the classroom. Further, while some reject online literacy practices as inappropriate, negative, or even harmful, many are seeing opportunities to connect these with in-school literacy practices. Black and Steinkuehler (2009) emphasized the value of adding these literacies—particularly those related to online social gaming—to student repertoires, and note that the "examination of what gamers actually do during play reveal that *gaming ... is not replacing literacy activities but rather* is *a literacy activity*" (p. 283). Further, these youth "actively and enthusiastically engage in reading and writing a wide range of literary (albeit popular) texts" (p. 283). In addition to youth reading and writing online, these literacy practices allow students to actively contribute their writing to a real audience with interested readers, who may encourage them to continue contributing and improving their writing.

Online Gaming as Transnational Social Spaces: A Study of Pet Society Nation

Online spaces provide sites for collaboration and discussion. Youth are increasingly engaged in gaming culture in a variety of ways. Online programs where youth are active provide "evidence of the complex, multilingual, and conspicuously multimodal nature of adolescents' online literate lives ... it is quite clear that the 'virtual' or online and 'real' or off-line distinction is an artificial one" (Black & Steinkuehler, 2009, p. 272). These social connections bring youth together with individuals from various nations, and they are able to create a virtual environment that would look much like the United Nations. These connections provide opportunities for a variety of learning and literacy experiences. Gee (2007) indicated that "when young people are interacting with video games—and other popular culture practices—they are learning, and learning in deep ways" (p. 215). Further, "Real learning comes from the social and interactional systems within which a powerful technology like video games is played, not from the game all by itself" (p. 215). Therefore, online games allow adolescents to see how they are tied to others, and how they can cross from their own understandings and places into the understandings and places of others.

Online game applications are becoming more and more popular with Internet users from around the world of all ages, but particularly for young adults. This section will examine one online game where adolescents can engage in these practices embedded within Facebook. Facebook itself is offered in 64 languages, and Playfish's Pet Society, which is available as an application within Facebook, has 14,000,000 players from around the world. Pet Society has its own Twitter feeds, website, forums, blogs, and e-mail lists. In addition to its official channels of communication, a Google search of "Pet Society" had over 25,000,000 hits, and a search of YouTube produced over 20,000 hits. Pet Society is a game in which users have an avatar (in the form of a pet) that they feed, bathe, house, clothe, and play with. Further, they are encouraged to visit, give gifts, and become friends with other pets. To make a leap of the imagination, Pet Society itself could be metaphorically considered a nation which users choose to join. Castles (2005) explained that a *"nation* is a cultural community of people who believe that they have a common heritage and a common destiny" (p. 302). So if a nation is considered a group of people who share a common culture, then the pets, and therefore the people controlling these pets, could be seen as belonging to Pet Society Nation. While this is an obvious leap from the textbook conception of a nation, it does help to understand how online spaces allow people to cross borders and demonstrates the point that online spaces may be transnational. The people, as their pet avatars, are crossing or transcending borders of their nation into transnational social spaces on the Internet. This phenomenon can be seen within the game itself, as well as in the game forums and fan sites.

Within the game, for instance, pets can go to a "café" to visit other pets from around the world. Once in the other pet's home, they are able to "friend" the pet. This pet's "owner" shares the common interest of the online game, which is why the two are becoming friends. However, becoming Pet Society friends also requires that the humans playing with these pets not only can see their online pet's home; they are also able to view their new (human) friend's Facebook profile page. Interestingly enough, many of these Pet Society users' profile pages feature several languages (one of which is frequently English), where people communicate with their friends from around the world. Topics range from Pet Society to politics to school. This could lead young people to consider how others view the world, and the issues that are important to them. Therefore, Pet Society opens up new ways for students to engage in transnational literacy practices, and for them to invest in the creation of popular culture. Black and Steinkuehler (2009) described the literacy practices of these online worlds:

> [A]dolescents and adults are engaged with copious amounts of reading and writing as part of their everyday lifeworld; they just happen to be doing it in spaces and with content that may not always be sanctioned by adults. Perhaps they should be, though. There is much concern expressed about youth culture's seeming engrossment in "merely passive" consumption of corporate-owner

and profit-driven content. From that perspective, the virtual worlds of fandom described herein look particularly promising, for it is through such affinity spaces that adolescents, through the very acts of reading and writing, transform increasingly "corporate owner" culture into the "raw materials for telling [our] own stories and resources for forging [our] own communities" (Jenkins, 1998, p. 32).

(p. 284)

While the literacy practices inherent within the online social worlds of adolescents may be under recognized as valid practices by adults, they provide a multitude of opportunities for educators.

Further, while Pet Society may allow youth to connect with individuals from other cultures, and to feel a bond with those individuals and cultures, it may be argued that it also reinforces some cultural stereotypes. Within Pet Society there are outfits, furniture, and foods for the pets to "buy" which are used to represent various cultures. These clothes have included a "tribal" outfit, a "cancan" outfit, a hula dress, a pharaoh's robe, a kimono, and more. Every week new outfits, foods, and other items are introduced. These are meant to be adorable and entertaining, and are quickly snapped up by users. However, while there is a notion that Pet Society is a transnational social space, it also seems to reinforce stereotypes about cultures. While the users are engaging in dialogue within and about the game, and they are creating a unique youth popular culture, they may also be contributing to the nationalistic, and at times, ethnocentric versions of the other cultures. The cultural practice within Pet Society that is particularly interesting to address in relation to transnationalism is capitalism and consumerism.

Online Social Networks and the Frequent Reinforcement of Capitalism and Consumerism

Although games may offer online transnational social sites, they may also serve to reinforce Western values of individualism, capitalism, and consumerism. The influence on consumerism is an important part of the study of transnationalism, because we can see how the exchange of goods and information between nations can affect the culture of both. Consumer culture adds new dimensions to this impact. Grewal (2005) explained new components of consumer culture, and noted that "the evolution of the global consumer and global advertising became key aspects of transnational culture" (p. 94). Therefore, despite the conversations and connections that are happening between members of different cultures, a "global consumer, marked by his or her recognition of global brand names, was identified by marketing agencies as a means to expand markets across national boundaries" (p. 94). Therefore, there are important issues of capitalism inherent in the study of online games as transnational social spaces.

Pet Society is a free application, but the culture of the game encourages players to earn coins (by visiting friends, competing at the stadium, digging for treasure, and selling produce grown in their gardens), shop, and give items as gifts to their friends. Pet Society even encourages players to have a positive influence the world, albeit through capitalistic practices. For instance, there is a "cash store" that allows players to purchase (with real money) virtual items for their pets, with a portion of the proceeds supporting the World Wildlife Fund. Therefore, the players obtain items for their pet while also donating money to charity. Further, players are also encouraged to "gift" items to their friends, which again reinforces friendships and ties among players, but through capitalistic means. The values supported by Pet Society are decidedly about consumerism. In fact, many of the discussion boards about Pet Society feature users attempting to buy or trade rare items from other players. Even with the presence of these capitalistic ideals, which are inherent within the game, ultimately users have— through their literacy practices—made Pet Society a place around which to make friends, create text, and bridge national divides. They have created blogs in which to discuss Pet Society, forums where users post in a variety of languages, and videos of their pets making friends with pets from around the world.

Despite the connections happening between adolescents, Grewal (2005) described how certain types of lifestyle can become normalized, even across cultures, as the "lifestyles of those within the nation-state become transnationalized across many national boundaries" (p. 90). Therefore, just because a person is not physically migrating across borders does not mean that her or his life is not affected by transnational markets. Global products, online social games included, may "sell" certain values to individuals across cultures. Grewal continued:

> Since market segmentation in the United States has used gender, race, ethnicity, and multiculturalism to sell products, and since products cross national boundaries, multiculturalism has also become transnationalized through global marketing practices by transnational corporations based in the United States ... Multiculturalism, as it was understood in the United States, was no longer solely a claim on civil rights but now a neoliberal corporate project of selling goods to a transnational consumer culture connecting many national identities. Within this project, multiculturalism also circulated as consumer culture in which immigrants created negotiated lifestyles from the "American lifestyle" that was so much a part of capitalist formation in the United States.
>
> *(p. 91)*

Providing a critical framework toward the positive and negative aspects of online social gaming practices in terms of a healthy transnational perspective offers many opportunities for discussion in composition and literacy classrooms.

Connecting Pedagogy to Online Youth Popular Culture and Social Practices

Popular culture offers an engaging way to begin discussions about transnational social spaces, literacy, and relations in the composition or literacy classroom. This pedagogy can be a way to help students bridge the gap between the traditionally nationalistic discourses so common in American culture. There are many implications and opportunities for teaching about consumerism, diverse literacies, and transnationalism using online gaming as a starting point. The youth engaged in online social spaces are not passive readers and writers, they are actively engaged. Rhodes and Robnolt (2009) noted that "the very relationship of author and reader has become muddied as readers create written work for mass consumption and contribute to the revision of online text" (p. 155). Many of the textual environments that surround online social gaming and a variety of other online environments encourage people to write together, as well as to update text, pictures, and graphics as needed to participate in the online gaming environment. These can be intriguing contexts through which to discuss collaborative authorship, as well as to examine varying senses of textual ownership across cultures. Further, online literacy practices are inherently social in that a variety of people are contributing, reading, and engaging in the texts. It is important to understand the broader context in which any type of literacy is situated; Gee (2007) explained, "Literacy in any domain is actually not worth much if one knows nothing about the social practices of which that literacy is but a part" (p. 18). Providing connections to the literacy practices that adolescents are already engaged in can help teachers use these environments to encourage students to make cross-cultural connections and to see how literacy practices vary from nation to nation, particularly when people are participating in transnational social spaces.

In these spaces, students are connecting with others, and are finding venues for their work. By communicating and publishing online they "have an integral, real connection to the global community. … incorporating digital literacy into the classroom can have important benefits by providing socially meaningful experiences for students" (Rhodes & Robnolt, 2009, p. 165). These communities provide valuable places for students to examine how literacies and popular culture are influenced by online communications, particularly within social gaming communities. Also, while online gaming itself may not make transnational connections transparent to students, they may begin to understand that there are a variety of people from a variety of nations engaged in conversations about the same topic. For instance, when students see a mixture of languages on a website they are interested in, this reinforces the fact that their object of interest is being discussed in languages possibly unknown to them, and that the language practices of individuals writing from that position may be quite different from their own. Therefore, online games can provide a non-threatening entrance to this discussion. From there, students may be able to engage in thinking about and considering the "Other." Gay (2004) said, "To engage in reflexive dialogue requires critical listening—to imagine yourself as the Other, to look, *really* look, at an Other's point of view, which requires suspending your 'I' for a little while. … The classroom, however, can be a space for the beginning of dialogue" (p. 237).

Ultimately, educators need to take opportunities to begin where students are, and to connect that with the critical thinking and understanding they are trying to promote. McGinnis, Goodstein-Stolzenberg, and Saliani (2007) stated that "educators need to consider the role transnationalism plays in the literacies and identities of their students, and view students as knowledgeable and active members of this fast-changing global culture" (p. 302).

Discussions of students' online activities, whether they are participating in fan worlds, online gaming, blogging, Internet chatting, Facebook, or the like, provide so many opportunities for the discussion of how texts are read within, as well as across, national borders. Texts are increasingly becoming global, which leads to important questions about how other nations' citizens influence the text that is created, as well as the multiple ways texts may be read. Queen (2008) explained that educators "must make visible the ways in which all of our knowledge is mediated—technologically, historically, geopolitically, culturally—and how profoundly that knowledge shapes, but also can be changed, by our encounters with others, down the block and across the globe" (p. 486). When we realize that our knowledge is created both within and across national borders, we open ourselves and our students to the idea that we are truly engaged in transnational communication. We have our feet planted within a nation, but we are influenced by other nations as well. We cannot ignore the positive and negative things that happen as globalization, in terms of the transnational movement of capital and culture, continues. Online social gaming can provide a peek at how consumerism can become pervasive, even when youth collaborate with people from other nations. However, it provides an enticing entry point to discuss multiple literacies. As Rallin (2004) explained, these types of discussions can help for "moving beyond local worlds, making connections, and constantly negotiating with the global in terms of accountability, responsibility, action" (p. 149). The online literacy practices of students are dynamic, interesting, and complex; by incorporating digital literacies into the curriculum, instructors offer new and innovative ways to connect students' interests with academic pursuits and conversations.

References

Black, R. W., & Steinkuehler, C. (2009). Literacy in virtual worlds. In L. Christenbury, R. Bomer, & P. Smagorinsky (Eds.), *Handbook of adolescent literacy research* (1st ed., pp. 271–286). New York: The Guilford Press.

Brittain, C. (2002). *Transnational messages: Experiences of Chinese and Mexican immigrants in American schools.* New York: LFB Scholarly Pub LLC.

Carter, S. (2008). *The way literacy lives: Rhetorical dexterity and basic writing instruction.* Albany, NY: State University of New York Press.

Castles, S. (2005). Citizenship and the other in the age of migration. In P. Spencer & H. Wollman (Eds.), *Nations and nationalism: A reader* (pp. 301–316). New Brunswick, New Jersey: Rutgers University Press.

Dobrin, S. I., & Weisser, C. R. (2006). Breaking ground in ecocomposition: Exploring relationships between discourse and environment. In P. Vandenberg, S. Hum, & J. Clary-Lemon (Eds.), *Relations, locations, positions: Composition theory for writing teachers* (pp. 258–290). Urbana, IL: NCTE.

Faigley, L. (2001). Understanding popular digital literacies: Metaphors for the Internet. In J. Trimbur (Ed.), *Popular literacy: Studies in cultural practices and poetics* (pp. 248–264). Pittsburgh, PA: University of Pittsburgh Press.

Gay, P. (2004). The politics of location: Using flare-ups to spark "reflexive dialogue" in the ever-changing classroom text. In A. Lunsford & L. Ouzgane (Eds.), *Crossing borderlands: Composition and postcolonial studies* (pp. 218–237). Pittsburgh, PA: University of Pittsburgh Press.

Gee, J. P. (2007). *What video games have to teach us about learning and literacy* (2nd ed.). New York: Palgrave Macmillan.

Glissant, E. (1997). *Poetics of relation.* Ann Arbor, MI: University of Michigan Press.

Grewal, I. (2005). *Transnational America: Feminisms, diasporas, neoliberalisms.* Durham, NC: Duke University Press Books.

Hattori, T., & Ching, S. (2008). Reexamining the between-worlds trope in cross-cultural composition studies. In L. Mao & M. Young (Eds.), *Representations: Doing Asian American rhetoric* (pp. 41–61). Logan, UT: Utah State University Press.

Hesford, W. (2006). Global turns and cautions in rhetoric and composition studies. *PMLA, 121*(3), 787–801.

Hornberger, N. H. (2007). Biliteracy, transnationalism, multimodality, and identity: Trajectories across time and space. *Linguistics and Education, 18*(3–4), 325–334.

Lam, W. S. E. (2005). Border discourses and identities in transnational youth culture. In J. Mahiri (Ed.), *What they don't learn in school* (pp. 79–97). New York: Peter Lang Publishing.

Lea, M. (2008). Academic literacies in theory and practice. In B. V. Street & N. H. Hornberger (Eds.), *Encyclopedia of language and education* (2nd ed., pp. 227–238). New York: Springer.

Lindgren, T., & Owens, D. (2007). From site to screen, from screen to site: Merging place-based pedagogy with web-based technology. In C. J. Keller & C. R. Weisser (Eds.), *The locations of composition* (pp. 195–214). State University of New York Press.

McGinnis, T., Goodstein-Stolzenberg, A., & Saliani, E. C. (2007). "indnpride": Online spaces of transnational youth as sites of creative and sophisticated literacy and identity work. *Linguistics and Education, 18*(3–4), 283–304.

Prensky, M. (2001). Digital natives, digital immigrants, part II: Do they really think differently? *On the Horizon, 9*(6), 1–9.

Queen, M. (2008). Transnational feminist rhetorics in a digital world. *College English, 70*(5), 471–489.

Rallin, A. (2004). (Im)migrant crossings. In A. Lunsford & L. Ouzgane (Eds.), *Crossing borderlands: Composition and postcolonial studies* (pp. 143–156). Pittsburgh, PA: University of Pittsburgh Press.

Rhodes, J., & Robnolt, V. (2009). Digital literacies in the classroom. In L. Christenbury, R. Bomer, & P. Smagorinsky (Eds.), *Handbook of adolescent literacy research* (pp. 153–169). New York: Guilford Press.

Street, B. (2003). What's "new" in New Literacy Studies? Critical approaches to literacy in theory and practice. *Current Issues in Comparative Education, 5*(2), 77–91.

Vertovec, S. (2009). *Transnationalism.* London: Routledge.

Warriner, D. (2007). Transnational literacies: Immigration, language learning, and identity. *Linguistics and Education, 18*(3–4), 201–214.

Yagelski, R. P. (2000). *Literacy matters: Writing and reading the social self.* New York: Teachers College Press.

6

THE "POPULAR" TURKISH ACADEMY

Tüge T. Gülşen

Education is a social and cultural process that enhances the knowledge of young people regarding the requirements for both being a member of a certain society and being integrated into the complex structure of the whole society. While schooling has always been considered a continuation of the present social order and its cultural patterns in institutionalized forms and practices, today Turkish students seem to shift between two different worlds of reality and find it even more difficult to relate what they experience and learn in school with their out-of-school experiences. The tension between school and culture outside the classroom has become even more complicated in higher education. With the rise of digital technology that directly influences educational practices globally, young people's literacy experiences have been transformed in Turkey. Moreover, the everyday social and cultural practices of Turkish students in the academy, who are participants in the popular culture shared and (re)constructed globally, have taken on new forms and functions that lead to different learning experiences and which manifest themselves in different educational expectations and cognitive, affective, and creative potentials.

This paper is an attempt by a teacher who has been part of the Turkish academy for twelve years to find a way to take students out of this conflict and to propose another approach, one that can bridge the gap between students' real-life learning experiences and academic learning. It is a compelling question, whether the products of popular culture can provide an alternative terrain where Turkish academics—who find the new generation "different"— could find resources and methods to make both teaching and learning more effective.

Learning Outside School in the New Information Age

Today, Turkish children and teenagers are part of a borderless global popular culture and are consumers of the commodities that are produced by and carried with that culture. In education, the main actors have transformed into new transnational individuals who encounter, produce, reproduce, and circulate multimodal texts in their everyday learning experiences and literacy practices.

With digital technology shared and used globally, the children and youth in Turkey not only use mass media but also participate in the production and distribution of cultural texts. Even far before they have received any schooling, children are highly competent in using not only personal computers, but also the Internet. Such a generation starts primary school with a vast range of linguistic and non-linguistic signs, in Turkish and in English, obtained via digital resources and stored in their memories. Today's children have become like walking cameras that are highly audio-visual. As a result, an infant in Turkey is likely to be able to interpret the linguistic sign "WC," which is not even Turkish, and the non-linguistic sign "portraits of a lady and a gentleman" on the door to a restroom. Such examples illustrate how children attain a great degree of literacy before school in visual representations.

Pre-school education, which used to be seen as a child caring period only for working mothers in Turkey, is undergoing a change accordingly. Compulsory pre-school education has already started being piloted in certain cities, and it will soon be compulsory for all children in Turkey. The state schools are establishing their pre-school units now, while private pre-school education has been a huge market in Turkey for a very long time. The private schools, which serve the needs of parents and children with better economic opportunities, are in such strong competition with each other that they do their best to attract their "customers" with highly advanced technology integrated into their curriculums. It is important to note that the students and their learning environment portrayed in this paper cannot be generalized to the ones in all mainstream state schools in Turkey, because the majority of state schools do not have enough funds to introduce technology into the curriculum, and they cannot provide children with the opportunities to develop their digital literacy skills. Moreover, the social and economic status of children is another important factor that affects their literacy development outside of schools. The differences could be another piece of future research to be conducted. Still, the multimodal materials and resources support a great number of children in that they are capable of using multimedia from very early ages.

Schooling starting from pre-school education, as the secondary socialization, takes different forms today. Even nursery schools have become terrains of global popular culture in Turkey. As children grow up, not only the modes and means, but also the popular representations and commodities change. The experience is the same; the products simply change. Students take on their new mediated identities, which are rather temporary but are always replaced by new ones, and they are part of the virtual societies, the new semiotic domains. Students are after new meanings and identities in social networking websites, and they can freely express their opinions and feelings in blogs, where they have already constructed a different language and discourse.

The digital world, wherever it is accessible, creates a new culture among both children and the youth. Certainly, it is important to note that the digital world is accessible only for the ones who are at a certain social and economic level, and, in Turkey, as in other parts of the world, not all children have the same opportunities. Children's preference of games is specifically illustrative. Walking in the streets in different districts of Istanbul, one can observe that even the games of children differ according to the socio-economic levels of the neighborhood. In the suburbs, one generally observes that children play in the streets, and their games are usually traditional ones like hide-and-seek, blind man's bluff, stuck in the mud, etc. In wealthy neighborhoods, by contrast, one can hardly see children playing in the streets, because they are usually sent to well equipped, specialized, high-tech institutions to keep up with the highly competitive education market, or taken to cinemas or shopping malls, where digital, mechanical toys are offered, or to amusement parks, where they spend their time playing with expensive popular toys in groups. Despite this inequality, today the Internet cafés (which are at stake because teenagers could have access to illegal websites or to games through which they could make money) and digital, satellite TVs are available to a great number of young people from different social and economic classes. One way or another, at different levels, they are part of the global culture, which reflects a "Western" production of the commodities of popular culture. Today, Turkish children at very early ages learn to see and understand images on screens, choose their preferences among global commodities, and decide to click or not to click on, drag or not to drag images. Their cognitive skills are developed accordingly; simply, their minds work quite differently than the minds of previous generations. My experience with my 4-year-old son is a relevant example to show how children attribute meaning to their world of reality. Marshmallows used to be uncommon in our childhood in Turkey, but as I was born in Germany they were part of my childhood. As my son was eating marshmallows, I said I used to love them when I was a child. He got really excited and asked if his grandpa was grilling marshmallows in the camp site, which is part of American and Canadian culture, but not Turkish. He was trying to adapt his favorite cartoon character *Caillou*'s experience to his culture and this was part of his learning of the world, which is not easy to define from a local perspective any more.

This picture of the new digital generation is certainly in the center of educational debates. Education today has to offer opportunities to attain digital skills which are "beyond the simple motor task of hitting keys with precision and speed" (Battro, 2004, p. 80) and require complex cognitive skills. Contrary to the many mainstream arguments that multimedia traps children in an unreal virtual world, causes them to have shorter attention spans, and hinders their individual social development, there are also strong views that through effective critical media literacy education, multimedia and online practices could benefit the development of young people (Battro, 2004; Gee, 2003; Davies & Whittaker, 1997; Sanger, Willson, Medeni, Miyata, & Sağsan, 2009; Stack & Kelly, 2006). Similarly, although the media is full of popular "superheroes" in violent cartoons, the popular TV channels still mass market alternative "heroes" such as *Dora and Diego* who involve the audience in their adventures to save the Earth, or *Caillou* who has the natural flaws, desires, and hopes of any 3 year old in the world.

Turkish children with such a rich potential can make use of various strategies and modes to achieve a task; however, as they proceed and enter the world of the academy, they do not seem to use these strategies and modes to achieve better because the Turkish academy requires different literacy skills that do not match their previous experiences.

Learning in the Academy

The children of the information age are surrounded by the digital resources and multimedia learning resources which they can make use of out of school, but such means are still not considered in mainstream education. It is evident that the research on literacy in Turkey still fails to adequately define the term *literacy* in the information age, because it neglects what students watch on television and what they read or do with computers. Literacy practices are confined to reading and understanding printed books only, and online academic resources, e-books, and databases are left out. In a recent article, university students' literacy practices were evaluated based on their reading of printed books. The findings indicated that the students spent almost half of their time watching television, listening to music, and using computers rather than "reading." Yet the article did not address what literacy practices students engaged in with computers (Odabaş, Odabaş, & Polat, 2008). Another research study conducted by Dengiz and Yılmaz in 2007 on habits of reading and library use in a number of primary schools in Ankara revealed that researchers still regarded libraries as places where students read printed books only.

Consequently, there is a mismatch between students' everyday literacy practices and formal schooling. Students are expected to read, understand, analyze, and internalize knowledge through printed books where the only alternative mode of representation is pictures, graphs, diagrams, etc. They have to confront the difficulty of adjusting their cognitive potential, shaped by multimodality, to a limited source of representations. Moreover, coming to university requires a wide range of new negotiations of other kinds by students. Becoming a university student is a difficult period of adaptation to a new micro-society that has its own rules, regulations, culture, and social practices, made even more challenging because the new approaches to children's education seem to be neglected in higher education in Turkey.

Education has already been seen as a scientific area in Turkey, but the main and only goal of the faculties of education is still defined as the education of prospective teachers (Erdem, 2008). Instead of faculties of education taking an active role in developing new teaching and learning methodologies, techniques, and alternative innovative curriculums to enhance quality learning in all educational terrains, they educate teachers to continue the status quo, without working on innovation. The issues of learning and teaching are not still handled by the experts on education in higher education in Turkey. No matter how new students are to the academic world, learners in higher education are treated like "expert" learners who can automatically grasp the concepts and whose cognitive development has already been completed. However, recent research conducted in the Institute of Cognitive Neuroscience, University College London, revealed that, contrary to previous findings that the human mind completes its cognitive development by the age of four, teenagers' brains continue developing far longer, into late adolescence and adulthood (Dumontheil, Apperly, & Balkemore, 2010). This research indicates that cognitive development from childhood to adulthood must be taken into consideration while designing curriculums. Thus, young people who start universities need to be approached with innovative pedagogic methods if they are to achieve more highly and complete their cognitive development.

Turkish students have to confront the high expectations of academics, who often neglect the fact that they still have to provide a learning environment for their students. Also, a great many academics in Turkey with whom I have had the opportunity to discuss this matter, take the term *pedagogy* as the study of children's learning only and neglect the fact that education, which also embraces higher education, is a science that requires certain methods and research. Learning and teaching, a step-by-step process at all levels, requires systematic design to attain deep learning. *Learning* involves not only gaining information but also internalizing it, so that the learner can retrieve and adapt the information when it is needed, a process which requires more than just memorizing. At the same time *teaching* goes beyond transmitting information from teachers to learners, to implementing a systematic programming that builds information in learners' minds step by step, helping them gain *knowledge* that they have processed, internalized, and possessed themselves.

Academics' intentions to stand in their students' shoes are generally limited to *their own* individual learning experiences, which could be very different from that of their students. There is an urgent need for a new academic environment in Turkey, where academics are expected not only to master their subject matter but also to become aware of the educational needs of learners.

Popular Culture in Education

Popular culture has always been in the center of the social, cultural, economic, and educational debates in Turkey. To discuss whether popular culture can provide a terrain where academics could find alternative methods and techniques for more effective education, it is essential to clarify how this paper views popular culture. Popular culture, which Grossberg (1992) describes as "merely the 'stuff' of every-day life" (p. 308), is taken as "a site of struggle, but, while accepting the power of the forces of dominance, it focuses rather upon the popular tactics by which these forces are coped with, are evaded or are resisted" and it "attempts to understand the everyday resistances and evasions that make the ideology work so hard and to maintain itself and its values" (Fiske, 1996, pp. 20–21). Thus, popular culture, which is "potentially, and often actually, progressive (though not radical)" (Fiske 1996, p. 21), is seen as the area where "the representation of social forces and values and the experience of them in everyday life" meet (Fiske, 1996, p. 133). These are the everyday practices out of which the encoder first produces meaning and then the audience (or decoder) produces and reproduces meanings in relation to other discourses. This is not to endorse the undeniably manipulative effect of commod-ities of popular culture, on young people especially, but it is rather an acceptance of the presence and reality of popular culture as part of the youth culture. The issue is how to find ways to utilize popular culture content and strategies in the area of education, because popular culture is the space where young people learn about and (re)construct the world of reality.

In the university, academic knowledge is considered to be "high" knowledge whereas knowledge gained from everyday practices engaged with the popular is regarded as "low." The Turkish academy seems to be far from the discussions around the place of the popular in education. There is little discussion of *critical pedagogy*, which criticizes traditional and progressive pedagogy for valuing the dominant culture's belief systems, and not considering the lower classes' and minority groups' values, and emphasizes "empowering" the disadvantaged in formal schooling. As part of critical pedagogy, several studies (e.g. Cook-Gumperz, 1986; Kress, 1994, 1997; Street, 1984, 1995) handle the issue of literacy development in relation to the social and cultural environment surrounding individuals, in which they practice literacy rather than using it as an instrument for the development of cognitive skills. So, literacy requires the questioning of the social and cultural variables surrounding literacy practices. That is, literacy practices are social acts of individuals, which shape and are shaped by the social and cultural environment surrounding them, and the individuals' own social backgrounds play a significant role in the process of making meaning through texts. Education then requires a curriculum that aims to teach socially organized knowledge.

While, in Turkey, literacy studies is an area that is often neglected and critical literacy has not been widely studied in the local context, outside of Turkey media literacy studies have mostly focused on mainstream education[1] or the field of ELT[2] so far, and have left higher education out. Turkish media studies researchers[3] have introduced the concepts of "media literacy" and "popular culture pedagogy," but the issue is still quite new. Media literacy education in Turkey started with an agreement between the Ministry of National Education and The Radio and

Television Supreme Council (RTÜK) in 2006, and a media literacy course started to be piloted in certain primary schools. In the following academic year, it became an elective course for grades 6, 7, and 8. The Ministry of Education has announced that the implementation will take place in almost all schools in Turkey. However, there are still numerous problems to overcome. First, the course is still an elective, so not many students take it. Second, there are no well-prepared course books available. Third, the teachers teaching the course are social sciences teachers rather than media specialists who hold teaching certificates. Finally, the content of the course focuses primarily on protecting children from the negative effects of media rather than creating a critical awareness of cultural texts and a critical approach to media.

Although the media literacy courses are at the center of the discussions about academic courses in Turkish universities, it seems that it is not one of the short-term goals of higher education in Turkey. And while higher education is to be perceived as a continuation of the social and academic development of young people, there seem to be two phases of students' education: Before Academy and After Academy. When young people enter university campuses, they are regarded by faculty as expert learners who are isolated from their cultural identities and cognitive potentials shaped by popular culture. However, these young individuals are still the same cultural beings who have to bring in their previous learning experiences and build upon them. The perspective of popular culture, as a terrain to offer democratic educational opportunities to young people in mainstream education, should be used to design academic programs in order to make education whole. That is to say, rather than rejecting the previous learning experiences of young people, higher education should provide a smooth transition to the world of the academy where they will certainly meet new approaches and methods of learning.

Popular culture as a social practice, the common ground where their meaning-making is shaped, as Mahiri (2001) puts it, urges the education practitioners to be:

> aware of the motives and methods of youth engagement in pop culture in terms of why and how such an engagement connects to students' personal identifications, their needs to construct meanings, and their pursuit of pleasures and personal power ... but the real challenge is to make these connections to and through changing domains of knowledge, critical societal issues and cognitive and technical skills that educators can justify their students will actually need to master the universe of the new century.
>
> *(p. 385)*

News in the media, in contrast to popular culture, for example, is usually seen as neutral and is believed to have a merely informative purpose, and this could be perceived as a connection between multimedia and education; however, news programs have become cultural commodities through which the media corporations "pursue stories about celebrities in an effort to increase their market share"

(Stack & Kelly, 2006, p. 18), which is also true in Turkey. Moreover, the issue of democracy in media has been at stake for a long time in Turkey, because the media corporations are in the middle of a political struggle. Business people that have close connections with the ruling party are taking over the most powerful media corporations with the support of the government, and manipulating public opinion about social and political issues. The issue has become even more critical recently as journalists opposing the policies of the ruling party have started to be arrested. The International Press Institute announced that there are currently at least 57 journalists in prison. In March 2011, for example, Ahmet Şık, who is both a journalist and an academic, was arrested with ten other journalists because of his unpublished book *The Imam's Army* which analyzes the Islamic bureaucratic structuring in Turkey. The U.S. and the European commission expressed their concerns over the arrests. Although a month of public pressure led to the possibility of his release, he and the rest of the journalists arrested remain in prison. Another Turkish journalist, Mustafa Balbay, who has been kept in prison for three years on charges of membership in an alleged organization, won a seat in the Republican People's Party, the main opposing party, in the elections in June 2011. However, his release was refused by the court. In a country where press freedom is at stake news can be a rich resource with which to teach critical reading skills, rather than using it simply as an information source. Thus, cultural commodities, regardless of their genre, should be the objects of education. In the world of multimedia, where the youth is surrounded by the global cultural commodities, education practitioners could enable students to explore their "social self-understanding" in Richards' (1998) terms. It is in this way possible to enable students to explore their own beings first and build bridges between themselves and formal education whose source of information is different from theirs.

Taking popular culture as a way to provide students from different social and educational backgrounds with educational opportunities could ensure education as a democratic practice and could also lead to a new understanding of popular culture in academic teaching, one that could give students access to "high" knowledge in the mode through which their cognitive development and learning has been shaped. Regarding the fact that audiences of popular culture are more sophisticated and critical than they are thought to be, it is fair to state that popular culture in the academy can be considered as a way to "recognize the power of the everyday." As such, we should try to reshape a studentship in the academic setting that embraces all students rather than excluding the majority, who are less able to access the "high" knowledge in its traditional modes.

Toward a New Understanding of Teaching in Higher Education

Universities are important and active in modern society, because modernity is associated with reason, and the complexity of modern society is manifested in rationality, which has taken its institutionalized form in universities. With modernity, higher education became more than cognitive learning within a particular discipline to internalize different modes of reasoning. Moreover, with advanced technology, gaining digital skills has an important role to play in helping people function in everyday life, at both academic and professional levels. Certainly, it is impossible to think of universities as places of production of knowledge isolated from social order. Thus, a new understanding of teaching in higher education needs to be adopted, starting with the identification of what students really need to learn today rather than romanticizing traditional forms of academic knowledge.

When considering the relationship between knowledge and production, a discussion of the pedagogy of academic knowledge should start with the employers' expectations, then consider the students' and academics' expectations for a university education. The expectations of the employers have a significant role in shaping the students' and the academics' roles at the same time. Although some institutions and some academics with a political view think that "capitalist forces are anti-intellectual" (Washer, 2007), and reject the concept of the university as a place primarily intended to teach students the skills that employers value, it is undeniable that universities today are there mostly to prepare young people for rivalry in the job market, and that students who attend university for purely intellectual self-development are the minority. Thus, the agenda for deciding which skills students should be equipped with preserves its importance. Washer (2007) identifies seven different skills that students need to develop gradually during their undergraduate years: "communication skills, working with others, problem solving, numeracy, the use of information technology, learning how to learn, personal and professional development" (p. 58). This updated list of required skills draws a new picture of academic knowledge and implementation because these skills cannot be achieved through traditional teaching and learning methods.

Today's reality calls for a movement that enables the key skills to develop students' learning of a discipline's subject matter and that encourages innovations in curriculum design and pedagogy in higher education. Today, the mode of learning has already been transformed by digital media. Do young people learning with new media therefore learn less than academics who learned from the printed page? Palfrey and Gasser (2008) assert that there is no concrete evidence that they learn less than the generation of the printed mode, nor is there data to suggest that they are smarter than the previous generations. Moreover, a recent study of young people demonstrated that young Americans do not read daily newspapers in a traditional way, but that they not only use the information in the fast digital flow but also contribute to the processes of distribution and reproduction of information, even across borders (Palfrey & Gasser, 2008). Similarly, in Turkey an increasing number of people, the majority of whom are young, prefer reading newspapers online, where they can post and receive recent news on social networks or blogs. People download online books and read them on their laptops, iPads, or iPhones that they carry wherever they go, and they watch and share videos published on YouTube. These videos can sometimes be a lecture given in a far-away university or in a conference. Learning has already become a digital experience that has no borders or limits.

The new society bases its productivity on information flow and the accumulation of knowledge. As far as my personal observations and experiences within academia are concerned, the most common complaint that is discussed in academic meetings or in everyday conversations among Turkish academics is how "ignorant" and "unmotivated" learners are in the university. According to academics, the new generation is "different" because they cannot understand what those certain texts mean, although those academics were quite confident in understanding and internalizing the same texts when they were students. To understand how the new generation differs, an outline of the characteristics of the youth is required. Some studies based on the American context characterize the new college students as "the millennial generation," but it is certainly not possible to generalize the current description of "the new college student" to all societies, and it also sounds stereotypical in itself. A recent experiment carried out in the Istanbul Bilgi University among students in the Department of Communication revealed that the students, a small group of millennial learners whose task was to remain "off-line" for only one week except for responsibilities related to their online studies, could not stand being away from social networks like Facebook and Twitter; the majority returned to using the Internet at the very beginning of the week-long research period. They confessed that they were addicted to the Internet, and described the digital world as a "virus" affecting their everyday practices. Accordingly, it could be considered that the millennial generation is "over-reliant on communication technology" and that they have developed "multitasking behaviors," which could result in the situation in which it has "shortened their collective attention span" (Elam, Stratton, & Gibson, 2007, p. 21). However, another point to consider is that they "gather information through a multi-step process that involves grazing, a 'deep dive,' and a feedback loop" (Palfrey & Gasser, 2008, p. 241), so that there is a mismatch between the process of reading printed texts and the digital ones. They cannot complete the tasks or follow the information flow on paper because they are used to motion, colors, sound, successive steps to follow, etc. Thus, when asked to retrieve the information during exams or discussions in the academic environment, such students are more likely to fail because the mismatch between the given mode and their cognitive learning skills may not allow learning to take place. The fact that they cannot concentrate on a printed text for a long time and understand it does not mean that they cannot learn at all; if they are given the same information in a different mode, they can process the information differently and learn it, in the end.

The generation that we welcome into the universities every year are multitasking learners. The main effect of multitasking on learning, it has been asserted, is that young people cannot pay attention to the information they have to remember and that they are distracted during the learning process. However, a study demonstrated that when students in one group were allowed to use their laptops during lectures and students in another group were not, those with their laptops were not affected by the disruption that was thought to be caused by laptops but by other factors like class structure, dynamics, and their level of competence in multitasking (Palfrey & Gasser, 2008, p. 192). Because academics do not have systematic methodologies to follow while designing their lectures, and digital sources remain outside traditional lectures, academics should design tasks to bridge what they explain to what students learn via computers. While in the past we talked about the importance of two-way interaction and communication between academics and students, today we need a three-way interaction involving multi-media communication, drawing on the reading and writing skills that students have developed outside the classroom through popular culture. In this way, students would be expected not only to listen to the lecture and follow the PowerPoint slides (which is not multitasking) but to be engaged in listening to the lecturer, following the slides, and finding information on the Web which could be used in answer to a question addressed to them or as a relevant example of a point being discussed. This would also enable both parties to take part in discussions about the relevance, reliability, and acceptability of information found via digital resources. Such discussions are particularly essential for learning in the academy, because digital sources to be used in learning are believed to lead to developing the habit of "copy and paste" in their academic writing, and a practice that reflects the difficulty in making decisions and being selective in the middle of the vast information flow.

Key to diminishing such effects of digital technology in education could be academic skills courses and critical media literacy. Rather than only criticizing digital media and young users for not being critical of information on the Web, academics should take an active role in guiding students in evaluating the information they access and teaching students what to accept and reject. In some Turkish universities, as part of the Turkish and English academic skills courses, students are taught how to access, select, analyze, and evaluate information via digital sources as well as with the printed media. However, it needs to be considered that such courses are support courses that help students to perform better in their departmental courses; lecturers in *all* departments should design their courses and assessment schemes so that students could practice these skills throughout their academic studies. This approach connects critical thinking with the digital media students use every day. Such a project would require the active participation of all instructors and academics in students' learning experiences. In Turkey, private higher education institutions, in particular, are promoting education opportunities that provide high-tech resources. They offer wireless Internet access on campuses, laptops, vast databases, e-books, DVD collections, SmartBoards, and online student pages through which students could participate in discussions. However, the higher education curriculums do not fully require students to utilize the high-tech resources. While these resources are available, the majority of lectures in departments are still traditional, and even when students are given special projects and assignments, they do not receive enough guidance about how to use their digital skills to attain academic learning. Young people are expected to participate in discussions and produce ideas with respect to what they read in classes; however, their communication patterns are also quite different today. It is my experience that whenever I share videos, quotations, news, and controversial issues through my Facebook account, a great many students on my list respond to them and express their view-points, while they remain silent if the same topic is opened to a discussion in class. I have many students who suggest opening *our own* groups on Facebook where we can discuss the subject matters further online. In that case, why not accept their invitation to join their terrains, where we can at least communicate with them? Does it really matter how they, actually we, do it as long as they learn and produce ideas? The social networks certainly create concerns over privacy; professors might not want to publish their private lives online, which is understandable. A recent article published in *The Chronicle of Higher Education* on 8 July 2011 announced a solution to the problem; a new social-networking platform, Google Plus, which will make it easier to communicate with sub-groups in someone's contacts in isolation from the other contacts in the list. While it is not always easy to control the messages, photos, and updates in Facebook, in Google Plus one can assign each new contact to a "circle" and can create as many circles as they like, and whenever they post an update they can easily select which circles get to see it. Google Plus might be used as a tool for education in the near future.

With a generation that learns about history through movies and popular doc-umentaries on the History Channel, scientific breakthroughs through programs on the Discovery Channel, mythology through cartoons or television series, politics and economics through popular news and discussion programs on TV or blogs that they participate in, academics still strive to convince them that they have to digest printed or at most "on-the-screen" academic texts presented through PowerPoint presentations or using overhead projectors. With a generation that gets so much information, and consumes it so fast that they cannot realize how much they acquire, academics try to make them internalize printed academic knowledge fast and apply it in different academic contexts. However, the outcome of this mode of curriculum implementation does not seem to be fulfilling the requirements of the market where competition is immense. Why learners in higher education cannot learn what they are expected to learn remains unanswered since academics rarely see the reality of their students' profile as learners together with their past learning experiences. Although we see the fast-moving images, screen-based information, and fast-consumed popular images as being *outside of* the academic context, they are actually *inside*, because they belong to our students. The learning that goes on outside of the institution is in a different direction from learning inside the university and creates confusion for them, often blocking their learning of academic subject matter. Thus, this paper simply offers a negotiation between the academy and the popular. It is not to say that the products of popular culture are to be part of the academic knowledge or that they should replace it. It is to offer the idea that products and modes of popular culture could help academics reach the minds of young people, who are newly introduced to the world of academy in their first year.

As one example, Turkish youth have started to reconsider the life and deeds of Mustafa Kemal Atatürk, the founder of the Republic of Turkey, with the release of the recent movies such as *Veda / Farewell* (2010) by Zülfü Livaneli and documentaries such as *Mustafa* (2008) by Can Dündar. These have had a stronger impact than the compulsory course "The History of the Turkish Republic and the Principles of Atatürk" has had in universities. After the release of these films and the discussions about their content and ideology on TV, it has been observed that the sales of books about Atatürk have also increased in Turkey. Certain popular commodities can sometimes motivate people to read books. Personally, whenever I hear the term "quantum," the image that appears in my mind is the demonstration that a physics professor in a popular Turkish movie *Organize İşler (Organized Jobs)* (2005) makes to her students in university. We cannot deny the fact that even the generation before the millennial generation undergoes a perceptual change and remembers visual, colorful, moving multimodal texts better than printed texts. It is to suggest that for example, rather than *banning* the movies produced based on the literary works, students could be encouraged to read the texts and watch the movies and be critical and analytical about both texts. Why not use certain popular characters for psychological analysis in psychology courses? *The Simpsons* have already taken their place in a book called *The Simpsons and Philosophy*, which makes it easier to understand philosophy. Don't you think it would make a difference to watch a documentary about the Frankfurt School to understand the ideas of the theorists? A series like *Boston Legal*, *Ally McBeal*, or *The Practice* could provide both academics and students with a resource for discussing fictional and real cases in Law Faculties—they might be most relevant to American students but could they not be compared with cases in the local context? The movie *The Wrestler* (2008) could be an influential medium to promote open discussions about using steroids in universities, where so many young people are affected by body images in the media. A series such as *Grey's Anatomy* (a Turkish version has also been produced with the name *The Doctors* on a Turkish TV channel), *ER*, or *Private Practice* could be used with prospective doctors in universities not only to compare fictional medical cases with real ones but also to discuss the ethics of medicine. What's more, online discussions and websites connected to these shows and movies include discussions and information that touch on the popular culture as well as many of the social issues involved. Students engaging in these online discussions could then talk of their ideas with other students in other cultures. Such an approach to learning in the academy does not mean replacing academic texts with popular culture products but simply offers a way to use them as tools to make academic knowledge more accessible. It is bridging the gap between learners' cognitive potential, shaped by multimodal, multistep learning tasks, and the printed texts. Such an approach would also enable learners to relate their cultural identities to their academic identities, and this would reduce their anxiety in accessing academic knowledge and make them open to learning new things because they will not feel as alienated.

It is time for academics and curriculum designers to think about where students come from, which skills they bring with them, and how they can be reached, rather than isolating them from the "real" academy; to talk about who students are rather than who they should be, and to consider alternative ways to make academic education more productive.

Conclusion

Popular culture, with its products and tactics, influences the lives of young people from the beginning. During childhood, television and computers replace numerous other activities and the people that children spend time with, and become the life savers of parents and caregivers when they do not have time and energy for children. The scenario that is globally repeated every day is that children are extensively exposed to the virtual realities of global commodities, and as they grow older, these realities on screens become *their* realities and facts in the sense that they learn through the medium of mass production and react to them as if they consider them the facts of life. When they become teenagers, their world is ruled by the commodities of popular culture. However, when they enter university, they are told by some people, the academics, that the realities of real life are different from theirs, which results in a gap between academic knowledge and students' everyday practices. At this point, there are two options for young people: they either strive to learn in the way that academics want them to but struggle to attain high marks, or quit because the academic tasks seem to be far above their capacity.

This paper is an attempt to reconcile this scenario. It is meant neither to glorify the situation young people are in nor to replace academic knowledge with popular texts, but to accept the situation and seek solutions to the inherent tensions. It is to accept that young people in universities have different realities and learn differently. It is to recognize that they may equate the discipline of law with *Ally McBeal* for example, and that academics could use the global commodities of popular culture to show how different the facts of the academy are. Rather than falling into denial, this paper proposes to look at *their* world of reality and to give students the opportunity to compare it with the world of academic knowledge, by using the cultural texts that they are acquainted with. In this way, *learning* in the academy can also be popular in the Turkish "popular" academy.

Notes

1. See for example: Buckingham, D. (Ed.) (1998) *Teaching popular culture: Beyond radical pedagogy*, [e-book] http://site.ebrary.com/lib/bilgi/Doc?id=5004634; Dolby, N. (2003) Popular culture and democratic practice, *Harvard Educational Review*, Fall, 73(3), Academic Research Library, 258; Mahiri, J. (2001) Pop culture pedagogy and the end(s) of school, *Journal of Adolescent & Adult Literacy*, Dec 2000/Jan 2001, 44(4); Morrell, E. (2002) Toward a critical pedagogy of popular culture: Literacy development among urban youth, *Journal of Adolescent & Adult Literacy*, Sep 2002, 46(1); Ciechanowski, K.M. (2009) 'A squirrel came and pushed earth': Popular cultural and scientific ways of thinking for ELLs, *The Reading*

Teacher, 62(7), 558–568; Thompson, M. (2008) Multimodal teaching and learning: Creating spaces for content teachers, *Journal of Adolescent & Adult Literacy*, 52(2); Williams, B. T. (2008) 'Tomorrow will not be like today': Literacy and identity in a world of multiliteracies, *Journal of Adolescent & Adult Literacy*, 51(8).

2. See for example: Cheung, C. (2001) The use of popular culture as a stimulus to motivate secondary students' English learning in Hong Kong, *ELT Journal*, Vol. 55(1), 55–56; Duff, P. A. (2002) Pop culture and ESL students: Intertextuality, identity, and participation in classroom discussions, *Journal of Adolescent & Adult Literacy*, 45(6); Ranker, J. (2007) Using comic books as read-alouds: Insights on reading instruction from an English as a second language classroom, *The Reading Teacher*, 61(4), 296–305.

3. Türkoğlu, N., & Şimşek, M. C. (2007) *Medya Okuryazarlığı (Media Literacy)*. Kalemus Yayıncılık, İstanbul; Bek, M. G., & Binark, M. (2007) *Eleştirel Medya Okuryazarlığı (Critical Media Literacy)*. Kalkedon Yayınları: İstanbul.

References

Bartholomae, D. (1985). Inventing the university. In M. Rose (Ed.), *When a writer can't write*. New York: The Guilford Press.

Battro, A. M. (2004). Digital skills, globalization and education. In M. M. Suarez-Orozco & D. Qin-Hilliard (Eds.), *Globalization: Culture and education in the new millennium*. Berkeley, CA: University of California Press.

Cook-Gumperz, J. (Ed.) (1986). *The social construction of literacy*. London: Cambridge University Press.

Dengiz, A. Ş., Yılmaz, B. (2007). 2004 İlköğretim Programı'nda Okuma ve Kütüphane Kullanma Alışkanlıklarına İlişkin Öğretmen Görüşleri/Evaluation of the 2004 program of the primary schools concerning the reading and library use habits by the teachers. *Bilgi Dünyası*, 8(2), 203–229.

Dumontheil, I., Apperly, I. A., & Balkemore, S. (2010). Online usage of theory of mind continues to develop in late adolescence. *Developmental Science*, 13(2), 331–338.

Elam, C., Stratton, T., & Gibson, D. D. (2007). Welcoming a new generation to college: The millennial students. *Journal of College Admission*, 195, 20–25.

Erdem, A. R. (2008). Küreselleşme Bağlamında Türkiye'de Eğitim Bilimlerinin Bugünü ve Geleceği/Today and the future of educational sciences in Turkey in terms of globalization. *Üniversite ve Toplum*, 8(4), 25–30.

Fiske, J. (1996). *Understanding popular culture*. London: Routledge.

Gee, J. P. (2003). *What video games have to teach us about learning and literacy*. New York: Palgrave Macmillan.

Grossberg, L. (1992). *We gotta get out of this place: Popular conservatism and postmodern culture*. New York & London: Routledge.

Harris, D. (1996). *Society of signs?* New York: Routledge.

Kress, G. (1994). *Learning to write* (2nd ed.). London: Routledge & Kegan Paul Ltd.

Kress, G. (1997). *Before writing: Rethinking the paths to literacy*. London: Routledge.

Mahiri, J. (2001). Pop culture pedagogy and the end(s) of school. *Journal of Adolescent & Adult Literacy*, 44(4), 382–385.

Medeni, T. D., Miyata, K., & Sağsan, M. (2009). Learning to reflect in online fantasy role-playing games. *Bilgi Dünyası*, 10(2), 139–162.

Odabaş, H., Odabaş, Z. Y., & Polat, C. (2008). Üniversite Öğrencilerinin Okuma Alışkanlığı: Ankara Üniversitesi Örneği /Reading habits of university students: The model of Ankara University. *Bilgi Dünyası*, 9(2), 431–465.

Palfrey, J., & Gasser, U. (2008). *Born digital: Understanding the first generation of digital natives.* New York: Basic Books.

Richards, C. (1998). Beyond classroom culture. In D. Buckingham (Ed.), *Teaching popular culture: Beyond radical pedagogy* (electronic edition): http://site.ebrary.com/lib/bilgi/Doc? id=5004634

Sanger, J., Willson, J., Davies, B., & Whittaker, R. (1997). *Young children, videos and computer games.* London: Falmer Press.

Stack, M., & Kelly, D. M. (2006). Popular media, education, and resistance. *Canadian Journal of Education, 29*(1), 5–26.

Street, B. V. (1984). *Literacy in theory and practice.* Cambridge: Cambridge University Press.

Street, B. V. (1995). *Social literacies: Critical approaches to literacy in development, ethnography and education.* London: Longman Group Ltd.

Taylor, G., Ballard, B., Beasley, V., Bock, H., Clanchy, J., & Nightingale, P. (Eds.). (1988). *Literacy by degrees.* Milton Keynes: SHRE & Open University Press.

Washer, P. (2007). Revisiting key skills: A practical framework for higher education. *Quality in Higher Education, 13*(1), 57–67.

7

DIGITAL WORLDS AND SHIFTING BORDERS

Popular Culture, Perception, and Pedagogy

Sandra Schamroth Abrams, Hannah R. Gerber, and Melissa L. Burgess

> I usually try to invade this one territory of Austria. I don't remember its name
> and usually they have a huge army that makes me fail, so when I listen to the
> podcast, they say that he [Napoleon] did not invade there, so [when I play
> *Rise of Nations*], I try to follow … what happened in real life up 'til the point
> where he failed in real life so I alter the plans—Robbie.

Instead of having his virtual army proceed as Napoleon did, 17-year-old Robbie
(all names are pseudonyms) went through Russia knowing that, in his game, Russia
did not have a winter, and he was able to succeed where Napoleon did not.
Robbie's rationale for his moves for real-time strategy game *Rise of Nations* reveals
the interconnection of his literacy experiences and the rich meaning-making
resulting from extracting and applying critical pieces of information to produce
his own, victorious, virtual re-creation of the Napoleonic Wars. Playing *Rise of
Nations* solidified Robbie's understanding of historical events, and the city-building,
simulation components of the game enabled Robbie to control the movement of
his troops, manipulate the progression of time, and evaluate the benefits and
consequences of his decisions. This active and critical application of knowledge
sharply contrasts with Robbie's perception of academic engagement: "If it's history
class, I have to make sure I remember it. That would be me learning."

★★★

Fifteen-year-old Davis, an avid gamer, spends most of his time online, playing video
games such as the massively multiplayer online game (MMOG), *Conquer Online*, or
Microsoft's *Elderscrolls* series game, or chatting with his friends about game-related
stories and storylines, which help him write his own novel collaboratively with

gamer friends. This novel writing often includes searching YouTube videos and reading game websites, walkthroughs, and other gamers' blogs. In class, Davis often converses with his friends about video game experiences, and, as in the virtual world, Davis dramatizes and transforms uni-dimensional worksheets into lively stories. Such "off-task" behavior seems wedded to Davis's perception that "much of my creative work takes place during school because there isn't anything else worth doing." Thus, creative play, dramatization, and exploration of game events serve as platforms for novel writing; gaming affords Davis multiple opportunities to network with friends and extend his knowledge of a passionate subject through reading, writing, listening, speaking, viewing, and presentation—central language arts practices.

★★★

Grayson, an 18-year-old college-level developmental reading student, further validates this divisive perception between in-school and out-of-school literacy learning. Grayson's reading class syllabus requires him to purchase a kit, disguised as an "advancement" in developmental reading, that contains a college reading text, a journal, a dictionary, and an Internet Access card that links to traditional reading passages and multiple choice assessments. Though the reading is online, Grayson "hate[s] doing Reading Road Trips" because his classmates and he are required to complete activities at the Reading Center, where ironically Grayson encounters isolated learning. However, when Grayson enters the multi-user virtual environment (MUVE) *Second Life*, from the comfort of his dorm, he finds the experience fun and immersive; he enjoys being able to "put myself in the boss's shoes so that I could understand what they look for in employees." Further, Grayson perceives the *Second Life* reading activities as collaborative and supportive, noting how it "feels like the instructor and classmates are right there with me." Because Grayson enjoys "chatting" with other classmates during activities, he does not necessarily view the *Second Life* experiences as learning.

Robbie, Davis, and Grayson call attention to their personal investment and immersion in online activities and the disassociation between digital and academic learning. A number of researchers (Goodson et al., 2002; King & O'Brien, 2002; Kress & Jewitt, 2003; Lacasa, Méndez, & Martínez, 2008) have noted the discrepancy between the literacy practices schools value and the literacy practices students engage in; many schools do not appear to address semiotic domains other than those of traditional texts (Alvermann et al., 2006; King & O'Brien, 2002), and classrooms are places where students typically face a "culture clash" with their teachers, school, and curricula (Delpit, 1995; Goodson et al., 2002).

Given the participatory and multimodal nature of media, such as MUVEs and video games, students are engaging in meaning-making activities that challenge the traditional schema for "learning [that] is related only to schoolwork, the content of the curriculum, and particularly those specific materials that have traditionally been present in the classroom: books, paper, pencils, textbooks, and so on" (Lacasa, Méndez, & Martínez, 2008, p. 342). Attention, therefore, has been centered on the need for curricula and practice to respond to technological and cultural changes, with advocates calling for the integration of MUVEs, video games, or the gaming experience into classroom instruction (Charsky & Mims, 2008; Gee, 2007; Lacasa, Méndez, & Martínez, 2008; Prensky, 2008; Sherblom, Withers, & Leonard, 2009), and the improvement of educator training to meaningfully incorporate technology into curricula (Boling, 2005; Labbo et al., 2003; Marsh, 2004). Because the focus has remained on educators and schools (a focus still necessary), the role of students' perceptions and understandings of texts has not been examined sufficiently, and there seems to be a hasty assumption that students will automatically acknowledge the academic value of their digital experiences.

Drawing upon qualitative and/or quantitative data from related studies of video gaming, MUVEs, and literate activities, this collaborative chapter juxtaposes secondary and tertiary students' perceptions of literacy with their digital practices. Two similar studies involving interviews with and observations of adolescent male video gamers, along with one study that observed and surveyed developmental reading students' use of *Second Life*, provide insight into how school culture in the United States may shape students' virtual literacy practices and collectively suggest how MUVE and video game experiences can impact students' understanding of academic texts or skills. In so doing, this work considers how school culture and popular culture mediate students' overt and embedded learning, and it explores the degree to which these students may validate their MUVE and video game experiences as "real" literacy practices in the face of traditional text-based assumptions of literacy. Further, this chapter calls for a cultural shift within the classroom to involve MUVEs and video games as important and relevant literacy practices; such a shift would foster an academic atmosphere that encourages and challenges students like Robbie, Davis, and Grasyon to integrate their knowledge gleaned from digital experiences to support and enhance meaningful learning.

Play, Learning, and Digital Worlds

Unlike other forms of media, MUVEs and video games involve "play," a term that complicates the discussion because it "inevitably raises concerns over standards and rigor, but only among those who have not participated in gaming or other digital discursive worlds" (Alberti, 2008, p. 268). Despite the research that suggests the academic benefits of play (Lim, 2008), acceptance of digital practices as learning experiences may be contingent upon one's exposure to and understanding of these practices. "Play" in video games helps players develop spatial and cognitive skills, anticipate flexibility and multi-tasking, read visual images, and learn through discovery (Greenfield, 1984; Gee, 2007; Green & McNeese, 2008; Schrader & McCreery, 2008).

In addition, the MUVEs may not have goal-oriented storylines or specific character roles, but they rely on user flexibility and creativity to design and build activities involving play, imagination, and exploration. In other words, student-driven learning and experimentation seem to be inherent factors in one's play in virtual spaces, especially by digital natives (Prensky, 2001, 2006) who seamlessly develop knowledge and skills that inform their interaction with and understanding of technology. Particularly important to this discussion is how technologically proficient students perceive their skills in relation to school, how school and online cultures shape students' perception, and how, if at all, students apply their digital knowledge outside of the virtual environment.

The examination of "play" through the MUVE and gaming lens reveals how students may tap into their diverse experiences (Sutton-Smith, 2001) and access their personal and collective funds of knowledge (Moll et al., 1992) or "historically accumulated and culturally developed bodies of knowledge and skills" (Moll et al., 1992, p. 133). For digital natives, their funds of knowledge include their experiences with and understanding of situated digital practices, which are ensconced in popular culture, and accessing these funds of knowledge to accomplish a task involves student-driven learning. Thus, a meaningful experience needs to have some form of currency—be it social, emotional, or intellectual—so the student can recognize the role of the knowledge and skills in relation to his/her life. As New Literacy Theorists (Barton, 1994, 2001; Gee, 1996, 2000; Street, 1995, 1999) explain, meaning is connected to context, culture, and perception. This concept of literacy in contemporary discussions (Barton, 2007; Gee, 2011; Street, 2010) underscores a socially and culturally situated notion of meaning-making, recognizing that literacies impact understandings and understandings impact literacies. Popular culture and community practice, therefore, naturally impact one's literacies. Though the virtual world is a global world, school culture and online practices in the U.S. appear to influence students' interaction with and perception of their virtual encounters; as this chapter suggests, the privileging of social or academic practices may impact the extent to which students envision their virtual literacy experiences extending into their real-world practices.

Online Popular Culture and School Culture: (Mis)Valued Practices and Text

Video games and MUVEs are platforms that challenge traditional environments for teaching and learning by offering and encouraging interactive collaboration, problem-solving, and team-based activities to which digital natives have grown accustomed. Online literacy practices may include critical, intertextual thought, but students don't automatically recognize the academic value of their online activities, even when engaging in traditional writing online (Witte, 2007). Much of this disconnect may be due to school culture, where "the theory of learning in good video games fits better with the modern, high-tech, global world today's children and teenagers live in than do the theories (and practices) of learning that they sometimes see in school" (Gee, 2007, p. 5). Despite the calls to include multimodal texts and students' out-of-school literacies, school-based literacy, which privileges traditional reading and writing (Vacca, 2005) and teacher-centered approaches, remains the norm in most American schools. Collins and Halverson (2009) contend that "the public schools in America are facing a crisis. The public is demanding higher standards from K–12 schools with policies that limit the variety of learning opportunities" (p. 3). As a result, an assessment-driven culture embraces a controlled context (and content) and traditional literacy, pedagogy, and practice are dominant in most schools (Solomon, 2009).

The schools that our participants attended represent two distinct cultures— suburban northeastern and rural southeastern communities. Garron High School, which Robbie attended, is situated in a middle-to-upper-middle-class neighborhood in suburban New Jersey; though the school was honored for its academics, the seven content-area classrooms I (Sandra) observed that were tracked for struggling students seemed based on the traditional, teacher-centered, desk-in-rows, print-text model. Unlike Garron, Sotheby High School, where Davis was a student, is located in a mid-sized college town in the southeastern U.S. and is considered the most ethnically and socioeconomically diverse school in the district. However, I (Hannah) observed how the diverse participants struggled with a traditionalist model. Finally, the university participants attended a four-year higher educational institution in southeast Texas, boasting high-technology use, doctoral research, and $250 million recent renovations. Despite these positive attributes, I (Melissa) observed that the institution's developmental reading courses rarely incorporated technology, and, like Garron and Sotheby, relied on traditional pedagogy and practice.

Students' Conceptions of Text

Given these schools' proclivity to cling to traditionalist methods and given that literacy and assessment are central to American school culture (Solomon, 2009), it seems logical that our participants identified texts and learning through a traditional lens. Further, given that as many as six out of ten students in postsecondary institutions require remediation (Bettinger & Long, 2009), we need to reconsider how students perceive and connect to texts. Digital natives may be technologically proficient and literate, but their exposure to traditional educational structures may shape their view of valued literacy practices in an academic environment (Abrams, 2011). Interview data from our two studies of adolescent males suggest that our avid video gaming participants understood literacy as separate from their out-of-school activities. The high school juniors in our studies echoed a traditional understanding of texts, relating reading and learning to books, school, and "words on a page." Further, Davis explained that school reading and writing were sometimes too difficult, and that he saw himself as a "poor" student because he read slowly, often unable to complete assignments. Meanwhile, he was engaging in collaboratively reading and writing his own novel based on characters from his gaming experience. This included researching, reading, and writing, as well as receiving peer feedback from his friends.

In addition, the students in these studies held a compulsory view of schoolwork and a passive view of learning; Robbie explained that he and his classmates "*have* to read this section, answer these questions" and "listen to what the teachers say, write down what they say." Furthermore, some teachers emphasized that students needed to follow explicit directions, as was evident in one teacher's mandate, "I would pay attention if I were you." Given the students' experiences with and perceptions of schooling, it comes as no surprise that the high school students did not initially recognize the relationship between their active learning in their virtual worlds and their receptive learning in their academic ones.

Applying Virtual Experiences to the Real World: Video Games

Students may not have been cognizant of their virtual learning experiences, and this may have been due to their understanding of valued academic texts and the overall public critique of video games (c.f. Padilla-Walker et al., 2009; Shibuya, Ihori, & Yukawa, 2008). Reports and discussions of video games and MUVEs used in the classroom (Hoppock, 2008; Hu, 2010; Salen & Zimmerman, 2004) help call attention to the possibilities these technologies present. After all, video games have "rich pedagogical potential" (Squire, 2009, p. 660), can bridge and complement traditional literacies (O'Brien & Scharber, 2008; Squire, 2009), and can provide a context for academic material (Abrams, 2009; Gerber 2009). Important to consider is the way in which students develop and utilize their digital practices and situated knowledge to engage in meaningful learning experiences.

As evident in the respective studies, the participants became increasingly aware of the ways in which their video game experiences helped inform their understanding of academic material. Much of this awareness stemmed from answering interview questions that prompted students to reflectively examine their literacies. The stories of gamers Robbie and Davis help to elucidate the rich learning that stemmed from their video gaming and the need for students to become more cognizant of the gaming–school connection.

His Story, His Learning: Robbie

Seventeen-year-old Robbie's shy and stoic manner made it difficult for me (Sandra) to examine his feeling or reactions, and his lack of class participation accompanied this outwardly unemotional demeanor. Despite Robbie's inconsistent schoolwork and placement in classes for academically struggling students, he was an avid reader and researched academic information outside school. As his history teacher noted, Robbie's "biggest fault is every once in a while he chooses not to do homework because he's probably spending his time reading, or playing on the computer … he'd rather be doing something else." It is possible that Robbie's disillusionment with school was also related to his social isolation at school. The culture at Garron High School included a strong social element and a number of cliques, to which Robbie did not appear to belong or attempt to engage; rather, he seemed to avoid opportunities to socialize by reading before class started, going home for lunch, and standing alone during the fire drill. Further, even after Robbie ironically helped to create the chess club, he rarely spoke with club members. In addition, as Robbie told me, at home, he kept to himself, and he devoted much of his time to reading historical reference texts, going online, playing video games, and listening to podcasts.

Gaming afforded Robbie the anonymity and opportunity to interact with others and develop historical knowledge in meaningful ways. More specifically, Robbie explained that his online experience playing *Battlefield 1942*, a World War II first person shooter computer game, informed in-class conversations about the war, thus providing a dimension to historic material (Abrams, 2009). Robbie explained how gaming enabled him to contextualize academic discussions: "Like when it says … this and that was a turning point in the war and after that I can picture like what happened in the battle and why such happened." Further, Robbie noted that other resources, such as websites, military podcasts, traditional encyclopedias and History Channel segments alerted him to military tactics and provided him with ideas for game play. In other words, Robbie's multimodal resources not only advanced his understanding of historic events, but also empowered him to experiment with a variety of strategies.

Experimentation wasn't the only element that contributed to Robbie's gaming and learning experiences. When I observed Robbie individually playing *Rise of Nations* in school, I noticed his game knowledge informing his decisions, "building a library to increase science and technology," and getting a "bonus from the granary" because he had farms. At times, Robbie would stop working on one section of his civilization to check in on his virtual researchers in the library and the woodcutter's shop, from which he could "get architecture and carpentry." Likewise, Robbie began to strategize, building a temple not only to gain "civic bonuses," but also to cause "attrition damage so if anybody tries to invade your territory they get automatically damaged." Because of time restrictions, Robbie only played for 25 minutes until we began the stimulated recall, when Robbie acknowledged that he first learned about the granary's function from the game, which provided a written "description that it [the granary] helps farms out." Further, Robbie explained that the granaries were important because "Egyptians are supposed to be like a farming society," something he remembered from seventh grade, when he "learned like Nile River, something about a Fertile Crescent area. So I figured that's got to be something with farming." Encountering information both in the game and in the classroom, Robbie made certain inferences about society and about the game that solidified his understanding of history and culture. What became clear is that the dynamic relationship among the mélange of Robbie's literacies provided him rich and multi-dimensional understandings of information he could connect to on a number of levels.

In addition to discovering information through reading and interpreting written text, images, sounds, and movements, Robbie took risks and socialized in a safe, self-chosen, virtual environment. He even became inspired to procure a Croatian-English dictionary in an attempt to understand his online, Croatian, *Battlefield 1942* teammates. In this way, the culture of Robbie's gaming world—collaboration, experimentation, and anonymity—supported his engagement in meaningful social and academic learning. Ironically, Robbie never thought that gaming helped him learn, possibly because school learning was rote learning. Therefore, it seemed logical that Robbie was not initially cognizant of the connection between his game playing and academic work. Interview data reveal how he encountered information in his games and eventually, after speaking with me, noticed the relevance of his gaming experiences in relation to school. The confluence of Robbie's literacy practices informed his game play and academic practices because Robbie's involvement was central to his understanding, an active and engaged learning experience that contrasted with his perception of school's traditional constructions.

His Story, His Learning: Davis

In the case of Davis, similar assessments can be made of how school's traditional constructions and conceptions of literacy can lead students to believe their own literate activities are not valid in the real world. Davis, an outwardly social, proud, and animated 15-year-old, was outspoken in social and academic arenas. During an interview, Davis's English teacher reported, "He is very smart and he likes for everyone to know that he is very smart. If he has an answer he wants to be loud and give it out … he is very social, but it seems like most of his friends are girls." Davis's social, interactive nature extended to virtual spaces, where he participated in massively multiplayer online gaming (MMOGs) experiences, online communication, and collaboration in researching and writing novels. He seemingly tried to recreate these social experiences inside the classroom, much to the teacher's chagrin.

Davis engaged in a more integrated and collaborative form of literacy outside of the classroom than while inside the classroom. When inside the classroom, he was often tasked with copying notes from overhead transparencies, independently completing worksheets, and reading classic novels, such as *A Connecticut Yankee in King Arthur's Court*, in order to complete the goal of taking weekly quizzes; however, while in the classroom he used his out-of-school gaming experiences to inform his collegial conversations with his peers to talk about issues integral to many standards taught and tested in the English language arts curricula: development of plot, sketching of characters, critiquing works, and writing novels and short stories—all in the name of developing his own novels and short stories.

Davis often was reprimanded to sit down, work silently, and pay attention, thus limiting his interactions with friends and the generation of ideas for novels through collaborative insight into reading, writing, listening, speaking, and presenting. When Davis's teacher thought he wasn't attentive to schoolwork, Davis often was engaged in work directly related to the English curriculum—discussions on writing a novel with a fellow novelist:

> Like the best thing about Gary [classmate] was that he was planning on writing a story about something he didn't quite understand, but that I did, which was sci-fi. So I gave him some ideas on that and what would work and weapon systems that would work [based on knowledge of weaponry from games he was playing] … and he had the idea to set my story in the middle of the Crusades [of which Gary had knowledge, given his affinity towards Biblical history], which we researched and found a period of 30 years not in history books which gave me complete control over what happened to my characters [designed/sketched from video game play].

Gary and Davis's collaborative classroom partnership allowed them to assist one another in deepening the ideas that they had for the novels; they accessed the areas for which they had individually developed deep affinities (science-fiction and history), while sharing an interest in a similar affinity group (Gee, 2007)—namely writing novels, playing video games, and building upon each other's existing funds of knowledge (Moll, Amanti, Neff, & Gonzalez, 1992). This allowed the friends to scaffold learning in a way that would afford individual success, while having the opportunity to act as resident experts about topics of passionate interest. This type of collaborative communication is pervasive and necessary for success in today's global economy (Trilling & Fadel, 2009). Yet, increasingly, this type of learning is often absent in the typical test-prep classroom where skill, drill, and worksheets dominate; sadly this is evident in Davis's perception of academic and professional writing. He explained, "well, what I do isn't actually writing."

Applying Virtual Experiences to the Real World: MUVEs

The students' voices resound with their disjointed views of learning in virtual and academic arenas. Similar to video games, multi-user virtual environments (MUVEs) provide a parallel world of learning and are increasingly popular among children of all ages; recognizing the didactic promise of online spaces, higher education institutions also are experimenting with a variety of virtual environments to enhance both teaching and learning experiences. With the upward trend in online distance education, there is an increase in such research in recent years (Burgess & Caverly, 2009). However, there is limited research on using virtual environments specifically in college-level developmental reading and writing courses, which are designed for those needing additional preparation for the tertiary literacy work load and standards. Some leaders in developmental education hesitate to promote virtual learning for college level developmental readers, citing high attrition rates due to the independent nature of this delivery mode (Boylan, 2002; Maxwell, 1992; Petrides et al., 2006).

Regarding virtual social communication, researchers have shown that traditional college-age students use, have knowledge about, and are comfortable with, a wide range of social technologies (Center for the Digital Future, 2007; Horrigan & Smith, 2007; Junco & Mastrodicasa, 2007). Steinkuehler (2008) posited that given the time young people spend in such environments and their importance for socialization, enculturation, and learning, situated spaces such as virtual environments should be part of the educational research agenda.

Educators must not assume, however, that all of their students are digitally literate prior to the integration of emerging technologies such as MUVEs. Therefore, it is imperative for educators to adequately assess students' digital literacies (as well as their own) and gauge current practices (Burgess, Price, & Caverly, in press). Through a study involving 80 tertiary developmental reading students, using the MUVE *Second Life* to teach critical reading concepts and skills, I (Melissa) examined students' digital literacies through a researcher-developed questionnaire that targeted an array of digitally related skills that many high school students are accustomed to using on a daily basis. Further, observation of students' collaborative reading activities in four *Second Life* virtual classes revealed the nature of students' digital literacy practices.

Findings from the study confirmed that the students were, indeed, digitally literate and further demonstrated digital literacy through their use of technological tools and/or sharing of information. More specifically, students, like Grayson, seemed to recognize how to manage and adjust various functions within *Second Life*, such as controlling camera focus and magnification, changing the environment settings from nighttime to daytime, and navigating terrain through flying, walking, running, and teleporting. Students utilized appearance functions (e.g. clothes, hair, body shape, eye color) to create their own persona while also using gestures (e.g. laughing, smiling, dancing) to interact with other avatars or virtual objects (e.g. golf cart, reading station) that existed on the island.

Students also understood how to adjust the volume settings for the headset and/or microphone, enabling them to better communicate with others using the voice chat tool. Along similar lines, students utilized the instant messaging, text, and voice chat functions within the MUVE to hold private conversations with another student (avatar) who was in close, virtual proximity. Further, instant messaging enabled students to share information and collaborate with others in their reading activity group, and some students used the snapshot function to take pictures of "themselves" and other avatars during the reading activities. Likewise, students shared information by uploading and/or downloading reading activities.

Embedded in this study are the implications that virtual spaces, such as *Second Life*, can be designed to promote literacy learning experiences that far surpass what the traditional classroom can offer. This type of platform is particularly attractive for educators who wish to have students create, inquire, and problem-solve, rather than engage in activities that have pre-set paths to reach goals and further produce educator-limited outcomes. Class meetings in MUVEs can provide students with opportunities to learn through their avatars' experiences, absorbing knowledge in environments that can range from traditional (desks, chairs, and lecture podiums) to informal and interactive settings. These unique environments have the potential to fuse the real and virtual toward creating what could possibly be the optimal learning environment that could spark imagination and creativity. Learning at this level ultimately will require taking risks by crossing and/or expanding the traditional, established borders, into worlds that allow the impossible to be very real and very possible.

His Story, His Learning: Grayson

The potential benefits of *Second Life* are evident in Grayson's learning. Prior to the second reading activity meeting in *Second Life* Grayson, a black-haired, blue-eyed avatar, explored the virtual island by taking a spin in the virtual university golf cart with two classmates he invited. During their exploration, they drove into the island's surrounding waters, saved themselves (and the golf cart), and returned to the virtual lecture hall, eager to share the story of the wild ride with classmates. Before his exposure to *Second Life*, Grayson expressed a dislike for reading because he could not understand multiple plots, advanced vocabulary, and inferencing multiple character viewpoints. However, in this *Second Life* class on point-of-view, Grayson seemed eager to learn as his group and he ventured off to the first of five reading stations, and he texted to a group member, "this is so cool, I wish we could have every class here."

Grayson was immediately attracted to the novel environment and his effortless navigation to each reading station. At each reading station, members of the group (each with a particular role) read various scenarios on point-of-view and entered their responses on a *Second Life* notecard, which they deposited into the island's "dropbox." One particular activity enhanced Grayson's learning, as it encouraged him to assume the role of a Human Resources employee interviewing three candidates for a position. A recent applicant for a real-life, part-time position, Grayson related to this experience *and* gained an alternate perspective of the interview process through the eyes of an interviewer. The transference of virtual-to-real life experiences solidified Grayson's understanding of point-of-view and introduced him to a world of playful learning that allowed him to explore, collaborate, role-play, and create.

A Necessary Cultural Shift

It is important for educators to harness and capitalize on the affordances of virtual-to-real experiences. However, in order to value and welcome students' out-of-school literacies into their classrooms, educators need to become familiar with the literacies they will be addressing (Labbo et al., 2003; Marsh, 2004). As Hawisher and Selfe (2004) contend, schools and teachers often do not validate these literacies:

> We fail to build on the literacies that students already have—and we fail to learn about these literacies or why they seem so important to so many students. We also fail, as we deny the value of these new literacies, to recognize ourselves as illiterate in some spheres. And in this intellectual arrogance, we neglect to open ourselves to learning new literacies that could teach us more about human discursive practices.
>
> *(p. 676)*

Along these lines, the teachers' experiences and comfort with digital literacies impact classroom practice (Goodson et al., 2002). Likewise, if educators *and* students do not understand or value learning mediated by digital practices, then schooling will continue to primarily maintain and privilege traditional texts and approaches.

As our studies suggest, we cannot make assumptions about our students' digital literacies. They may be engaging in virtual worlds, but they may not be conscious of their learning in these spaces. Initially, Robbie did not think he learned from video gaming, and Davis did not recognize his virtual writing as a practice valued by school. Though Grayson's *Second Life* reading activities were required for school, he distinguished them as "fun" in comparison to the traditionally grounded Reading Road Trips. Further, as Melissa's study reveals, students are engaged in meaning-making activities even as they accomplish routine tasks, such as selecting an avatar, focusing on a particular image, and communicating during reading activities. Not only is it important for educators *and* students to recognize the skills developed through virtual practices, but it is also necessary for the connection between the virtual world and the actual classroom to become part of an ongoing, class conversation.

The aforementioned studies reveal the need for dynamic applications of digital skills and understandings. Although digital literacies can be used to extend and amplify traditional writing assignments or multiple choice questions, educators need to build upon the collaborative, experimental, creative, and problem-solving talents that have emerged from video game and MUVE experiences. Gleaning insight from our participants' feedback, we are suggesting that across digital genres and spaces—from real-time strategy games to first person shooters to massively multiplayer online games to multi-user virtual environments—students are involved in critical and meaningful learning. And, given that video game and MUVE spaces and games continue to shift because of technological advancements and consumer demands, we contend that educators need to go further than acknowledging students' lives outside school; educators need to make digital literacies relevant, included, and applied in the classroom—regardless of the platform. Ultimate success hinges on a milieu of creativity and respect and the ability and support to consider alternative ways to integrate students' digital literacies without suffocating innovation with traditional assessment.

There needs to be a cultural shift inside the classroom that helps students understand how, what, and why they are learning in the virtual world. Educators need to consider the stories of Robbie, Davis, and Grayson, and ask themselves: How can I use a video game to support student learning? How can I use virtual learning in place of a worksheet? How can collaborative journaling activities include blogging and online learning groups through Skype or *Second Life*? And, how can I incorporate such technology without necessarily using traditional models of teaching and assessment that continue to plague our educational system at all levels? There are multiple answers to these questions, but before educators can begin to answer them they need to recognize ways popular culture texts, such as video games and MUVEs, can mediate learning in virtual spaces and not dismiss video games or MUVEs because they involve "play." If educators *and* students help each other understand and find relevant connections between digital literacies and academic practices, students, like Davis, Robbie, and Grayson, will be empowered in both virtual *and* academic spaces.

Conclusion

This chapter calls attention to the perceptions and practices of students inhabiting a virtual world—in either a video game or an MUVE—in an effort to highlight the ways in which the participatory cultures of gaming and online environments nurture active scholarship and contribute to the development of academic learning. What becomes evident is the disassociation between school literacy and digital literacy practices, and there needs to be a shift in school cultures to help students become more aware of their meaning-making activities, how they are learning, and the implications and applications of their skills and knowledge developed in the virtual world. All too often students and teachers view digital and academic literacies as dichotomous practices. Robbie, Davis, and Grayson seem trapped in a mindset, supported by their educational system, that refuses to equate play with learning.

Although there has been more attention given to including digital literacies in learning (Kajder, 2010; Knobel & Lankshear, 2010; NCTE Framework, 2008), traditional models of teaching and assessment seem to cloud educational approaches that don't even come close to the engagement and daily demands of our digitally charged world. We should help students harness the energy, proficiency, and enjoyment of virtual experiences and explore the multi-disciplinary applications. Student feedback will empower teachers to apply these new understandings most effectively, without forcing content or turning what students enjoy into "school work." In the virtual spaces, Robbie, Davis, and Grayson were seemingly autonomous learners, not subject to school-based assessment or judgment. Carefully, their "play" needs to be more widely accepted as an effective avenue for learning and achievement. Perhaps then educators will more consistently and productively integrate video games and MUVEs into the classroom, valuing digital literacies and virtual environments and their contribution to innovative learning, enriching practices, and rewarding careers in today's and tomorrow's global economy and society.

References

Abrams, S. S. (2009). A gaming frame of mind: Digital contexts and academic implications. *Educational Media International, 46*(4), 335–347.

Abrams, S. S. (2011). Video games in the classroom: Harmonizing traditional constructs and digital experience. In M. S. Khine (Ed.), *Playful teaching, learning games: New tools for the digital classroom* (pp. 39–49). Rotterdam: Sense Publishers.

Alberti, J. (2008). The game of reading and writing: How video games reframe our understanding of literacy.*Computers and Composition, 25,* 258–269.

Alvermann, D. E., Jonas, S., Steele, A., & Washington, E. (2006). Introduction. In. D. E. Alvermann, K. A. Hinchmann, D. W. Moore, S. F. Phelps, & D. R. Waff (Eds.), *Reconceptualizing the literacies in adolescents' lives.* Mahwah, NJ: Lawrence Erlbaum Associates.

Barton, D. (1994). *Literacy: An introduction to the ecology of written language.* Oxford: Blackwell.

Barton, D. (2001). Literacy in everyday contexts. In C. Snow & L. Verhoeven (Eds.), *Literacy and motivation* (pp. 23–37). Mahwah, NJ: Lawrence Erlbaum Associates.

Barton, D. (2007). *Literacy: An introduction to the ecology of written language* (2nd ed.). Oxford: Blackwell.

Bettinger, E., & Long, B. T. (2009). Addressing the needs of underprepared students in higher education: Does college remediation work? *Journal of Human Resources, 44*(3), 736–771.

Boling, E. (2005). A time of new literacies: Who's educating the teacher educators? *Teachers College Record.* Retrieved 8 March 2007, from www.tcrecord.org

Boylan, H. (2002). *What works: Research based best practices in developmental education.* Boone, NC: Continuous Quality Improvement Network/National Center for Developmental Education.

Burgess, M. L., & Caverly, D. C. (2009). Techtalk: Second Life and developmental education. *Journal of Developmental Education, 32*(3), 42–43.

Burgess, M. L., Price, D., & Caverly, D. (in press). Digital literacies in multi user virtual environments among college level developmental readers. *Journal of College Reading and Learning, 41*(2).

Center for the Digital Future.(2007). Online world as important to internet users as Real World? Los Angeles, CA: USC Annenberg School for Communication. Retrieved from http://www.digitalcenter.org/pdf/2007-Digital-Future-Report-Press-Release-112906.pdf

Charsky, D., & Mims, C. (2008). Integrating commercial off-the-shelf video games into school curriculums. *TechTrends, 52*(5), 38–44.

Collins, A., & Halverson, R. (2009). *Rethinking education in the age of technology.* New York: Teachers College Press.

Delpit, L. (1995). *Other people's children: Cultural conflict in the classroom.* New York: The New Press.

Gee, J. P. (1996). *Social linguistics and literacies: Ideology in discourses* (2nd ed.). London: Taylor & Francis.

Gee, J. P. (2000). Teenagers in new times: A new literacy studies perspective. *Journal of Adolescent & Adult Literacy, 43*(5), 412–420.

Gee, J. P. (2007). *What video games have to teach us about learning and literacy* (2nd ed.). New York: Palgrave Macmillan.

Gee, J. P. (2011). *Social linguistics and literacies: Ideology in discourses* (4th ed.). New York: Routledge.

Gerber, H. R. (2009). From the FPS to the RPG: Using video games to encourage reading YAL. *The ALAN Review, 36*(3), 87–91.

Goodson, I. F., Knobel, M., Lankshear, C., & Mangan, J. M. (2002). *Cyber spaces/social spaces: Culture clash in computerized classrooms.* New York: Palgrave Macmillan.

Green, M. E., & McNeese, M. N. (2008). Factors that predict digital game play. *The Howard Journal of Communications, 19*, 258–272.

Greenfield, P. A. (1984). *Mind and media: The effects of television, video games and computers.* Cambridge: Harvard University Press.

Hawisher, G. E., & Selfe, C. L. (2004). Becoming literate in the information age: Cultural ecologies and literacies of technology.*College Composition and Communication, 55*(4), 642–692.

Hoppock, J. (2008, June). Playing to learn: Video games in the classroom. *ABC News.* Retrieved from http://abcnews.go.com/Technology/story?id=5063661&page=1

Horrigan, J., & Smith, A. (2007). A typology of information and communication technology users. Washington, DC: Pew Internet & American Life Project. Retrieved from www.pewinternet.org/PPF/r/213/report_display.asp

Hu, W. (2010, May). Avatars go to school, letting students get a feel for the work world. *The New York Times.* Retrieved www.nytimes.com/2010/05/07/nyregion/07avatar.html

Junco, R., & Mastrodicasa, J. (2007). *Connecting to the Net.Generation: What higher education professionals need to know about today's students.* Washington, DC: NASPA.

Kajder, S. (2010). *Adolescents and digital literacies: Learning alongside our students.* Urbana, IL: NCTE.

King, J. R., & O'Brien, D. G. (2002). Adolescents' multiliteracies and their teachers' needs to know: Toward a digital détente. In D. E. Alvermann (Ed.), *Adolescents and literacies in a digital world* (pp. 40–50). New York: Peter Lang.

Knobel, M., & Lankshear, C. (2010). *DIY media: Creating, sharing, and learning with new technologies.* New York: Peter Lang.

Kress, G., & Jewitt, C. (2003). Introduction. In C. Lankshear, M. Knobel, C. Bigum, & M. Peters (Series Eds.) & C. Jewitt & G. Kress (Vol. Eds.), *New literacies and digital epistemologies: Vol. 4. Multimodal literacy* (pp. 1–18). New York: Peter Lang.

Labbo, L., Leu, D. Jr., Kinzer, C., Teale, W., Cammack, D., Kara-Soteriou, J., et al. (2003). Teacher wisdom stories: Cautions and recommendations for using computer-related technologies for literacy instruction. *The Reading Teacher, 57*(3), 300–304.

Lacasa, P., Méndez, L., & Martínez, R. (2008). Bringing commercial games into the classroom. *Computers and Composition, 25*, 341–358.

Lim, C. P. (2008). Spirit of the game: Empowering students as designers in schools? *British Journal of Educational Technology, 39*(6), 996–1003.

Marsh, J. (2004). The techno-literacy practices of young children. *Journal of Early Childhood Research, 2*(1), 51–66.

Maxwell, J. A. (1992). Understanding and validity in qualitative research. *Harvard Educational Review, 62*, 279–299.

Moll, L. C., Amanti, C., Neff, D., & Gonzalez, N. (1992). Funds of knowledge for teaching: Using a qualitative approach to connect homes and classrooms. *Theory into Practice, 31*(2), 132–141.

NCTE framework for 21st century curriculum and assessment (2008). National Council of Teachers of English. Retrieved from www.ncte.org/governance/21stcenturyframework

O'Brien, D., & Scharber, C. (2008). Digital literacies go to school: Potholes and possibilities. *Journal of Adolescent & Adult Literacy, 52*(1), 66–68.

Padilla-Walker, L. M., Nelson, L. J., Carroll, J. S., & Jensen, A. C. (2009). More than a just a game: Video game and Internet use during emerging adulthood. *Journal of Youth and Adolescence, 39*(2), 103–113.

Petrides, L., Kerglani, A., & Nguyen, L. (2006). Basic online education literature. *League for the Innovation in Community College.* Retrieved from www.league.org/league/projects/beo/files/Literature_Review.pdf

Prensky, M. (2001). *Digital game-based learning.* New York: McGraw-Hill.

Prensky, M. (2006). *Don't bother me, Mom—I'm learning!* St. Paul, MN: Paragon House.

Prensky, M. (2008). Students as designers and creators of educational computer games: Who else? *British Journal of Educational Technology, 39*(6), 1004–1019.

Salen, K., & Zimmerman, E. (2004). *Rules of play: Game design fundamentals.* Cambridge, MA: MIT Press.

Schrader, P. G., & McCreery, M. (2008). The acquisition of skill and expertise in massively multiplayer online games. *Educational Technology Research & Development, 56*(5–6), 557–574.

Sherblom, J. C., Withers, L. A., & Leonard, L. G. (2009). Communication challenges and opportunities for educators using Second Life. In C. Wankel & J. Kingsley (Eds.), *Higher Education in Virtual Worlds.* Bingley, UK: Emerald.

Shibuya, A., Ihori, A. S. N., & Yukawa, S. (2008). The effects of the presence and contexts of video game violence on children: A longitudinal study in Japan. *Simulation & Gaming, 39*(4), 528–539.

Solomon, P. G. (2009). *The curriculum bridge: From standards to actual classroom practice* (3rd ed). Thousand Oaks, CA: Corwin Press.

Squire, K. (2009). Video-game literacy: A literacy of expertise. In J. Coiro, M. Knobel, C. Lankshear, & D. Leu (Eds.), *Handbook of Research in New Literacies* (pp. 635–669). New York: Lawrence Erlbaum Associates.

Steinkuehler, C. A. (2008). Massively multiplayer online games as an educational technology: An outline for research. *Educational Technology, 48*(1), 10–21.

Street, B. V. (1995). *Social literacies: Critical approaches to literacy in development, ethnography, and education.* New York: Longman.

Street, B. V. (1999). Literacy and social change: The significance of social context in the development of literacy programmes. In D. A. Wagner (Ed.), *Future of literacy in a changing world* (pp. 55–72). Cresskill, NJ: Hampton Press.

Street, B. V. (2010). New literacies, new times: Developments in literacy studies. In B. V. Street & N. H. Hornberger (Eds.), *Literacy: Encyclopedia of Language and Education, vol. 2* (pp. 3–14). New York: Springer.

Sutton-Smith, B. (2001). *The ambiguity of play.* Cambridge, MA: Harvard University Press.

Trilling, B., & Fadel, C. (2009). *21st century skills: Learning for life in our times.* San Francisco, CA: Jossey-Bass Publishers.

Vacca, R. T. (2005). Let's not minimize the "Big L" in adolescent literacy: A response to Donna Alvermann. In J. Flood & P. L. Anders (Eds.), *Literacy development of students in urban schools* (pp. 202–204). Newark, DE: International Reading Association.

Witte, S. (2007). "That's online writing, not boring school writing": Writing with blogs and the Talkback Project. *Journal of Adolescent & Adult Literacy, 51*(2), 92–96.

8

THE PARTICIPATORY MEME CHRONOTOPE

Fixity of Space/Rapture of Time

Lynn C. Lewis

In 2003, a band called O-Zone had a runaway pop hit, a single titled "Dragostea Din Tei" that hit number one that summer on the European music charts. The trio, from Moldavia, also released a video, which, in a scene reminiscent of popular renditions of Beatlemania, begins with three young men running to a plane. They are wearing tight white pants and colorful open shirts. The lead singer has suspenders hanging down and his shirt is open to the waist. The cabin door closes, and as the plane takes off, the single's Europop dance beat pounds out in simple 4/4 time. The following shots focus on the men clowning around in the cockpit, dancing on the wings of the place, and dancing around a hotel room. These shots are interspersed with sudden inexplicable anime style stills of the band. In other words, the video is eminently forgettable. The song, however, did not fade into one hit wonder obscurity. Something else happened.

In December 2004, Gary Brolsma, a New Jersey teen, plugged in his webcam and lip synched his own music video using "Dragostea Din Tei" as the soundtrack. Eyebrows dancing, lips quirked just right, he mouthed the words: "Numa Numa …"

Within days, the Numa Numa Dance had surged across the Web. As Brolsma explains:

> I'm just a regular guy that sits in front of his computer bored out of his mind messing around on the Internet looking at funny videos and other websites to pass the time. The video was originally intended to make a few friends laugh by just goofing off. It only took one take and about 15 minutes to put all together. A lot of people ask me if I planned the video out or took multiple tries with it. The real answer is … no. A week or so after I finished the video, I decided to throw it up on Newgrounds.com just for the heck of it, thinking it would get blammed (automatically deleted for a low scoring

video). Little did I know it would explode in the views, and would touch so many people.

(Newnuma.com, n.d.)

Typical in narratives explaining the genesis of Internet memes, Brolsma's recounting focuses on the randomness of the phenomena: "little did I know …" as well as its immediacy: "explode in the views …" and, as I will emphasize in this essay, its speed—that is, the culturally dominant phenomenon of pleasure in speed and the concomitant privileging of artifacts demonstrating speediness. If it is fast, it is good.

Detecting the prevalence of pleasure in speed is easy: from advertisements promoting fast food, cars, computers, loan approvals, and Internet access, to FastWeb for college scholarships, and speed dating for the lonely, to films extolling speed such as the *Fast and the Furious* series, *Fast Five*, *Speed Racer*, and others. These artifacts not only exemplify the cultural passion for speed, but also demonstrate the inextricable relationship between technology and speed: technology that supplies more speed—is fast—is good. If, as Knobel and Lankshear (2007 p.1) suggest, literacy is best investigated through interrogation of "the contexts of social, cultural, political, economic, historical practices," then examining how the pervasive speed context affects composing practices is critical.

Indeed, the uncritical privileging of speed, redolent of determinism, sponsors problematic identity constructions. Paradoxically, speed also sponsors collaborative composing spaces allowing for anyone with Internet access unique opportunities in participatory authorship. This chapter investigates this uneasy space in a concrete instantiation: the Internet meme.

Meme Foundations

As Knobel and Lankshear (2007b) point out, Internet memes refer to widely spread concepts or cultural artifacts. The concept of the meme is derived from Richard Dawkins' 1975 book *The Selfish Gene*. Referring specifically to brain development and evolution, Dawkins posited that the meme phenomenon helps explain how information and ideas are transmitted. Knobel and Lankshear (2007b) focus rather on the power relations and social networks evidenced through Internet memes. However, they see memes as "recognizable, bounded phenomena that have material effects on the world and can be scrutinized" (p. 201). Drawing on Dawkins' categories of fidelity, fecundity, and longevity, Knobel and Lankshear (2007b) develop a typology of online memes in order to outline the characteristics of this "new literacy practice." For Dawkins, memes that are easily reproduced and circulated demonstrate fidelity while memes that circulate widely and over a long period of time exemplify, respectively, fecundity and longevity. Blackmore (2000) similarly applies these terms in order to describe how memes spread culture. For Blackmore, memes are inventions and she argues that language itself was developed in order to spread memes. While Blackmore differentiates between the creativity of memes and simple imitation or contagion, she does not address the active participatory Internet meme—the meme that is continuously remixed in dozens of iterations and sent speeding across the Web.

Like Blackmore and Dawkins, Knobel and Lankshear (2007b) employ fidelity, fecundity, and longevity in order to select and define meme phenomena in their empirical study, but they focus on online memes. Similarly, I examine online memes, but focus instead on participatory Internet memes. Some Internet memes are extraordinarily fertile, inspiring widespread remixing and evolving into participatory occasions. In addition, as I will argue below, they both reify identity and construct authorship within the same moment. In other words, a participatory Internet meme "explodes in the views" with representations of identity that are typed and familiar: the computer nerd, for example, is a frequent trope, as this chapter will demonstrate. Yet, paradoxically, this meme will also invite creativity, humor, and carefully constructed parodies. These remixes, too, sprint globally across the Web.

I argue that interrogating such participatory Internet memes provides insight into new literacy practices. Why do some memes spark mass participation? What are the characteristics of the images and texts that populate such memes? What do meme remix composing practices suggest about twenty-first century language and literacies? This chapter seeks to respond to these questions. In it, I explore three particularly long-lived and well known participatory memes: the Star Wars Kid; Numa Numa Dance; and Snakes on a Plane.[1] I begin by developing a theoretical framework in order to interrogate the meme context. I build on Knobel and Lankshear's (2007b) description of meme characteristics and draw on work by Bakhtin (1990). In particular, I focus on the characteristics of meme time and space, arguing that the unique qualities of that context offer valuable insights about identity—and the ways in which a cultural passion for speed may obscure critical issues of ethics.

Fidelity and the Meme Chronotope

Because of the increasing ease of access to technologies that allow authors to circulate their compositions—think how easily Brolsma created and uploaded his Numa Numa Dance—fidelity on the Internet depends more and more on qualities other than easy reproduction and circulation. For Knobel and Lankshear (2007a), fidelity is due to kairotic susceptibility; in other words, a cultural production becomes an Internet meme when it emerges at a time and within a space that privileges its reproduction. I argue that speed, normalized and therefore under-interrogated as cultural value, informs kairotic susceptibility in participatory Internet memes.

In his essay "Forms of Time and Chronotope in the Novel," Bakhtin describes the changing nature of chronotopes in the novel through an exploration of their use of space and time, and an exploration of how the two are fused. I draw on

Bakhtin's useful analysis of the chronotope as "[t]he intrinsic connectedness of space and time" in order to parse the complex relationship between Internet memes and susceptibility. Bakhtin (1990) applies the chronotope metaphor in order to analyze the generic characteristics of novel characters and argues that it allows a fuller interrogation of both meaning and the dialogical relationship between reader and writer. For example, in a novel in which chance determines the sequence of events, Bakhtin's Greek adventure-time chronotope controls initiative so that a hero is at the mercy of the gods, resulting in a flat, two dimensional character. Bakhtin is able to explore the ways in which language creates this chronotope—this time/space context. Since memes not only produce their own time/space context, but also depend upon language for their circulation, Bakhtin's chronotope can, I argue, help decipher what it is that memes are doing.

While Bakhtin (1990) focuses on the chronotope in literature, he notes that he borrows the concept from Einstein and that it aptly describes other cultural phenomena as well. Within the Bakhtinian chronotope the inseparability of time and space suggests a method of investigation in which "time, as it were, thickens, takes on flesh, becomes artistically visible; likewise, space becomes charged and responsive to the movements of time, plot, and history" (p. 84). Bakhtin's description evokes the Internet meme.

Bakhtin's description of the novel and the experience of falling into a novel—how a novel's time and space feel to the rapt reader—is familiar. He emphasizes the ways in which language creates, "makes artistically visible" or concrete, a particular sense of time and space. This strategy provides a pathway into thinking about memes. As with the novel, the audience falls into the meme. Like the novel, the meme concretizes a particular time and space. What, then, is that time and space like?

A viewer experiences the meme in a moment—an obvious difference from the experience of a film or novel. The viewer also recognizes the meme in a glance. I gave a conference presentation on memes and showed a short clip from the Numa Numa Dance meme. At the moment I clicked on the meme, the audience smiled, nodded, and laughed. Whether or not they had seen the meme before, they fell into its moment, its time and space. I argue that the space of the Internet meme remains fixed, seemingly outside of time. In fact, it engenders its own original time/space, running from beginning to end endlessly, forever reborn as new audiences discover it and, significantly, forever remixed within the ahistorical speed culture moment. I describe this phenomenon as the meme chronotope and explore its characteristics below.

The Numa Numa Dance meme is one minute and forty seconds long and consists of a grainy shot of Brolsma's head in the lower third of the screen, tan walls, a blue curtain, window air conditioning unit, blurred top of a bed, and the corner of a brown armoire in the background. The simplicity of the objects in the shot, Brolsma's everyman clothing, operate to ensure recognition and the stability of the chronotope. These objects are fungible: the many recognizable remixed features of this meme depend upon the repetitive chant of the song and the lip-synched mime of its hero. In other words, particular elements of the meme always appear in remixes while others are replaceable and unimportant to the meme.

The Star Wars Kid meme similarly operates within the stable chronotope, with fixed and fungible objects inviting remix. The Star Wars Kid meme is one of the most well-known and heavily remixed phenomena on the Web. The story goes like this. In April 2003, four classmates of Ghyslain Raza, a 15-year-old French-Canadian tenth grader, discovered a video. Ghyslain had recorded himself twirling a pretend light saber—in fact, a golf ball retriever—and making Star Wars fight noises. The boys digitized the video and uploaded it to Kazaa, a file-sharing network. Within a staggering two weeks, the video had been downloaded millions of times. Internet denizens redigitized the film to make it "funnier," with Benny Hill soundtracks, flatulence noises, and other amusing sound effects, and those copies were posted and downloaded worldwide. By mid-May, Ghyslain was everywhere—and he was humiliated. As numerous news articles attest, Ghyslain stopped going to school within a month. In July, his parents filed a lawsuit against the boys who had stolen and uploaded the video (Star Wars Kid Files Lawsuit, 2003), which was later settled out of court. Ghyslain himself was reported on numerous websites, including waxy.org, the first website to host the video, to have been either treated for depression or hospitalized (though he is now a law student in Montreal). The familiar speed-pleasure rhetoric emerged immediately in every commentator's remarks about this meme phenomenon.

Like the Numa Numa Dance, the Star Wars Kid video demonstrates the meme chronotope. Its props are few: a purple curtain covers two perpendicular walls, a crumpled yellow pile of fabric in the corner—possibly Ghyslain's jacket—and a golf ball retriever. The hundreds of remixes of this video inevitably include the golf ball retriever or similar object. For example, in "Undercover Star Wars Kid," the golf ball retriever morphs from oars to spears to electrified oars and back again as the figure of the whirling teen is whisked from scene to scene. The figure of the boy is essential to the meme but the other props are not. Similarly, fecund participatory memes such as the Dancing Baby, This Land is Your Land, Louituma, and Hitler Rage videos repeat this pattern. Something is fungible. Something is not.

Space in the meme chronotope, then, resembles space in the Bakhtinian adventure-time Greek novel in which place matters only insofar as it provides a frame for the action. Time does not change the heroes of these memes but rather "[I]n this chronotope, all initiative and power belongs to chance. Therefore, the degree of *specificity* and *concreteness* of this world is necessarily very limited" (Bakhtin, 1990, p. 100). The meme chronotope possesses an "interchangeability of space"; only a few objects are essential to meme recognition, a quality that encourages the participatory remixes endemic to the genre. The rhapsodic narratives describing the emergence of the memes, such as Gary Brolsma's description of the creation of the Numa Numa Dance, depend upon the assumption that chance has created the meme artifact. Further, the content of the memes—the boy caught playacting a

Star Wars battle, the man mugging to the Moldavian pop song on his webcam—also insist upon chance as instigator of the meme. Indeed, the most remixed memes on the Web universally possess this characteristic.[2]

However, this is not to suggest that the contexts within which these memes originate lack relevance. As Knobel and Lankshear (2007b) point out, "[t]he successfulness ... seems attributable in a significant way to the match between the meme and recognizable events or issues in the larger world (and confirmed by analysis of the system invoked by or embodied in the meme)" (pp. 218–219). Still, the meme itself demonstrates fixity in time. The characters within these iconic participatory memes are stable and inflexible, fixed both in and outside of time. As in the adventure-time chronotope, "this most abstract of all chronotopes is also the most static. In such a chronotope the world and the individual are finished items, absolutely immobile. ... What we get is a mere affirmation of the identity between what had been at the beginning and what is at the end" (Bakhtin, 1990, p. 110).

This fixity of identity and static placement in space promotes participatory remixing, while the ahistoricity of speed ensures these memes' constant rebirth. Rhetors easily identify what objects, gestures, and language need to be remixed and what may be omitted. The recurring of the simple pattern, like the constancy of the 4/4 beat in pop songs, is easily reproducible. Kairotic space/time susceptibility hinges upon fixity and simplicity—a paradoxical notion hinting at the complexities of time in a postmodern technological age. Nevertheless, memes do not operate outside of economic systems. To see them as new media objects untethered to the information economy would be to strip them of context, though the impulse to do so may be strong because of their peculiar relationship to time.

As Jameson (2003) suggests in his ironically titled essay "The End of Temporality," "[I]t is the system that generates a specific temporality and that then expresses that temporality through the cultural forms and symptoms in question" (p. 718). For Jameson, that system is late capitalism and, unquestionably, memes operate as cultural forms whose temporality or chronotope exists within and reifies the capitalist system. Gary Brolsma has his own website, newnuma.com, devoted to selling Numa Numa Dance products such as t-shirts, coffee cups, hats, bags, buttons, and dog coats. Brolsma also offers clips of his band and the chance to buy and download their music through a link leading to Apple's iTunes store. While Ghyslain has no website, he and his family did receive a settlement for their lawsuit and he also received an iPod and money from a group of fans. These instances also reveal the continuing influence of participatory culture. In fact, in the case of the Star Wars Kid meme, fans worried about Ghyslain's psychological pain not only donated money to a fund for him, but also started a petition for him to be given a part in the next *Star Wars* film. The petition is still available online with 148,624 signatures as of late 2011.[3]

A connection between memes and capital is particularly evident in the Snakes on a Plane meme, which I discuss below. However, I develop the concept of the meme chronotope not only to demonstrate these well-established links. Unlike

Dawkins' (1989) first concept of meme, Internet memes are typically textual, aural, and visual. This is meme-language—and operates within the meme chronotope as a code fixed in time. Jameson (2003) argues:

> [B]ut to position language at the center of things is also to foreground temporality for whether one comes at it from the sentence of the speech act, from presence or the coeval, from comprehension or the transmission of signs and signals, temporality is not merely presupposed but becomes the ultimate object or ground of analysis.
>
> *(p. 706)*

By their nature, memes privilege language—oral, aural, visual, and textual. They also insist on their own temporality and cannot exist without speed. Their fecundity—their breadth of circulation through global cyber networks—rests on their recognizability. In other words, the identities they construct and represent—the depth of their magnetism—increases when characters are instantly familiar. The Snakes on a Place meme is a productive example.

Fecundity and the Image

When the not-yet-released movie *Snakes on a Plane* erupted into the blogosphere in the spring of 2006, and swept into YouTube remix space, the title of the film first became a pop culture expression denoting fatalism, as in "Nothing we can do—it's snakes on a plane," and then an acronym SoaP. The term constructed the identities of the participants in the phenomena as sophisticated cynics, world-weary, but connected to the networked heart of the creation of a movie. This is a B-film, which attracted enormous attention on the strength of neither plot nor character nor winning portrayals by talented actors. Rather, its title alone led to catchphrases, websites, music, and ardent, blogging fans. Here a strange efficiency can be traced, for the Snakes on a Plane phenomenon arose with such minimal input that the phenomenon occurred even before the film was finished. A script doctor who turned the film down referred to the title in his blog. Those four words, a title without finished script on a networked blog, sped through the Internet universe attracting the excited attention of Internet inhabitants at an exponential rate.

Participatory authorship denotes this meme in particular. For example, when New Line Cinema wanted to change the title of the film to *Pacific Airflight 121*, fans (as well as Samuel L. Jackson, the film's star) reacted with horror. New Line not only changed the title back to *Snakes on a Plane*, but also reshot and added some film scenes in order to ensure that the film received an "R" rating. In other words, the Internet community's views of what the film's title denoted shaped the content of the film. Almost giddy with the speed and circulation of the phenomenon the world news media, too, jumped into the Snakes on a Plane phenomenon, with headlines such as "The shape of fangs to come? Snakes on a what?" from the *Daily*

Telegraph (July 2006), or "Is huge hype the hiss of death for Snakes?" from the *Toronto Star* (April 2006). The *Sunday Star* (April 2006) offered up "Scales of the Unexpected" while the *New York Daily News* (August 2006), referring to film star Samuel L. Jackson, gave readers "Wham, Bam—Thank You Sam."

The phenomenon went global because of the necessary speed which characterizes the Internet and upon which this cultural phenomenon's reach depends. With one click, bloggers could post rants, raves, and demands. With one click, they could sign a petition and send it on to everyone they know. And send it on they did. Inspired by the absurdity of the concept, Internet insiders set about composing the film—and New Line Cinema immediately paid attention.[4]

The SoaP phenomenon appears first as pure spectacle, occurring because the idea of snakes on a plane amuses and the four-word title evokes response. The acronym, SoaP evokes quickly the snakes' spectacle on blogs, on webpages, and in emails. There appears to be no content—only a visual moment flickering across the cultural landscape. Yet, the creative remixes it inspired argue that there is significance. Like the Star Wars Kid and Numa Numa memes, SoaP possesses chronotopic characteristics: its static time and recognizable motifs capture attention. Simple objects: snakes, a hero, and a plane, and a repetitive catchphrase: "I've had it with these motherfuckin' snakes on this motherfuckin' plane." But remixes include "Snapes on a Plane"—a reference to the ambiguous hero-villain character, Professor Snape, in the Harry Potter series; "All Your Snakes Are Belong to Us"—a remix of an older meme based on *Zero Wing*, a Japanese video game poorly translated into English; and "Snakes on a Plane Early Auditions" in which a comic imitates famously macho actors Joe Pesci, Robert DeNiro, and Jack Nicholson, trying out for the part of the hero. These remixes are accessible and seen by any global citizen with Internet access.

KnowYourMeme.com (n.d.) reports that SoaP remixes follow a particular formula:

1. Start with the title: *Snakes on a Plane*
2. Next, alter it while keeping the same flow, but changing the meaning. Example: *Snakes love John Coltrane*
3. Throw in a bad MS Paint drawing of a snake, an image of Samuel L. Jackson, and a Jackson-esque action movie catchphrase to tie it all together. Example: *That's some smooth jazz, motherfucker!*

Both in spite and because of formula, these memes are fecund. Indeed, the remixes summarized above demonstrate that this meme, like the Star Wars Kid and Numa Numa Dance, became deeply fertile. Interestingly, the SoaP meme, which occurred before the release of the film, was valued because of the *imagined* visual spectacle: snakes on a plane.[5] In this sense, chronological time is contested.

The catchphrase SoaP itself is meant as an acknowledgment of powerlessness in the face of the inexorable along the lines of "bad stuff happens." Instead, one just says, "What are you going to do—snakes on a plane." The SoaP phenomenon's speedy arrival into popular culture appears as if generated from those outside the production process, isolated from the producers of the film. The bloggers' action had an effect because the film's real stakeholders, the owners of New Line Cinema, redesigned their film not for the sake of aesthetics, but rather so that the film might generate higher profits.[6] As in the Star Wars Kid and Numa Numa Dance memes, speed reifies the market.

Still, I argue that the phenomenon does not only exemplify the hegemony of capital. SoaP exemplifies the fidelity of the meme: the absurdity of its premise functions as a kind of backtalk to the narratives of terror and war prevalent in this post 9/11 historical moment. Snakes dropping from air vents, slithering across the cabin floor, and driving poisonous fangs into unsuspecting flesh are a subtle reminder of the faceless and mysterious terrorists who appear out of nowhere and turn airplanes into deathtraps. The culture of fear provided the kairotic opportunity. SoaP also offers a useful glimpse of the ways in which memes construct identity. This process promotes the fecundity of successful memes. I examine this phenomenon in the following section.

Identity Construction

Vivian (2007) argues that "[a]n image is a mode of action, a material practice." That is, he sees image as verb rather than noun (p. 479). In the case of Internet memes, images act to construct identity in particular ways. For example, in SoaP, the images used to promote the film deliberately evoked black male sexuality in hyperbolic stereotypical terms. The image is familiar and therefore helps ensure the meme's fecundity. Typed identities are more easily fungible—they serve to promote participatory remix. Jackson's placement as hero is also recognizable—indeed, the catchphrase, "Enough is enough! I've had it with these motherfuckin' snakes on this motherfuckin' plane," was written by bloggers and envisioned in YouTube videos because it recalls his roles in other films.

Representations of Jackson as a black, aggressive alpha male, in both text and visuals, mirror stereotypes and reduce gender and race to their least complicated, most problematic form so that they are easily identifiable within the rush of speed culture. A movie still selected for wide distribution in newspapers and on the Internet shows Jackson holding a dead snake. His grasp on the snake is casual. The photograph is framed so that the phallic shape of the snake, its position against Jackson's black leather-clad body, evokes stereotypical black male sexuality. He is, however, connected by phone to an expert who will, presumably, tell him how to handle the problem. The white phone is familiar and makes the image of Jackson less threatening. His power is mitigated; the gleaming light on his head assures his audience that he is on their side.

The Internet community's play with Jackson's image is intertextual, that is, based upon particular well-known roles such as Mace Windu in the *Star Wars* series.

Jackson is typed within a particular context so that questions of race or difference are erased. Race, represented visually in a meme, becomes flattened and broadened. Nuance in a meme is pointless. Thus, the familiar typed image of the geek in both the Numa Numa Dance and Star Wars Kid memes. In a real sense, these images' mode of action is offering a safe Other.

The particular body of Ghyslain became the object of ruminations, flames, and sympathetic postings because he fitted the generalized identity of the nerd. He wore glasses. He was chubby. He wore a long button-down shirt untucked over baggy pants. He moved clumsily, swung and spun his golf ball retriever, and made the swishing sounds of a light saber with enormous earnestness.

But to what extent does this hold true for non-English speaking countries? Do participatory memes flourish in part because of typed identities? Since YouTube crosses borders, do typed identities as well? Clearly any response to these important questions must begin with the caveat that despite the flattening effects of globalization and the arguably deep penetration of American pop culture across borders, contexts—and kairotic susceptibilities—vary. Nevertheless, two approaches to these questions suggest that typed identities do appear in fecund non-English speaking participatory memes.

First, a search on the YouTube and Know Your Meme websites reveals a number of participatory memes that depend on the nerd identity. For example, the Angry German Kid meme features a chubby German teen, apparently angry at his video game, yelling and pounding on his keyboard. Audience responses to the meme, in both English and German, poke at the boy's weight, glasses, and video game obsession just as they do Gary Brolsma and the Star Wars Kid. I discuss audience response in more detail below.

Second, a Google image search for the nerd concept—the awkward teen boy in glasses—demonstrates image after image. Search for "Japanese nerd" (*otaku*) or "Indian nerd" or "Chinese nerd" and the result is the same. Many of these images are hosted on American sites but enough of them are not that the reasonable conclusion is that the nerd identity is a recognizable trope across borders. Memes flash into existence and cross borders so immediately that they appear to be nationless and as the Internet penetrates more deeply into global lives, they will affect conceptions of identity at an increasing rate. Memes that last longer and spawn more remixes therefore become especially effective.

Generalized or typed identities are characteristic of fecund and long-lived memes for three reasons. First, speed inheres to the meme chronotope. Memes are patterns, meant to be immediately transparent so that their circulation is rapid. The conditions of reception—how the audience will read the meme—are strictly observed: memes are invariably brief because they are read in a moment, a glance of attention. For example, the "Rick Rolled" meme—a clip of 80s pop star Rick Astley, hair styled in a high pompadour, singing his 1987 hit "Never Give You Up"—became a bait-and-switch meme, probably around 2006 (according to Wikipedia and KnowYourMeme.com). Audiences click on a link, expecting it to lead them to a particular site only to be subjected to Astley's video. The prank assumes a glance will be enough for the Internet user to know he/she has been had.

Second, it invites identification. As Kenneth Burke (1974) argues about the appeal of identification, type recognition allies the audience so that participation from both audience and remixer remains a norm. Burke links persuasion and identification directly: strategies of identification make persuasion stronger. "Persuasion," says Burke, "in turn involves communication by the signs of consubstantiality, the appeal of identification" (p. 62). For Burke, consubstantiality allows individual identities to exist at the same moment in which they identify with others. Participatory meme audiences not only recognize typed identities such as the geek or the Jackson persona, but they use these typed identities in their remix projects. SoaP complicates the processes of identification within speed culture because it demonstrates the ways in which visual markers may become what Fleckenstein has defined as a "habit of seeing."

Fleckenstein (2003) draws heavily from Burke in order to identify the "habits of seeing." Deconstructing these habits is the necessary first step towards demystifying codes of image and word and the narratives they construct. Fleckenstein identifies three dominant habits of seeing in contemporary culture: the habit of spectacle, the habit of surveillance, and the habit of antinomy (the Burkean concept of breaking up patterns to form new methods of organization and seeing). These cultural habits inform the construction of identities and regulate their boundaries (pp. 55–58). Participatory meme chronotopes, spectacles dependent upon the glance, offer typed identities as opportunities for remix. They depend upon habits of seeing— and appeals to identification. These habits of seeing are no longer local, but rather global. Types are recognized globally as they sweep through virtual spaces—the fixed and fungible awkward twirling of the Star Wars Kid and the eyebrow quirking lip synch of the computer nerd appear in remixes from industrialized countries across the globe.

However, for the SoaP meme, the typed Samuel L. Jackson hero figure has not demonstrated the same fertility and longevity as the Star Wars Kid and Numa Numa typed nerd figures. It is, perhaps, more connected to a particular kairotic opportunity—the post-9/11 fear culture. In fact, this meme has claimed longevity through the repetition of its title. I argue, however, that the results of this strategy are the same.

Lingering in media traces, for the moment without evanescence, the phrase "snakes on a plane" reappears over and over. Each time a snake really does get loose on a plane, a movie theater, a train, or any other unexpected locale, the event appears in the news, "Snakes on a ..." Here language marks the meme chronotype. The phrase evokes identification with not only a particular cultural moment, but also a habit of recognizing and making safe the exotic Other. The particular semantic nature of this meme—this phenomenon—reveals what Bakhtin (1990) calls "its artistic meaning." As he argues, "These artistic meanings are likewise not subject to temporal and spatial determination. We somehow manage to endow all phenomena with meaning, that is, we incorporate them not only into the sphere of spatial and temporal existence but also into a semantic sphere" (p. 257). Thus, Bakhtin links semantic meaning inextricably to the chronotope and, whether it is a text or image sign the meme chronotope reveals, "Consequently, entry into the sphere of meaning is accomplished only through the gates of the chronotope" (p. 258).

Integral to the meme chronotope, and its ability to circulate meaning, is ubiquitous speed. Speed informs the SoaP phenomenon. That is, speed made possible a moment in time during which SoaP could sprint across the globe. At the same moment, it created a space in which anyone with a camera and a computer could make parody or music or script lines. However, participatory memes are not only rich sites of remix: their permanence on the Web interface ensures their long, if not immortal, presence. The meme chronotope is ageless—outside of chronological time—because of its participatory nature.

Participatory memes offer evidence of Burkean identification through audience responses. Here I depart from Bakhtin (1990), who chose not to examine the "complex problem of the listener-reader" (p. 257), because audience is key to understanding the global nature of participatory memes. Audience interaction with memes is an expected part of the meme experience, marked by the processes of identification described above. Indeed, audience/listener-reader can be tracked because sites offering memes and their remixes also provide space for viewers to comment.

For example, when the Star Wars Kid meme appeared, Internet posters referred to the video in one of two ways. Either they made fun of him, as in one user's comment that "Some of you might be forced to admit the same thing. But there is one important difference between you, me, and this dork. He did it on video" (as cited in Felperin, 2003, p. 13). Or, they admired his sincerity because they recognized its familiarity: "'I personally feel like he is like me and all of my friends,' said Andy Baio, 26, a Web developer in Los Angeles" (as cited in Harmon, 2003). While these comments underscore how identification motivated the rapidity of the Star Wars Kid meme, they also suggest how the performance of typed identity invites audience alliance and social bonding. Cynthia Lewis (2007) closely links performance and identity and argues that memes perform repeatedly and therefore construct identities efficiently. As she explains, "[M]emes themselves both construct and are constructed by group identities through repeated performances. And again, in this case, the performances are dependent on the intertextual chains that exist through the textual history of the meme" (p. 232). Recognition, once again, emerges as a key term: identification narrows to recognition because of repeated performance.

While remix potential ensures the life of online memes, audience responses ensure their agelessness. Internet memes are not evanescent for two reasons. First, they recur. This seems paradoxical: the rapid cycle and profusion of memes belies my position here. However, within that exclusive community of the Web with deep access, time moves in waves rather than sequentially. This is not so much the loss of history that postmodernist theorists lament, but rather new time. Web pages rarely go away. They may be rediscovered. YouTube and similar video sites only purge videos under particular circumstances such as privacy or copyright issues and therefore function as historical databases. The Star Wars Kid meme re-emerged on one website as recently as December 2008, and posters commented in the same vicious language as they had in 2003:

> hey if this kid loses some weight he could become the subway guys apprentice stick to world of warcraft and viva pinata and dungeons and dragons there is nothing more homo then swingin a stick around on the internet cuz people are watching the only way it wouldnt be homo is if you were a girl or a baseball player but this is straight up gay ur parents must be proud.
> *(www.youtube.com/watch?v=HPPj6viIBmU)*

The homophobic virulence of the comment is marked. However, I also note that the commenter's chief concern appears to be the fact that Ghyslain is in a public space where "people are watching." The repeated, performative aspects of the nerd identity give the commenter license to indulge in hate speech. He assumes that Ghyslain has chosen to perform to an Internet audience and only girls and baseball players have this viewer's permission to indulge—an odd mix—that suggests the commenter feels performance should be reserved to those meant to be watched in public spaces. Presumably, the gaze is reserved to the athletic and other objects of desire.

Memes also linger in intertextual traces. Television shows such as *The Colbert Report*, *Family Guy*, and *The Simpsons*, as well as t-shirts, websites, text messages, and news media reports deploy both catchphrases and images from memes. Knobel and Lankshear (2007b) refer to this as "idiosyncratic spins" and cite the Star Wars Kid as well as other early memes, such as All Your Base and Lost Frog (p. 208).[7] Composing work, then, especially in the Web world, keeps memes alive. However, the Star Wars Kid meme also lingers because of the ethical issues that it raises.

Ethical concerns are prominent in stories about the Star Wars Kid meme. For example, worries about the ethics of Ghyslain's emergence as the Star Wars Kid led to the elision of his last name from news reports at the time. (The concern did not extend to the three boys who uploaded the video, however, and their surnames appear in both Web and news texts.) However, the story of the Star Wars Kid meme became an object lesson about privacy in the age of the Internet. As recently as May 2008, the London *Sunday Times* featured a story titled "A Simple Way to Avoid Being the Next Star Wars Kid," in which Oxford University professor Jonathan Zattran argued for instituting certain Web codes so that images are distributed only with the permission of the subject. Yet these concerns about identity and privacy obscure the ways in which identification is functioning here:

the nerd as object of patronizing pity, the nerd as object of sympathy, the nerd as object lesson.

Social bonding through participatory Web memes can be traced in the YouTube video of "Japanese Numa Numa." At first glance, the video appears to feature five schoolgirls in plaid skirts, singing "Numa Numa." After a moment, the viewer notices that the singer in front—the one with the flower behind his ear—is in fact a man. "Hebrew Numa Numa" features three girls in full make-up in front of a mirror, and three men in white shirts and pants, jockeying to use the phone to speak to the girls. Like Brolsma, the six use their facial expressions to mug to the song, which has been translated into Hebrew. The viewers' responses to these videos are similar—the Japanese girls and Hebrew singers are object lessons in the fundamental oddities of their respective countries.

Yet, predictably, there are some cultural differences in the texts of these memes. The Moldavian lyrics of the song, "Dragostea Din Tei," tells the story of a young man attempting to reach a young woman on her cell phone. Curiously, both a Vietnamese Numa Numa and the Hebrew memes pay attention to the meaning of the lyrics, unlike the American remixes which treat the lyrics as nonsensical and amusing sonic accompaniments to Gary Brolsma's exuberant mugging.

The audience responses, however, tellingly demonstrate the typed character identification mechanism described above. For example, the texts from April to July 2011 focus on the Jewishness of the characters, some in admiration ("Jews are so intelligent" wrote one viewer in Spanish), and others less so ("they are all terrorists making bombs" wrote another in English). An Israeli poster comments drolly that "They are not conservative Jews," and an American girl who identifies herself as twelve writes that she no longer considers herself to be Jewish although she likes the food. The Jew as type dominates these viewers' responses. It is as if they need something—a familiar phrase, an evocative image, a song phrase—to show that they belong and identify with the audience.

Recognizing catchphrases and the intertextual mixing and remixing of image/ text is essential for entry to the meme zone. It is, as Knobel and Lankshear (2007a) emphasize, a new literacy in which recognizing, and indeed producing, effects depends upon the ability for fast humor. It is dependent on recognizably fixed identities, the nerd for example, in order for the satire to circulate widely. In sum, identification affects the speedy dissemination of Internet memes, yet speed culture itself affects the formative power of the images populating Internet memes.

The Numa Numa Dance meme, the Star Wars Kid meme, and the Snakes on a Plane meme—as well as the more recent Bed Intruder Song meme—suggest ways in which identity and identification are complicated within global speed culture. Each represents rich sites of analysis. Identifying the threads binding these phenomena together reveals how speed culture is constructing identity—and the complexity of new literacy practices in an era dominated by speed. As Virilio (2005) remarked, "[s]peed has become the privileged measure of both time and space" (p. 134).

Notes

1. Each meme circulates through the YouTube website, and while an analysis of YouTube is outside the scope of the present chapter, the interface functions as a nationless virtual space inhabited by anyone with computer and Internet access. Indeed, YouTube itself reports that "70% of YouTube traffic comes from outside the United States" and its most frequent users are from 25 different countries, using 38 different languages (YouTube statistics page).
2. Some websites such as Know Your Meme purport to create memes; however, to date this has met with limited success
3. See www.petitiononline.com/Ghyslain/petition.html
4. New Line Cinema's responsiveness to the Internet hype directly contrasts with Lotus Corporation's lack of interest in the blogosphere's world described by Laura Gurak in the 1997 book *Persuasion and Privacy in Cyberspace*. As Gurak explains, Lotus's failure to take seriously Internet protests about a proposed product, Lotus Marketplace, ultimately contributed to the product's demise.
5. According to Wikipedia, this includes the straight-to-DVD release of a parody of *Snakes on a Plane*, titled *Snakes on a Train*, three days *before* the actual release of the film.
6. Although the film has not generated enormous profits as hoped by New Line, its marketing products have. These include a book, a comic book, a CD, posters, and a number of different promotional sweepstakes and contests. In addition, the viral videos and song clips posted by bloggers are to be gathered into a DVD available for purchase through Automat pictures.
7. All Your Base refers to a meme begun in 2001 when the beginning of a Japanese video game titled *Zero Wing* was uploaded to the Web. The Japanese was translated into absurdly bad English which included the catchphrase "All Your Base Are Belong to Us" and quickly was remixed into Photoshopped versions of the Hollywood sign, advertisements, and all kinds of documents. The phrase continues to be remixed and reappear including during the Snakes on a Plane phenomenon, with the phrase, "All Your Snakes Are Belong to Us." The Lost Frog meme occurred when a programmer uploaded a copy of a child's note posted on a Seattle street corner asking for help finding his lost frog and stating his determination to find it. The Lost Frog note was remixed onto official banners, posters, and on sky advertisements, and was even remixed into an All Your Base Are Belong To Us remix.

References

Blackmore, S. (2000). *The meme machine*. New York: Oxford.
Bakhtin, M. M. (1990). Forms of time and of the chronotope in the novel. In M. Holdquist (Ed.), *The dialogic imagination: Four essays by M. M. Bakhtin* (pp. 85–258). Austin, TX: University of Texas Press.
Brolsma, G. About/FAQ. In *Numa network*. Retrieved from www.xeornx.com/numanetwork/about.htm
Burke, K. (1974). *A rhetoric of motives*. Berkeley, CA: University of California Press.
Dawkins, R. (1989). *The selfish gene*. New York: Oxford University Press.
Felperin, L. (2003, July 4). Film: when the world strikes back. *The Independent*. London. 13. Retrieved from www.lexisnexis.com.argo.library.okstate.edu/hottopics/lnacademic/
Fleckenstein, K. S. (2003). *Embodied literacies: Imageword and a poetics of teaching*. Carbondale, IL: Southern Illinois University Press.

Harmon, A. (2003, May 19). Compressed data: Fame is no laughing matter for the "Star Wars Kid." *New York Times*. Retrieved from www.nytimes.com/2003/05/19/technology/19VIDEO.html

Know Your Meme. (n.d.). *Internet Meme Database*. Retrieved from http://knowyourmeme.com/memes

Jameson, F. (Summer, 2003). The end of temporality. *Critical Inquiry, 29*(4), 695–718.

Knobel, M., & Lankshear, C. (2007a). Sampling "the new" in new literacies. In M. Knobel & C. Lankshear (Eds.), *A new literacies sampler* (pp. 1–24). New York: Peter Lang,

Knobel, M., & Lankshear, C. (2007b). Online memes, affinities, and cultural production. In M. Knobel & C. Lankshear (Eds.), *A New Literacies Sampler* (pp. 199–228). New York: Peter Lang.

Lewis, C. (2007). New literacies. In M. Knobel & C. Lankshear (Eds.), *A new literacies sampler* (pp. 229–238). New York: Peter Lang.

Social Media News and Web Tips—Mashable—The Social Media Guide. (n.d.). Retrieved from http://mashable.com/

Star Wars Kid files lawsuit. (2003, July 24). *Wired*. Retrieved from www.wired.com/culture/lifestyle/news/2003/07/59757

Vivian, B. (2007). In the regard of the image. *Journal of Advanced Composition, 27*(3–4), 471–503.

Virilio, P. (2005) *Negative horizon: An essay in dromoscopy*. New York: Continuum.

YouTube—Broadcast Yourself. (n.d.). Retrieved from www.youtube.com/

Zattran, J. (2008, May 4). A simple way to avoid being the next Star Wars Kid. *Sunday Times*. London. Retrieved from http://technology.timesonline.co.uk/tol/news/tech_and_web/the_web/article3866927.ece

PART II

Constructing Identity in an Online, Cross-Cultural World

9

FACELESS FACEBOOK

Female Qatari Users Choosing Wisely

Mohanalakshmi Rajakumar

The use of social media in the Middle East is undisputed after the revolutions of Tunisia and Egypt, both staged early in the first two months of 2011. The organizations of protests in both countries via Twitter and Facebook, as well the prominent role of Egyptian Google executive Wael Ghonim as the face of the Egyptian revolution, brought to bear the unmistakable fact that social media are not just for entertainment but can be adapted to the needs of any population by the common decisions of their users. Yet Facebook does not have binary justifications: it is not only a tool for coed commiseration in Europe and North American or a popular uprising vehicle in the Middle East and North Africa. The United Arab Emirates, Qatar, and Bahrain have the highest penetration per total population of Facebook users in the Middle East (Dubai School of Government, 2011, p. 17) and there is very little social unrest or political disaffection in these emirates.

This chapter will address the ways in which gender, social class, and ethnicity affect Qatari women's use of social networking sites on the Internet by examining not only their Facebook profiles but also their other social networking behaviors including wall posting and messages as ways of understanding female Internet personas. Most of the analysis draws from survey responses by students who are current Facebook users. Of central interest are the parameters within which web content is created and circulated by young women in Qatar; in most cases they are willingly opting out of certain actions so as to honor the expectations of their families. Also central to the discussion will be the ways in which women may be circumventing these restrictions to promote and participate in lively digital communities.

The countries on the Arabian Peninsula—including Qatar, the United Arab Emirates, Saudi Arabia, and Oman—enjoy a wealth and political stability unique in the Middle East (with the notable exception of Yemen). Since the discovery of oil in the late 1970s and the rapid development of Qatar's economy since 1995, the small peninsular state, which is situated just above the Kingdom of Saudi Arabia, has expanded from a mostly nomadic Bedouin population to a growing urbanized country, due to host the world at such events as the World Cup in 2022 and aspiring to other events such as the summer Olympics. Accompanying such unprecedented growth is a younger generation that has known much more wealth and opportunity than the ones that came before. Due to its geographic and cultural positioning, Qatar continually balances between the desire to emerge as a global player in the arts, sports, and medical innovation, with its socio-religious background as a Muslim state. Situated between the conservative Saudis to the South and the liberal emirate of Dubai to the East, Qatar consistently attempts to forge its own path. The citizens are no different in the ways they negotiate this juxtaposition between modernity and tradition.

Petrodollars and oil wealth have made the Gulf monarchies headliners in the Western media as they funnel billions into educational programs such as the Qatar Foundation for Education, Science, and Community Development or Kalima, the translation project to increase the number of classic English titles in Arabic. In the case of Qatar, there are twin sides to this growth and modernization; six American universities have set up branch campuses in Doha, Qatar, as part of the QF Education City initiative and most of the classrooms have significantly more female than male students. While this generation of women enjoys roles in public life not available to their mothers or grandmothers, there are still social and cultural mores which most families prefer their daughters to adhere to out of deference to local customs, even if these restrictions are lifted when not in Qatar.

Gender and Modernity in the Qatari Context

Modernity for the Qatari young person can be a very vexed question because it represents opposing values to that of traditional Gulf culture. These traditions are often sources of national and familial pride. Yet the juxtaposition of language and modern/Western practices against those of family, home, and country, put the young person at a paradoxical interchange between consumption of modern goods and services (including state-funded English education) as well as restraint in terms of behavior, dress, and conduct as they adhere to values rooted in a Muslim/Arab/Arabic speaking culture.

Affluence is a talisman in this part of the world where social standing and family ties contribute to a person's *wasta* or personal influence. An individual would never want his or her actions to affect the reputation of the family; for female Qataris their behavior has significant gender-specific boundaries.

The use of socially appropriate terms is an example of an important traditional tenet still used in this incredibly complex society permeated by class and cultural distinctions. In general practice, no female Arab student or unmarried female would be called "woman" for example, because this connotes a female who is married and, more important, has had sexual knowledge of a man. And none of the males are "men," because they haven't fathered their own families and aren't heads of households; this holds true for Muslim and Hindu students whose socially conservative cultures define sexuality only within marriage. Students are "boys" and "girls" and even maybe more so because over ninety percent of these students still live at home with their parents. The milieu of the Middle East respects the family and privileges the family relationship over that of "outsiders." Students stay at home until they are married to start their own families—unless they go abroad for school, and it is very difficult for a female Qatari student to gain permission to do so. Often she is accompanied by a member of her family or has a brother or other male relative working or studying nearby.

In Qatar, as well as other Gulf states, non-related women and men are socially gender segregated after the onset of puberty, sometimes even within the extended family. Qatari society is still very kinship based and those who have connections to Arab ancestors enjoy a higher status than those who may have Iranian or other Arab origins. The family structure retains an emphasis on patriarchy in some instances, as citizenship is largely defined by a father's nationality. A Qatari woman who marries a non-Qatari man cannot pass citizenship to her children without applying for it legally through the government.

For Qatari women ladies' night means complete freedom as they discard the *hijab*, the veils that cover their hair in observance of Islamic dictates for female modesty. In the same way a woman only covers her hair when outside her house, or when non-relative, marriageable male guests come inside, the distinction between public and private is divided along the traditional lines of family life (Joseph, 2000). This very specific and physical definition of inside versus outside, and the appropriate behaviors in each space, have been tested with the advent of modernity and technology.

The Public/Private Online Space

Yet the Internet is one arena, perhaps because it is inside the home, where women can both express themselves and yet restrain themselves because of social conventions around photography and dissemination of images of female citizens older than adolescents. Hence social networking sites such as Facebook or even blogs are applied in different ways. The contrast is a marked one: while American college students are posting compromising photos of parties, relationships, or outings—perhaps unthinkingly—from their smart phones at all hours of the day and night, female Qatari college students, and indeed Muslim women of all ages in Qatar, often do not use any images at all on their pages. This is not due to a lack of technology or ability, as the populations are fairly similar in their degree of middle-class affluence and technological savvy. Instead of a photo of herself in a bathing suit or embracing a friend or even just a self-portrait, a Qatari female user's profile photo is most often that of a younger relative, favorite celebrity, or object. Many women in Qatar do not use their full names or photos to identify themselves with their Facebook profiles, blogs, or Twitter accounts.

For most of the respondents to this survey, they choose to use Facebook in a way that was socially and culturally acceptable to their friends, acquaintances, and families. For this reason it is not surprising that all the respondents' families knew they had Facebook accounts and most of them had had their accounts for a year or more.

For this research, a link to a ten-question survey was circulated via Twitter, BlackBerry Messenger, and of course, Facebook. Respondents were told their answers would be used as part of a project to explore Qatari women's use of Facebook. These three technologies, Twitter, BlackBerry Messenger, and Facebook, are amongst the most popular social media in Qatari society. Twitter is a growing social platform in Qatar with the introduction of Doha Tweetups sponsored by Virgin Mobile, a cellular company in Qatar. Users tweet in English and Arabic and many who circulated this survey had 1,000 followers or more. The BlackBerry Messenger service is a unique live chat system, offered only on the BlackBerry phone to subscribers for free. Via this service one can send broadcast messages including jokes, invitations to personal events, and surveys. Facebook outreach included messages to students at various universities in Qatar, as well as recent graduates, in order to solicit a wide cross-section of responses. In all instances, Qatari women were resending the original survey to their friends and family, requesting them to respond, which is one of the most effective ways to engage people who are situated within a highly family oriented social network. There were 100 respondents to the survey overall.

"I Keep an Interesting Face"

Surprisingly, during the survey collection two potential respondents could not answer any of the questions because they did not have Facebook accounts at all nor had they ever had them. When asked why, one of the respondents did not point to the challenges of keeping the public private; rather she was more worried about her ability to manage interactions with her digital identity:

> There isn't a specific reason why I don't use Facebook. When the initial upheaval took place for this new cyber social network in my society (school and amongst family) I wasn't interested or swayed to own an account. I enjoy using the Internet but I know I won't be faithful to updating my account and keeping it interesting for my list of friends. I feel content with keeping in touch with my direct friends and family through the phone and messaging because I think it's simply easier and faster. That doesn't mean I believe Facebook is useless or silly. If I gave myself a chance to open an account and get connected with my friends I am sure I will get addicted to it.

The young woman is a junior at one of the American universities in Qatar Foundation and a wife and new mother; she perceives Facebook as not merely a means of her connecting to others, but for them to gain an understanding of her. Her inability to "be faithful" and to "update [her] account and keep it interesting for [her] list of friends" highlights her perception of Facebook as a way to construct and maintain an identity as a lively and active person. For this particular non-user, her decision is driven by the speed and rapidity by which she can connect with her friends and for this reason, "the phone and message ... [are] simply easier and faster." Not surprisingly, her responses to the survey for this study were sent via her iPhone.

She's not incorrect in her assumption that Facebook users in Qatar update their status frequently; nearly sixty percent of the respondents said that they changed their profile status regularly. Seventeen percent said they changed it daily. Perhaps she also knows something about how Qatari women like to use their accounts; nearly ninety-five percent of the respondents said that they comment on other people's walls, revealing that exchanging comments throughout the week is a recurring behavior on this particular network.

Language Choice

Language is another significant part of identity construction and, for Qatari nationals in general, the issue of languages used in their country is a complex one. In the last ten years the State of Qatar has undergone tremendous development and modernization in various sectors, which many believe has had an impact on Qatari culture and tradition. With the establishment of various English-medium private schools, the Qatari primary and secondary school reform which has led to the establishment of English-medium independent schools, and the birth of Education City with six American universities, English has become a part of daily Qatari life.

While knowledge of English is a commodity that carries with it various economic and social benefits, the spread of English in Qatar and throughout the world has created several tensions. Some question whether the spread of English in the world has led to global bilingualism or English imperialism, and particularly in Qatar, whether the emphasis on English-medium education may lead to the loss of Arabic and a preference for Western ideas and practices rather than Muslim values and traditions.

If the choice of language used by survey respondents on their Facebook accounts is any indication, these anxieties may be somewhat warranted. Eighty-eight percent of those surveyed said that the language they use to communicate with others on the site is English. Thirty percent indicated they used transliterated Arabic; that is, Arabic words spelled phonetically with Roman letters. Only seventeen percent said that they used Arabic script when interacting on Facebook. This may be a factor unique to Qatar due to the emphasis on education in English, as a Facebook Arabic beta site is in fact growing and doing well with members from many countries in the Middle East.

"I'm Afraid"

The other significant category of responses came in reply to the question of whether or not female users had photos of themselves on their accounts. Overwhelming, eighty percent of respondents said "no." When asked why, their responses echoed a common theme: in such a public forum, they were not sure where their photos would end up or by whom they would be seen. Even while veiled or appropriately dressed, the respondents felt uncomfortable with the thought of having their images floating on the Internet via their Facebook accounts.

When the respondents tried to explain their choices, their theorizations pointed to the consequences of their actions and reputations on their larger familial and social circle:

> It's kind of a rule here in Qatar; girls usually don't put up photos of themselves. I used to till my mom advised me to stop because lots of rumors go around in Doha and stuff.

> It is a long story ... bottom line is that I do rarely post pictures of myself just to let people whom I am friends with from abroad to know who are they friends with & trust me. But afterward I just take them off as whenever pix are online, they are online! And we all know how creepy some people can be (talking from an experience!).

> I am afraid of sharing my photos with others, even my friends. I don't imagine having my photos at half of the country's houses. I also don't guarantee if men look at my photos.

The consequences for these women are greater than compromised employment opportunities or judgment of their choices by others; they could be sanctioned by their friends, families, acquaintances, and strangers for images they post of themselves online. Choosing not to put up photos on Facebook may seem ironic but for them it is a form of protection against criticism. It is an active and conscious choice to circumvent any negative attention that may result in sanctions against their other social choices. The respondent who mentions "my mom advised me to stop" indicates no ill will or feeling of oppression at not putting up photos. Instead she reads this move as a protective gesture, whereby her mother is shielding her from the "rumors going around Doha and stuff." The vagueness of the terms signifies the extent to which photos, the people depicted in them, and the act of displaying them can be misconstrued in such a small community. The ensuing grief, the respondents seem to be saying, is simply not worth it.

The issues of privacy and cultural acceptability were also raised in response to the question regarding why users chose not to have photos of themselves on their profiles. In each response, however brief, one can see that it was in fact a conscious choice: "Cultural reasons," as one person put it briefly; or "Social restrictions!" as another respondent commented. The explanations consistently pointed to the reactions to the photos within the wider community within which the user lives: "Cultural reasons. Friends might post group photos which are not tagged; mostly associated with university events."

Another common theme was uncertainty over where the photos go once they are posted online; of particular concern was the viewing by any non-relative males. This fear is directly linked to the importance of modesty amongst unmarried women and the continuing notion that a woman's face is an embodiment of her reputation and—by extension—that of her family's. Therefore someone who posts a photo online is risking not only someone making fun of an unflattering photo; she could also draw unwanted attention to herself if she presents herself as attractive:

> I don't trust people's actions in certain moments.

> Cultural restraints ... Many people believe that someone else having your picture is not a good thing as they can show it to their brothers or male relatives.

> I am afraid of sharing my photos with others, even my friends. I don't imagine having my photos at half of the country's houses. I also don't guarantee if men look at my photos.

> Because I'm worried people stealing pictures.

> Because I have male friends on Fb.

There are a few who express concern over how these photos influence people's perceptions of them when they are not there to defend themselves:

> I use Facebook as a method of staying in touch with friends who live all over the world. There are photos of me in people's albums, but I refuse to have a profile picture because that is the one thing everyone in the world can actually see, besides your name, no matter what else you limit. The idea of that is pretty scary; do I want people I've never been introduced to, to know exactly what I look like from a social networking site? To me it's less of a cultural thing as a Qatari woman and more of an identity matter, a right to my own privacy really.

This user might find agreement with Facebook users in other parts of the world who have unlisted profiles or who only communicate with specific people via their account; the issue of privacy, she explicitly states, is not to do with her national or gender identity, but more with exercising her right as an individual to be seen only when she chooses.

Others are not as articulate but describe the effect of social norms or a form of peer pressure as opposed to familial pressure:

> Personal decision of not to be seen by others (personal privacy).

> I would love to put my own photo in my profile, but somehow I feel it's not socially acceptable.

132 Mohanalakshmi Rajakumar

I have only Manga pictures.

As a Qatari woman it's not allowed to show our photos in public.

While posting photos rated as a non-behavior for most of the respondents, using their real names was not a problem. Perhaps having no photos of themselves made them feel more comfortable in creating profiles as themselves. Only two of those surveyed indicated that they used identities other than their own. One explained that she used her real first name, so that her friends could recognize her, and Qatar as her last name. When asked why they chose not to use their real names, both declined to respond.

The introduction of such vast wealth to a minority national population has created access to the best that modern society can offer. The challenge for the young women of Qatar is how to negotiate amongst the wide range of choices such access provides them. For many of the female users of Facebook, they are doing so in a deliberate and thoughtful way to protect themselves from social sanction.

These responses by Qatari women are not that different from Arab women in Qatar in general as a recent study with students at Northwestern University in Qatar found. After interviewing forty-two female students, aged 18–22, League and Chalmers (2010) published their research as a chapter titled "Degrees of Caution: Arab Girls Unveil on Facebook," in the book *Girl Wide Web 2.0: Revisiting Girls, the Internet, and the Negotiation of Identity*. Their study found that most of the respondents also referred to family over the course of the interviews as factors in the decisions they made about their online identities. Perhaps a recent status update on Facebook by a young Palestinian woman sheds some light on the findings in League and Chalmers' study. A college age woman, whom we'll call Lubna, posted:

> not under any circumstances I will accept any GIRL 2 call out ppl with names or use such words on a website !! remember who u r, ur religion, ur morals & where u come from ... it's a social network with lots of coworkers, teachers, colleagues & male friends so BEHAVE and use words that reflect how u were raised!!!

Clearly Lubna is expressing the idea that female Muslim users of Facebook have certain shared sensibilities about what should and shouldn't be posted on Facebook, outside the realm of photos into "words" that indicate her "morals." This type of social policing is what Qatari women said they were avoiding when being careful about what they posted on their or the walls of others.

Throughout the Arab world, the demographic of users is one of the highest amongst teens and college age students and recent graduates as the Arab Social Media report by the Dubai School of Government shows (2011). Most users in the Arab world are between the ages of 15 and 19 and there are approximately 21.5 million Facebook accounts in the region (p. 4). The Gulf Cooperation Countries, including

Qatar, Yemen, Bahrain, Oman, the Kingdom of Saudi Arabia, and the United Arab Emirates, have the highest percentage of Facebook users per population—only exceeded by Lebanon (p. 4). Yet while the global trend is for more female users than male, in the Arab world this is reversed with a ratio of 2:1, with more males than females on Facebook. This reversal is likely due to many of the social considerations discussed in this chapter.

Conclusion

This study highlights the creative approaches to Facebook used by female Qatari users to interact within the social norms to which they wish to adhere. A Western-centric interpretation of the faceless Facebook profiles discussed here would describe these women as being forced not to display photographs or other distinguishing features about themselves. Rather, the reader is encouraged to see their faceless Facebook profiles as a choice, a demonstration of agency on the part of the participants in this study as well as non-Qatari Arab women who refrain from specific behaviors as a form of conscious image management. They demarcate the differentiation between what one does in public and private with an acute awareness of information, photos, and other details shared on Facebook—a medium that tends to serve as a public diary for many of its global users. A hyper-awareness of Facebook details is exercised by Arab women who wear hijab in a way that, perhaps, non-hijab wearers or non-Muslims do not exercise. This dichotomy between the public and private self is a significant marker of female Qatari identity in contemporary society; one might watch *Desperate Housewives* at a friend's or cousin's house for example, but never be seen in any of the revealing dresses worn by many of the actresses in public.

By displaying photos of younger family members or designer items, these users are in control of who has access to their likeness and by default control over a critical aspect of how their identity is accessed and understood by other users—male and female. The choice not to be seen in a public sphere like the Internet (and also newspapers or videography) is an active and conscious one, in stark contrast to the ubiquitous nature of contemporary personal photography amongst other Facebook users in the same age group but of other cultural backgrounds. These women are seeing subjects, while at the same time remaining unseen by strangers and non-relative males and females.

The study by League and Chalmers (2010) further expands the examination of social norms for female Arab users of Facebook. Future studies could examine the growing numbers of users on Twitter, as well as existing technologies which are on the rise, including Tumblr, and the continued use of blogs in the Middle East as a means to express oneself. The discussion provided here contributes to what will hopefully be a growing body of work on the dynamic world of Arab women.

References

Dubai School of Government. (2011). *Arab social media report*. Retrieved from www.dsg.ae/LinkClick.aspx?fileticket=-WvgLGPQ9G0%3d&tabid=1163

Joseph, S. (2000). Gendering citizenship in the Middle East. In S. Joseph (Ed.), *Gender and citizenship in the Middle East* (pp. 3–30). Syracuse, NY: Syracuse University Press.

League, R., & Chalmers, I. (2010). Degrees of caution: Arab girls unveil on Facebook. In S. R. Marzzarella (Ed.), *Girl wide web 2.0* (pp. 27–44). New York: Peter Lang Publishing.

10

RUSSELL T DAVIES, "NINE HYSTERICAL WOMEN," AND THE DEATH OF IANTO JONES

Laurie Cubbison

The Internet has fostered the growth of an active participatory popular culture, especially among fans of science fiction and fantasy, and this development has brought to the forefront the emotional and intellectual investment that fans make in their favorite narratives.[1] This investment often makes for a contentious relationship between the writer/producers who create and control a popular story and the fans who not only consume the official narrative but also use that narrative to foster their own creativity. In this essay, I examine a particular conflict that arose when producers made significant changes to a television program, including the death of a favorite character, in terms of its implications for the relationship between authors and audiences in the age of participatory popular culture. My case study focuses on the *Children of Earth* mini-series of the British Broadcasting Corporation (BBC) program *Torchwood*, whose producers made major changes in genre, characterization, and target audience, angering many fans who expressed that anger[2] via online social networking sites. In my analysis of this case, I draw on Roland Barthes' distinction between the work and the text—the commodity and the conceptual field—in order to explore the basis of the conflict that developed between author and audience.

In "From Work to Text," Roland Barthes (1977) recognizes the commodification of an author's creation as a work distinct from the conceptual field of the text:

> the work can be seen (in bookshops, in catalogues, in exam syllabuses), the text is a process of demonstration, speaks according to certain rules (or against certain rules); the work can be held in the hand, the text is held in language, only exists in the movement of a discourse (or rather, it is Text for the very reason that it knows itself as text); the Text is not the decomposition of the

work, it is the work that is the imaginary tail of the Text; or again, *the Text is experienced only in an act of production.*

(Barthes, 1977, p. 157)

The work thus is affected by market forces. It is bought and sold, produced as a physical object. The text, on the other hand, is experienced in the shared symbolic discourse between author and audience:

> The logic regulating the Text is not comprehensive (define "what the work means") but metonymic; the activity of associations, contiguities, carryings-over coincide with a liberation of symbolic energy (lacking it, man would die); the work—in the best of cases—is *moderately* symbolic (its symbolic runs out, comes to a halt); the Text is *radically* symbolic: *a work conceived, perceived and received in its integrally symbolic nature is a text.*
>
> *(Barthes, 1977, pp. 158–159)*

As Graham Allen (2000) points out, "Barthes distinguishes between two kinds of readers: 'consumers' who read the work for stable meaning, and 'readers' of the text who are productive in their reading, or, to put it in Barthes's terms, are themselves 'writers' of the text" (pp. 69–70). This formulation of the distinction between a narrative as work and a narrative as text is particularly useful for discussions of media fans and the products they enjoy, as very often their enjoyment consists of writing and re-writing their favorite narratives, in ways that challenge those with legal ownership over those works. Jenkins (2006) points out that "Fans are the most active segment of the media audience, one that refuses to simply accept what they are given, but rather insists on the right to become full participants" (p. 131). Jenkins observes that participation is often a fraught concept, with media companies viewing "participation as something they can start and stop, channel and reroute, commodify and market" (p. 169), even as fans resist being commodified. The relationship between television series producers and their fans, in particular, highlights these issues as the market forces influencing production and distribution of the work affect the emerging text, with *Torchwood: Children of Earth* providing a useful example of the kind of conflict that can result.

Case Study: *Torchwood*

A spin-off of the long-running science fiction series *Doctor Who*, *Torchwood* features a group of people monitoring a dangerous rift in time and space centered on Cardiff, Wales. The program's writer/producer is Russell T Davies, known for creating *Queer as Folk* and for reviving *Doctor Who* in 2005. The Torchwood Institute, the Cardiff rift, and the character of Captain Jack Harkness originated on the revived *Doctor Who* and became the basis for a science fiction series in the investigative team mode. Seasons one and two of *Torchwood* featured a main cast of five: immortal time traveler Captain Jack Harkness (John Barrowman), and his staff: Gwen Cooper (Eve Myles), Dr. Owen Harper (Burn Gorman), Toshiko Sato (Naoko Mori), and Ianto Jones (Gareth David-Lloyd). As led by producer Davies and actor Barrowman, both of whom self-identify as gay, *Torchwood* is unique among science fiction television series for featuring both heterosexual and homosexual relationships, in particular the same-sex relationship between Harkness and Jones, a relationship that became extremely popular with many *Torchwood* fans.

During its first two seasons, *Torchwood* located itself narratively within the standard genres of science fiction television. Like *The X-Files* and *Buffy the Vampire Slayer* before it, *Torchwood* used a monster-of-the-week structure, in which each episode features an alien or supernatural event to be investigated, with a seeded story arc, in which narrative developments are sprinkled across episodes and culminate in the season finale. *Torchwood*'s legacy from *Doctor Who* meant that in its first two seasons it featured adventure narratives, with occasional dark undertones, that emphasized the participation of the main cast. Elsewhere, science fiction television was heading in the direction of increasingly dark narratives with political themes, with the new version of *Battlestar Galactica* leading the way. While *Torchwood* often contained dark storylines, the full implications were rarely explored on screen.

The first season ended with Captain Harkness departing for points unknown, only to appear in the season finale of *Doctor Who* before returning to Cardiff at the beginning of *Torchwood*'s second season. In the finale of the second season, the characters of Dr. Owen Harper and Toshiko Sato, the team's medic and technician respectively, were killed off, their actors leaving the show. *Torchwood* ended the second season in April 2008 with only three of its main cast remaining: Jack Harkness, Gwen Cooper, and Ianto Jones. As is often the case, many fans reacted to the events of the season finale by continuing the story on their own, supplementing the official narrative canon with their own versions of how the survivors would cope with their losses. Even though many fans eagerly supplement the official narrative with their own stories, they generally privilege the canon, or the narrative provided by the author, over other narratives with those characters in that setting (Busse & Hellekson, 2006, p. 10), whether produced by fans or by the writers of tie-in novels.

When discussing the development of *Torchwood* as a television program, it is not enough to discuss the progress of the narrative; one must also consider the progress of its production and distribution. It is in the production and distribution that one most clearly sees the commodification of the work. *Torchwood*'s movement from one BBC network to another led Matt Hills (2010) to refer to *Torchwood* as a brand in search of an audience ("Brand *Torchwood*"). The program had initially aired on BBC Three, a UK niche network, during its first season, and then moved to BBC Two for the second. The program became quite successful among science fiction television audiences and gathered a global audience, becoming, for instance, one of BBC America's most popular evening dramas. A television program such as

Torchwood is developed with an audience in mind and pitched to networks based on that audience, but programs aimed at a niche audience and telecast on a niche network can become popular enough to claim a more mainstream audience on a more mainstream network, thus the move from the niche network BBC Three to BBC Two, and eventually BBC One, the flagship network with the broadest audience in the UK. But a move to the mainstream often forces changes to the text that can alienate the original audience. In the process of moving to BBC One, Davies was offered a five-part mini-series instead of the usual thirteen-episode season (Davies & Cook, 2010, p. 356). The change in format set up a change in the kind of story that could be told, and *Torchwood*'s niche audience wasn't prepared for the effect these changes had on the text of their favorite program.

The conflict at the center of this case study arose when *Torchwood*'s third season, a five-part mini-series titled *Children of Earth*, was telecast on BBC One the week of 7 July 2009, fourteen months after the end of the second season. *Children of Earth* had been scheduled to air in Britain and Australia for five consecutive nights from Monday to Friday, with its American broadcast scheduled for two weeks later on BBC America. A major difficulty for contemporary producers of global popular culture is the inability to completely control distribution of the work. The distribution of television programs is based on a system of regional licensing and coding, with a great deal of money riding on licenses for popular shows in the major media markets. That system is being undermined, however, by online media fan communities who are not willing to wait until all their members can legally access the program before discussion starts and stories are written.[3]

The forms of popular culture most prominently affected by the breakdown in this system are American and British television programs and Japanese anime and manga, and these media genres often share fans, with *Doctor Who* and *Torchwood* fans being just as likely to be fans of *Supernatural* and *Saiyuki*. The impetus to break down the existing system is due to the desire on the part of fans to cope with the problem of spoilers. Not only do fans pursue information about the narrative prior to its initial telecast (Jenkins, 2006), pestering producers and actors during convention appearances for example, but once an episode has aired in its primary market the discussion begins in online communities, even if many members of the community are not able to view it. Downloading developed as an act of narrative self-defense. The only way for an avid fan living outside the originating country to preserve the experience of the text is to gain access to the work as quickly as possible, so as not to be locked out of the discussion.

These issues, at play in global participatory popular culture, are illustrated by the fan anticipation that preceded the UK broadcast of *Torchwood: Children of Earth*. Given the fourteen-month hiatus between the end of the second season and the telecast of *Children of Earth*, fans were eager for news on the developing narrative: Would new team members replace those who had died? How would the relationships of the survivors develop? Who would survive the mini-series? The fan fiction writers had filled in the gaps, but *Torchwood* fans were eager to see how the canon narrative would develop narrative possibilities raised by the finale of the second season. Meanwhile, the actors, writers, and producers were promoting *Torchwood* at fan conventions, their every word analyzed for hints about the story of *Children of Earth*. In fact, early speculation about the fate of Ianto Jones was the result of fan parsing of Gareth David-Lloyd's use of the past tense to refer to his character at one convention, only to be countered by fans citing John Barrowman's statement at another[4] that fans would be happy with the development of the relationship between Jones and Barrowman's character, a statement that led to fans feeling betrayed by the actor when they did learn of Jones' death.

By the time "Day One" was broadcast on BBC One (and later that day on Australian television), fan anticipation and anxiety was at a fever pitch. Even though the mini-series was scheduled to air on BBC America two weeks later, fans in the United States were using bit.torrent and YouTube to download the episodes. Virtually the only way for a *Torchwood* fan in the United States to remain unspoiled would have been to shut down all communication with her online friends and communities until the program had aired legally in her region.

Spoilers reporting the death of Ianto Jones began to circulate early on 9 July 2009 when a poster on the forums of the Internet Movie Database[5] claimed to have received an early shipment of the *Torchwood: Children of Earth* DVD set and learned from it that Jones died in the episode to air that evening. The rumor spread quickly through the LiveJournal and Twitter social networking sites, confirmed by other British fans who had also received early delivery of their DVD sets. Anxious and angry fans bombarded the blog and Twitter sites of James Moran, the scriptwriter for the third episode (Moran, 2009a), asking for confirmation that he refused to provide. As the member of the production staff with the most noticeable online presence, Moran became the lightning rod for early fan reaction. Later that day, the episode finally aired on BBC One, and the fandom erupted, with hashtags for *Torchwood* and Jones showing up on Twitter's list of top trending topics. Meanwhile the BBC's copyright lawyers seemed to be trawling YouTube for illegally uploaded copies of the episodes, working overtime to prevent the "Day Four" episode from being viewed. As the *Children of Earth* concluded, some fans were satisfied but more were angry and grieving, declaring that they would never watch *Torchwood* again.

The speed with which social networking spread the rumors and reactions encouraged a highly emotional response over a reasoned response. Twitter, in particular, with its speed and the limited length of its messages, fostered a sort of mob reaction (known as a Twitter storm) in which outrage is propagated and reinforced across the Internet. When studying social networking, one must remember that such storms are not contained within a single site. Users participate simultaneously in a variety of global sites, from such major sites as Facebook and Twitter, to smaller sites such as LiveJournal and the discussion forums of particular websites. Thus, news moves quickly, and once it makes the jump from a smaller site such as the Internet Movie Database Forum to a global site such as Twitter, the news and the reaction to the news cannot be contained.

Fan Expectations Versus Production Decisions

While significant, Ianto Jones' death was just one of the reasons given for the outrage. The intense reaction to *Children of Earth* on the part of *Torchwood*'s most avid fans resulted from the mismatch between fan expectations and the decisions made by the producers and writers. Production decisions with regard to the genre, plot, and characterization of *Torchwood* took the narrative in a different direction than fans expected.

In its first two seasons, *Torchwood* seemed on the surface to belong to the television genre of investigative teams, the premise being a group of people with specialized skills working together to solve particular problems, similar to such shows as *CSI* and *NCIS*. For these other series, the plots only occasionally affect the main cast directly, but *Torchwood*'s plots often featured the main cast as participants in the events rather than solely as investigators (Vermuelen, 2010). This focus on the part of the writers resulted in plots that were largely internal. In the episode "Adrift," for instance, the plot is ostensibly about a missing person's case; the focus, however, is less on the mother and her missing son and more on Gwen's disillusionment with what Torchwood can accomplish as an organization. Many other season one and two *Torchwood* episodes take a similar approach, developing an episode's plot in order to focus on the main cast. Even so, while the focus remained on the main cast, that did not mean that the relationships between the characters received much screen time. The developing relationship between Jack and Ianto was glimpsed here and there, but particulars were left to the viewers' fan fiction. As a result, fans who had written extensively about the two, exploring as many aspects and potentialities of the relationship as they could imagine, developed a sense of ownership of the characters and their relationships, even as the fan fiction writers' disclaimers acknowledged Davies' and the BBC's legal ownership of Jack and Ianto.

The change in genre changed the plot structure as well. Fans perceived the *Torchwood* cast as having been dropped into a *State of Play* type plot, as opposed to the plot being primarily focused on the *Torchwood* characters, as the previous seasons had. In *Triumph of a Time Lord*, Matt Hills points out that the political thriller was one genre that *Doctor Who* had not attempted (Hills, 2010b, p. 7), so it is interesting to see Davies taking *Torchwood* in that direction, and pre-production reports of series four seem to indicate that direction will continue, even though it is known to alienate many of the program's longtime fans.

In terms of characterization, *Children of Earth* expanded the cast in ways that stretched the narrative and pointed it in a different direction from the first two seasons. *Children of Earth* introduced extended families for both Jack and Ianto (although the third season seemed too late for these family members to be given their first mention). The political context within which the Torchwood Institute operated was shown, and the narrative focused much of its screen time on the actions of political players, such as John Frobisher, a government official, and his staff.

The most significant, but by no means the only, fan objection to *Children of Earth*, was the death of Ianto Jones, an extremely popular character amongst the fans. Rumors that Jones would die in the series had actually been circulating on LiveJournal for several months, not just during the week of the broadcast, but as early as February 2009, with fans convincing themselves that their favorite character would remain safe. During the "Day Four" episode, however, Jones accompanied Harkness into a government building to confront the alien threat that then killed him. Among the objections was the belief that Jones' death was not heroic, as it didn't accomplish anything in the fight against the alien, serving the narrative only by bringing his lover to the point of despair.

Meanwhile other fans read the death within the context of other character deaths and objected on the basis that it continued a pattern common within popular television of killing off gay characters, an issue that served to focus discussion at afterelton.com, a popular culture news and views website for gay men (Skibinskaya, 2009). Because *Torchwood* featured a variety of same-sex relationships and interactions, many GLBTQ fans had begun to see the program as a televisual safe place, a safety that they perceived as being violated in *Children of Earth*. Media fans have long interpreted close male friendships romantically, referred to as "slash," and much of the scholarship into fan fiction focuses on the tendency to write sexual relationships between male characters (Bacon-Smith, 1992; Jenkins, 1992; Kustritz, 2003). *Torchwood* is unusual in that a male same-sex relationship similar to that generated by fans was part of the ongoing plot. As a result, *Torchwood* attracted not only slash fans but also young GLBTQ fans who longed for a television program that featured the characters and relationships with which they identified. However, some fans were discontented with the portrayal of homosexuality in *Children of Earth*: Ianto is shown as being uncertain about his sexuality and his importance to Jack, and Ianto's brother-in-law is shown to be using casually homophobic slurs.

I suspect that some of the reaction to this aspect of *Children of Earth* is due to differences within the GLBTQ fan community, as many self-identified GLBTQ fans tended to side with Davies on this aspect of the program, while others tended to be angry with him. Some fans accused Davies, one of the most powerful gay writer/producers in the television industry, of being homophobic. On LiveJournal, whose users are predominantly female, older fans seemed to side with Davies, while younger fans tended to view Jones' death as indicative of homophobic portrayals of gay characters. Polina Skibinskaya's essay "Death By 'Torchwood': Captain Jack, Ianto Jones, And The Rise Of The Queer Superhero" (2009) at afterelton.com, a site whose readers are predominantly but not exclusively male, argued that Jones' death was a "marker on the continuing road to true gay empowerment—a road that has frequently been two steps forward and one step back." But the essay's comments placed *Torchwood* and Jones' death in the context of Davies' previous work on the British version of *Queer as Folk* as well as other depictions of gay men, leading the commenters to take a much more cynical view of *Torchwood* as not only having not lived up to its billing as providing positive portrayals of gay men[6] but rather privileging the heterosexual relationship of Gwen and her husband over the relationship between Jack and Ianto.

The treatment of Ianto Jones' sexuality was not the only issue for his fans, however. Many fans identified with him on other criteria, from personality to occupation, and these fans were also invested in Jack and Ianto being in a committed relationship, but *Children of Earth* disappointed them when it showed Jack resisting the "couple" label and Ianto reluctant to pursue the issue. These fans were also disappointed that while Ianto declared his love for Jack during his death scene, Jack did not do the same, causing the fans to reinterpret the relationship in ways that disappointed them. At least one fan fiction writer expressed the sense that she could no longer write Jack as having any degree of commitment to Ianto, since the canon narrative had undermined the relationship.

Fans also objected to the changes they perceived as having been done to Jack's characterization, with some fans expressing distress at his actions in "Day Five."[7] It is important to note, however, that Jack had been shown in several episodes to be the only one capable of making the decision to sacrifice the one for the many. Thus, one may argue that Jack's actions in "Day Five" are in character, but his actions, combined with the change in direction of the program, resulted in a darker narrative than many fans were prepared for, leading to a need on the part of these fans to confront their reactions to the darkness of the narrative.

The intense reaction of these fans immediately brought them into conflict with the writers of *Children of Earth* over the relationship between author and audience in terms of control of the narrative, raising such questions as: What is the author's responsibility to the story? What is the author's responsibility to the audience? What is the audience's responsibility to the author? What is the audience's responsibility to the story? As fans reacted to the series, their emotional reactions were being directed at those with authorial responsibility for the program. The blog and Twitter feed of "Day Three" screenwriter Moran provided the only Internet presence of the production staff. Fans bombarded his sites with their emotional reactions, to the point that he shut down the blog for a while, saying: "I write what I write, for whatever the project might be. I have the utmost respect for you, and honestly want you to like my work, but I can't let that affect my story decisions" (Moran, 2009a). Moran went on to challenge the right of the fans to expect a story to go the way of their expectations, adding that:

> Everybody wants different things from a story, but this is not a democracy, you do not get to vote. ... [T]he ONLY person I need to please is myself, and the ONLY thing I need to serve is the story. Not you.

Moran then sets the author as the arbiter of the story:

> I will do my work to the very best of my ability, in an attempt to give you the best show, the best movie, the best story, the best entertainment I possibly

can. Even if that means that sometimes, I'll do things you won't like. ... It's all in service of the story.

(Moran, 2009a)

Davies echoed this commitment to the story in several interviews, including one with afterelton.com:

I don't mean to say I take any joy in upsetting the audience. But we're talking about drama here. Powerful drama isn't just there to make you smile. ... Drama should make people uncomfortable. I've always happily done that.

(Jensen, 2009)

Here Moran and Davies are constructing *Children of Earth* as an entity in itself as opposed to an installment in an existing narrative, and indeed that is one of the objections that many avid fans had to *Children of Earth*, that it seemed to be a new story into which *Torchwood* characters had been dropped. The tension between cult and mainstream status that Hills (2010b) discusses in relation to *Doctor Who* is also at work in relation to *Torchwood*. *Children of Earth* is a bid for the mainstream audience that rewrites many aspects of the series that most appealed to the cult audience.

In claiming the right of the author to serve the story, Davies and Moran disregard the role that production issues played in shaping the narrative, as described in Davies' book with journalist Benjamin Cook (2010). *The Writer's Tale: The Final Chapter* consists of a series of email messages between Davies and Cook discussing the writing and production of *Doctor Who* and its two spin-offs, *Torchwood* and *The Sarah Jane Adventures*. The emails document Davies' writing process as he develops his initial ideas and follows them as they become stories, then scripts, and finally finished programs. In reading through the emails, it becomes clear that the shift to the five-part format, the unavailability of actors, and other issues necessitated changes to the story that Davies had initially planned to present in the third season.

Producing the Work/Creating the Text

I want to unpack this dual role of writer and producer further because the two roles indicate the dual relationship the author has with the program. The producer is always conscious of the work, even as the writer is conscious of the text. When it comes to television production, given a conflict between the writer and producer roles, the producer wins. Can a given scene be produced in an affordable way? Will the actors who portray the characters intended for the scene be available?[8] Can the necessary special effects be created, given the budget? These concerns play into the story the producer is able to tell, regardless of the story the writer might wish to present. As Davies indicates, "The plotting [of *Children of Earth*] is a whole science in itself, and fascinating. It's a story being written according to the transmission and cast workload. But then that's often the case on *Doctor Who*. Production rules" (Davies & Cook, 2010, p. 412). The text is servant to the work, even as it is being conceived.

For fans, who concern themselves only with access to the commodity, the work is of secondary importance, far behind the text, which is granted primacy. That is not to say that fans are not aware of the role of commerce and production concerns in the creation of their favorite texts. Fans often refer to the Doylist versus Watsonian interpretations of a text (Watsonian versus Doylist, 2010). The former refers to interpretations of developments as rooted in production concerns, such as Conan Doyle's desire to kill off Sherlock Holmes in order to move on to other projects. The latter refers to interpretations rooted in the narrative itself, as in Holmes dying in a confrontation with Professor Moriarty at Reichenbach Falls. The Doylist reading is extradiegetic, while the Watsonian reading is intradiegetic. Doylist readings are rooted in the collection of production news that fans carry out while waiting for the program to air. The long delay between the end of *Torchwood*'s second season and the telecast of *Children of Earth* led to an intense tracking of the progress of production, with a great deal of speculation on the role of BBC decision-making in determining aspects of the series. The ability of fans to follow the blogs and Twitter accounts of the stars and scriptwriters, as well as the ability to distribute fan-shot photographs of filming, fostered an intense awareness of production decisions that might even be considered as a form of oversight that reinforces a sense of investment in the program. A casual fan, not hooked into the social networks which propagate production news, would end up with a very different experience of the resulting narrative than those fans who have been tracking the production through both official and unofficial channels. Such a fan, for instance, would be unaware of the convention statement by Barrowman that raised fan expectations for the development of the relationship between Harkness and Jones, but that same fan might come to *Children of Earth* with a Watsonian set of expectations of tone and characterization based on the previous *Torchwood* seasons, expectations also violated by *Children of Earth*.

While fans recognize and do engage in Doylist readings, they tend to find Watsonian readings more engaging. Fan fiction writers in particular engage with the text intradiegetically. They explore the gaps and potentialities within a narrative without regard for whether or not the resulting story can be produced and telecast in a viable way. If extradiegetic issues force changes of genre and audience on a text/work, how much can the text change and still be considered the same text? Unlike a novel or a film, a television program is an ongoing narrative, with extradiegetic factors and influences that shift over time. An actor dies. The program moves from one network to another. The conditions of production present at the time of the program's launch change over the course of the production of the series itself, and those changes affect the story that can be told, even if the title, cast, and setting remain the same. Meanwhile, longtime viewers cling to their sense of the program as they've experienced it over the years:

The attachment of fans to television programs, actors, and the characters they play grows with time and is particularly acute in the case of a long-running series that has been followed for many years. Faithful fans have watched their favorite characters go through legal battles, physical problems, sexual alliances, and emotional angst.

(Costello & Moore, 2007, p. 135)

A common response among fans of *Torchwood* to *Children of Earth* was that it was a good story, but it wasn't *Torchwood*, that the *Torchwood* characters and setting seemed to have been tacked on to an entirely different narrative. Davies admits as much, saying

A long time back, we stared, all of us together, at the emptiness of Episode 5. We had no solution. Nothing. We had bits of plot, but no story, no essence, no real reason for the show to exist. So, I took a deep breath and … well, I gave away one of the best ideas I've ever had. The point being, it wasn't a *Torchwood* idea. It was a notion I've had in my head for about 20 years, and a series that I've always been dying to write.

(Davies & Cook, 2010, p. 413)

The narrative characteristics that define *Torchwood* as a text in the minds of these viewers transcended the title and presence of *Torchwood* characters as markers. So if a title and the presence of the cast aren't sufficient to mark a new season's episodes as part of the same text, the same program, what was it that detracted from the text? What aspects of *Children of Earth* seemed to place it in a different category? For *Children of Earth*, the change in genre and setting seemed to be key factors. *Children of Earth* changed the genre of *Torchwood* from monster-of-the-week science fiction to a political thriller mini-series, a change which highlights one of the unique narrative aspects of television.

In an ongoing narrative such as a television program, a key issue is the relationship between an episode and its season, and the season in relation to other seasons. How does the current narrative connect with prior narratives under the same title, and how does it set up the future within the overall narrative line of the program? An unbounded narrative leaves the plot open for continuing episodes, while a bounded narrative seems to leave the story with nowhere to go. *Children of Earth* as a mini-series came across as a stand-alone program rather than as part of an ongoing serial narrative. Many fans objected to *Children of Earth* on the grounds that they did not see where the program could go from that point: the headquarters was destroyed, most of the original cast was dead, and the group's leader was departing for parts unknown. For a bounded narrative of the sort Davies, Moran, and the other writers seemed to want *Children of Earth* to be, such a storyline was appropriate. Within the context of an ongoing series, however, it violated the expectations that fans had for the existing story. As Rebecca Williams (2010) observes:

> Given … fans' emphasis upon long-standing fandom, detailed knowledge of the show, and emotional attachments, it is often the rewriting of the show's history and key characters that fans most resent and which they read as a betrayal by TPTB or a violation of the expected behaviours of their position within the broadcasting field.
>
> *(p. 284)*

Thus, while Davies and Moran see themselves as acting according to the story they wished to tell, fans saw a larger story comprised of not only *Torchwood* as a whole, but also, I would argue, one that encompasses their own fan fiction. By diverting the canon away from the larger story, the authors rewrote that story in ways that left some fans disgruntled.

Fans Take the Story Into Their Own Hands

Many of these fans turned to their own writing in order to process cognitively their feelings about the implications of the canon narrative on their favorite characters and relationships. When writing fan fiction about an ongoing serial narrative, fans are always in danger of being jossed[9] if the canon narrative goes off in a different direction, but that does not invalidate the fan fiction. Rather it temporalizes the fan fiction, positioning the fan-written story at a particular point in the narrative, a pivot point in the construction of an alternate universe. As Kristina Busse and Karen Hellekson (2006) point out, "The source of texts in many cases are serial, in progress, and constantly changing, as are the fan stories set in these universes" (p. 7). When the canon narrative heads in a direction that fans resist, fan fiction can be a method whereby fans come to accept that direction, or conversely, continue to resist it.

In this case, almost as soon as "Day One" had aired, fan fiction writers had begun to decide how they would process *Children of Earth* through their writing. By the end of the week, three strains of fan fiction were emerging from the reaction to the series. Writers of "denial fic" chose to deny that the events of *Children of Earth* had taken place, though some incorporated information about Jack and Ianto's families into their stories. "Fix-it fic" writers chose to rework the events of *Children of Earth* in such a way that the dead characters survived. Still other writers processed the narrative through *Children of Earth*-compliant fan fiction in which those characters remained dead, and the story was meant to explore Jack's recovery from the trauma of *Children of Earth*, or else the story was meant to show how Gwen might rebuild a new Torchwood Institute, visualizing ways in which a fourth series might be developed from the events of *Children of Earth*. A closer study of fan fiction written following *Children of Earth* would be intriguing if it could reveal whether fans who initially wrote denial fiction later processed the events in the narrative more closely in line with the canon.

Writing fan fiction, however, was not the only way in which disgruntled *Torchwood* fans reacted to the events of *Children of Earth*. On 10 July 2009, a memorial to Ianto Jones appeared in a corner of the Roald Dahl Plass/Mermaid Quay area, one of the program's Cardiff filming locations, according to Melissa Beattie (2010), who is cataloging the memorial as an archaeological site. Beattie sees the memorial as an experiment in community archaeology for a virtual community. Contributions to the memorial include such items as fan-drawn pictures, letters to the character, Twitter transcripts, and many other objects which represent either the character of Ianto Jones, or the relationship between the Jones and Harkness characters.

As a result of the conflict over *Children of Earth*, the relationship between Davies and the disgruntled fans became highly contentious, with both sides using harsh language to characterize the other. Michael Jensen of afterelton.com reported that:

> Curious if his appearance at Comic-Con, as well as the passage of a little time had softened his point of view about the fan reaction, I asked Davies if he stood by all of his previous statements. He did so emphatically saying he believed the "controversy" over Ianto's death was bascially [sic] "nine hysterical women."
>
> *(Jensen, 2009)*

Already angry fans became furious, viewing Davies' words as disrespectful to the audience, and they promptly began to count off just how many "hysterical women" they were. Many stated their refusal to watch any new version of *Torchwood* without Ianto Jones that might follow on *Children of Earth*.

Although many suspected that *Children of Earth* would be the series finale for *Torchwood*, in June 2010 the BBC and Starz Entertainment announced the return of *Torchwood* in a new format, announcing that "While previous series were based on location in Cardiff, Wales, this new installment will see storylines widen to include locations in the U.S. and around the world." Interviews with Davies and other writers brought to the new multi-national project indicated that the fourth season of *Torchwood* would continue in the same direction as *Children of Earth*, as a political thriller grounded in science fiction. Fan reaction to the news split along the same lines as reaction to *Children of Earth*, with fervent Ianto fans vowing not to watch the program without him, and others mourning the loss of the local Cardiff focus of the new series.[10] However, even as some fans vowed they would never watch again, others were using the initial story hints as the basis for yet more fan fiction. *Torchwood: Miracle Day* began airing on Starz in July 2011. Interestingly, for this series, the episodes were shown first in the United States and aired a week later on the BBC. Except for occasional scenes set in Wales, the story is primarily set in the United States, confirming fan fears about the loss of the Cardiff focus.

As this case study of the reaction to *Torchwood: Children of Earth* illustrates, a television program is necessarily commodified, throwing the tension between text and work into high relief. The writer/producer, although often cast as an auteur, depends on the screenwriters, cast, and technical crew to produce the program, which is then distributed through various networks and home video companies. Even as the writer claims the primacy of the story, the production of the work forces changes that could be seen as compromising the integrity of the text. In turn, the tension between author and audience grows as new installments are evaluated against the standard of the existing text. When the audience finds that the new installments do not cohere with the existing text, then author and audience may come into open conflict over their shared guardianship of the narrative. This conflict is fostered by the global participatory culture that breaks down not only the barriers between audience groups across the world but also that between audiences and authors, leading to a situation in which a television program's audience can no longer be seen solely as its market share within its originating country but as an international collection of highly networked and highly vocal fans.

Notes

1. I want to thank Kim Gainer, Frank Napolitano, and Renee Dickinson for their many helpful suggestions during the writing of this essay.
2. In order to protect the privacy of the fans, I have chosen not to cite any particular individual post. The description of fan behavior is based on my observation of various online fan communities, particularly those on LiveJournal.com, as well as various fan-fiction archives.
3. The British Broadcasting Corporation has since changed its global distribution for fan favorite *Doctor Who*, moving to a same-day telecast in both Britain and the United States for the 2010 Christmas special and the 2011 series.
4. Convention reports are typically written up by fan attendees and posted by them to the relevant fan communities in order to present the latest news for discussion.
5. The post in question is no longer available, although many references to it remain on the torch_wood community on LiveJournal.com and comments to James Moran's blog.
6. Afterelton.com has found the controversy over the death of Ianto Jones to be a topic guaranteed not only to recur but also to generate many pages worth of comments whenever it is raised. The site's March 2010 poll of "Top 50 Gay Characters of All Time" featured Jack Harkness in the top spot, and Ianto Jones ranked third.
7. The plan Jack developed to defeat the aliens involved the sacrifice of his grandson.
8. For instance, Freema Agyeman and Noel Clarke, members of the *Doctor Who* cast, were scheduled to reprise their roles, but became unavailable for *Torchwood: Children of Earth* when they were cast in other projects, according to Davies and Cook.
9. The verb "to joss" derives from Joss Whedon, the writer/producer of such television programs as *Buffy the Vampire Slayer*, *Angel*, *Firefly*, and *Dollhouse*. The term refers to the effect on fan fiction when the writers of a program take the plot of the canon narrative in an unexpected direction.

10. Stephen Lacey at the University of Glamorgan and Melissa Beattie at Cardiff University have both been studying Welsh identity in relation to *Torchwood*, an issue that is explored to a degree in *Torchwood: Miracle Day* as Gwen is shown to be asserting her Welsh identity in an American context.

References

Allen, G. (2000). *Intertextuality*. London: Routledge.

Bacon-Smith, C. (1992). *Enterprising women: Television fandom and the creation of popular myth*. Philadelphia, PA: University of Pennsylvania Press.

Barthes, R. (1977). *Image, music, text* (Stephen Heath, trans.). New York: Hill and Wang.

Beattie, M. (2010, June). *"Ne memoria excidat": A study of the impromptu Ianto Jones memorial in Cardiff Bay*. Paper presented at Investigating Torchwood: Text, Context, Audiences. University of Glamorgan, Cardiff, Wales.

Busse, K., & Hellekson, K. (2006). Introduction: Work in progress. In K. Busse & K. Hellekson (Eds.), *Fan fiction and fan communities in the age of the internet* (pp. 5–32). Jefferson, NC: McFarland.

Costello, V., & Moore, B. (2007). Cultural outlaws: An examination of audience activity and online television fandom. *Television & New Media 8*(2), 124–143.

Davies, R. T. (Producer). (2008a). *Torchwood: The Complete First Season*. [DVD]. London, U.K.: BBC Worldwide Ltd.

Davies, R. T. (Producer). (2008b). *Torchwood: The Complete Second Season*. [DVD]. London, U.K.: BBC Worldwide Ltd.

Davies, R. T. (Producer). (2009, July 6–10). *Torchwood: Children of Earth*. [Broadcast]. London, U.K.: BBC One.

Davies, R. T., & Cook, B. (2010). *The writer's tale—The final chapter*. London: BBC Books.

Hills, M. (2010a, June). Brand *Torchwood*: Theorizing intertextual rifts and resonances in the Whoniverse. Paper presented at Investigating Torchwood: Text, Context, Audiences. University of Glamorgan, Cardiff, Wales.

Hills, M. (2010b). *Triumph of a time lord: Regenerating Doctor Who in the twenty-first century*. New York: I. B. Tauris & Co. Ltd.

Jenkins, H. (1992). *Textual poachers: Television fans and participatory culture*. New York: Routledge.

Jenkins, H. (2006). *Convergence culture: Where old and new media collide*. New York: New York University Press.

Jensen, M. (2009, July 31). *Torchwood*'s Russell T Davies makes no apologies—for anything. Retrieved 4 September 2010 from Afterelton: www.afterelton.com/TV/2009/7/russeltdavies

Kustritz, A. (2003). Slashing the romance narrative. *The Journal of American Culture 26*(3), 371–384.

Moran, J. (2009a, July 9). Torchwood. Children of Earth. Day Four. Retrieved 4 September 2010 from *The Pen Is Mightier than the Spork*: http://jamesmoran.blogspot.com/2009/07/torchwood-children-of-earth-day-four.html

Moran, J. (2009b, July 12). Stepping Back. Retrieved 4 September 2010 from *The Pen Is Mightier than the Spork*: http://jamesmoran.blogspot.com/2009/07/stepping-back.html

Skibinskaya, P. (2009, October 28). Death by "Torchwood": Captain Jack, Ianto Jones, and the rise of the queer superhero. Retrieved 30 December 2010 from Afterelton: www.afterelton.com/TV/2009/10/death-torchwood-queer-visibility

Vermuelen, J. (2010, June). Quaint little categories: The positioning of fandom towards *Torchwood* and their subsequent reaction to representations of death. Paper presented at Investigating Torchwood: Text, Context, Audiences. University of Glamorgan, Cardiff, Wales.

Watsonian versus Doylist. (2010, August 14). Retrieved 30 August 2010 from TVtropes. org: http://tvtropes.org/pmwiki/pmwiki.php/Main/WatsonianVersusDoylist

Williams, R. (2010). Good neighbours? Fan/producer relationships and the broadcasting field. *Continuum: Journal of Media & Cultural Studies 24*(2), 279–289.

11

LEAPFROGGING IN THE GLOBAL PERIPHERY

Popular Literacy Practices of Nepalese Youth Online

Ghanashyam Sharma and Bal Krishna Sharma

Stories:

While impatiently waiting for a traffic jam to clear, Ratan (all people and school names in this chapter are pseudonyms) flipped open his cell phone and looked up Facebook updates. One of his friends, who was stuck in the same traffic jam about a kilometer ahead had just updated his status: "Omg, I can't reach Tahachal by 9 am today. This traffic is screwing my exam!" Ratan turned into a small alley, took a different route, and reached the exam venue, on the other side of Kathmandu, on time.

"For the last class project, my group embedded some cool TED videos on our Facebook page and discussed them for developing our own project." In an email interview, Deepesh told us that because his group "looked at the best and latest scientific developments in the world," his project team "simply amazed" their teacher with the work that they produced through web-based collaboration. Deepesh also added that he derives great benefits from the access that he has to a global community of people and resources in the field of electronic engineering.

Another participant in our research, Ashma, said that she chose to work for a significantly small salary at a local cyber cafe in the town of Birtamod because that would allow her to network with her friends and relatives around the country and abroad, as well as to create and share media with them.

The college students who shared the above stories with us belong to the contemporary generation of Nepalese youth for whom the possibilities of discovering, creating, and sharing knowledge have exploded due to convenient access to the World Wide Web, through which they learn about, participate in, and appropriate global popular culture and literacy practices. In this essay, we will discuss how the increasing access to global popular culture and literacy practices, which Nepalese youth have through new technologies, has enabled them to bypass severe material limitations; to undermine traditional hierarchy characterizing the access to and the use of knowledge; to develop new "glocal" cultures; to bring about a convergence of multiple forms of literacy; to blur the boundaries between in- and out-of-school literacy practices; and to create and share knowledge through popular culture activities using new media, which we call "popular literacy."

Radical Overtures: Context and Overview

A country that became open to the outer world through the establishment of diplomatic relationships as late as the 1970s, Nepal has witnessed unprecedented political and educational developments as well as cultural transformation. Following radical political changes that occurred, especially in the last two decades—including the establishment of a parliamentary democracy in 1990 and a decade-long communist insurgency (1993–2005) that resulted in the complete overthrow of the monarchy and the declaration of a secular state in 2006—the use of digital technologies and the access to the Internet have exploded, even though the country has remained economically poor and politically gridlocked in the process of creating a new constitution. In a society where a single Internet connection was first made at the National Institute of Science in 1993 and access to the Web was first commercially available around 1997–1998 (Montgomery, 2002), the number of Internet subscribers increased 31.5 times from 30,000 in 2003 to 945,000 in 2010 (Nepal Telecommunications Authority, 2003, 2010). This dramatic increase in the use of the Internet, which has significantly contributed towards a cultural transformation, is particularly striking because the last decade of Nepalese socio-political life has also been characterized by extreme political instability which has severely affected industry and business, power supply for daily needs, and the country's economic growth in general. This transformation is most visible in the rapid increase of participation in global popular culture by young people and the tremendous impact that participation has on their literacy lives.

This chapter is a discussion of how young people in Nepal, especially high-school and college students in urban areas, are adopting and appropriating global popular culture; how material and political conditions shape their popular culture and literacy practices online; and how both global and local cultures influence their literacy practices in and out of school. The research behind this writing began with about 400 high school- and college-going young people whom we contacted through their teachers, using email, and through direct Facebook invitations. A total of 156 individuals responded to an online survey, and we later observed online networking activities of about 200 participants, including those who took the survey, with their permission. The young people (16–22 years) were mostly from the capital city of Kathmandu and other metropolitan areas, but many of them also came from rural backgrounds. The ratio of women to men was about one to two, and most participants belonged to the middle and upper middle classes that are educationally privileged. The anecdotes we include here come from follow-up interviews with twenty-one participants who discussed their experiences and ideas about popular culture and literacy, via email and Skype conferences. Through these stories about the interplay between the forces of global popular culture on the Web and the unique political/cultural conditions of a country that is undergoing radical changes, we intend to shed light on how material, technological, and socio-cultural forces shape the adaptation of global popular culture by local youth around the world. We also highlight how the contact of local and global popular cultures through the Web gives rise to multiple literacies in the domains of education, new media, and social and political life.

Benefiting from Challenges: How Nepalese Youth Overcome Material Limitations

It is 9 p.m. on a Saturday evening in Kathmandu, and because it is the dry season, more than half the city is under "load-shedding"—which means a scheduled power cut due to shortage of supply in relation to demand. Deepesh has prepared to work online with his engineering project group by charging his laptop battery in advance. The family of Garima, another member of the group, happens to own a personal generator as an alternative source of power. Rijan is at Sarita's place today because of load-shedding in his residential area, and the fifth member of the group, Keshab, is using a laptop with a solar panel to join the project discussion tonight. This group of electronic engineering students starts the discussion by watching a few TED videos on subjects such as "robotics, wireless electricity, shiftables, augmented reality mapping, special effects in movies and photosynth" which Deepesh and Sarita had linked to the group's Facebook page. When their Internet connection is interrupted, or when it cannot smoothly stream the videos for some of them, they use the conferencing feature of their cell phones to keep listening to the material. During the following discussion of the videos that they watched or heard together, the group starts taking notes and drafting paragraphs, using Google Documents, for their project, which they decide to title as "The Importance of Wireless Electricity in Nepal."

As we write about the limiting material conditions through which young people of our country are engaged in global popular culture and literacy practices, we become conscious about how we take for granted the availability and affordability of technology, as well as political stability and security, in the society where we now live. Sitting at our desks in Louisville, Kentucky (Shyam), and Honolulu, Hawaii (Bal), we are using an advanced collaborative writing software that is installed on personal computers that are supported by extremely reliable Internet connections and uninterrupted power supplies. We are using audio/video devices to talk and the files that we want to share reach each other in the blink of an eye, while we synchronously compose these sentences. In contrast, our fellow Nepalese at home experience up to fourteen hours a day of power shortage, their Internet connections transfer about a hundred times less data per second, few of them can afford the devices that we have access to, and all of them live in a strikingly unstable political condition. However, restrictions posed by material, political, and often cultural forces do not completely prevent them from using the technologies and appropriating the cultural and literacy practices, as the examples above illustrate. In fact, the limitations seem to force them to find or develop alternative ways to access the technologies, creative ways for responding to the local political conditions, and the desire to perform both local and global cultural identities. Thus, when one of the members of this group told us about this incident as an example of how they "bypass" material and technological restrictions, we were amazed at how people develop ways to transcend limitations as long as they have the motivation or reason to do so.

Nepalese scholars of popular culture, literacy, and technology have discussed how larger social and political forces shape or influence individual citizen's experience and success with literacy, access to global popular culture, and use of new technologies. For instance, in his article "Literate Lives Across the Digital Divide," Pandey (2006) tells a personal story, reflecting on how an individual's "literacy learning is imbricated in the larger politics of a society" (p. 246). After the latest political transformation and crisis in the country the advent of highly advanced technology, which sharply contrasts with the dismal political condition, has brought about an extremely intriguing situation. On the one hand there is an extreme shortage of power supply with which to recharge laptops for instance; on the other hand, there are technologies like the wireless modem with USB connection which allow people to travel the country with laptops and be able to connect to the Web. Similarly, while a high quality Internet connection is not only rare outside the cities but also extremely uneven and unreliable even in urban areas, there are cyber cafes even in smaller towns and many villages across the country. And, while the political crisis has greatly intensified the economic disparity between the few rich people and the rest of the society, electronic devices are now available at previously unimaginable prices. Thus, in spite of the severely limiting material conditions and extremely uneven distribution of resources, the increased access to the Internet has connected Nepalese youth to global popular culture and thereby helped them redefine and develop local cultures based on networking, while also allowing them to engage in cross-cultural conversations. The upsurge in the availability of digital technologies is likely to help Nepalese youth continue to make stunning achievements even against the extreme limitations imposed by material and political conditions. This seeming paradox of social progress is visible in many kinds of situations: for example, many people in the countryside own a cell phone before even seeing a traditional/wired telephone, use a laptop or even a tablet computer before using a desktop, have a wireless modem before seeing cabled connection, use webcams that are integrated within laptops before using any device called a camera, or possess a solar-panel laptop before getting to use a traditional form of electricity. Such bypassing of material limitations through the "leapfrogging" of technology use is a phenomenon that manifests itself in the socio-political, cultural, and literacy lives of Nepalese youth, which we will further explore in the following sections.

Appropriating the Global: Emergence of Glocal Cultures

Growing up in a small village from where she had to walk for ten hours to Pokhara, the nearest town that had a high school, Pabitra would have never imagined that ten years later she would be doing what she does today: using Skype, she talks to family members and relatives who live in the Netherlands, Australia, and the U.S., as well as her parents back in the village, who have Magic Jack connected to a laptop that she bought for them. She celebrates the Tihar (brother's day), by giving blessings to her brother in Sydney using video call. She also uses online social networking for updating an increasing number of diasporic Nepalese in the world about her country's political ups and downs and she enthusiastically updates herself about world politics, popular culture events, sports, and science and technology; and she organizes cultural events using Facebook pages.

Pabitra is just one example of a social phenomenon whereby the younger generation is not only participating in global popular culture and developing a sense of global citizenship, but also drawing on the cultural practices of other societies around the world and using information technologies in order to create new cultural practices locally by also building on traditional cultural resources. Pabitra participates equally enthusiastically in global popular cultures when she constantly updates herself about the FIFA World Cup Football, or when she listens to Michael Jackson's music in tribute to the singer when he dies. Such convergence of global and local cultural practices has been called "glocalization" by some scholars (Gabardi, 2000). This convergence of literacy practices has been made possible by the breaking of barriers between formal and informal literacy practices, traditional culture, and modern/popular culture as well as the access to networked spaces that allow different modes of expression.

Access to advanced technologies is the means for this generation to express its sense of connection with global communities and also to renew local cultures. There are political and cultural reasons that motivate those practices. First, social networking is a characteristic feature of the Nepalese society. Similarly, the Nepalese society has traditionally had a positive attitude and acceptance of cultures from outside, especially Western cultures, education, and ideas of progress. Finally, the lack of strong feeling about the country's socio-political history and institutions probably contributes to the relative attachment to global popular culture and sense of global citizenship. Because these means and motivations undergird the local–global interplay of popular culture and literacy practices, they deserve further elaboration.

Located in the extremely rough terrain of the Himalayas, Nepalese society is still composed of small and tight-knit village communities where people live heavily interdependent social lives, are severely lacking in access to transportation, and have not had modern means of communication until very recently. Perhaps these same historical forces shaped a culture of sharing, collaborating, and networking through meeting in the village square. Choutari—a raised platform under a large tree where the community comes together to chat informally, share and transmit knowledge, adjudicate legal issues, and so on—best symbolizes the traditional culture of social networking and collaborative problem-solving. The traditional Nepalese society also conducts its religious, cultural, and political life in especially communal ways. The rapid pace of urbanization, mass internal displacement of population due to political insurgency, and a diasporic movement of a vast number of Nepalese youth to places across the globe in the last few decades created a crisis in the traditional networking culture. This vacuum was quickly filled by the availability of communication and networking technologies. Such a political and cultural necessity perhaps explains the exponential increase of Internet service and a similar acceleration in the pace of adaptation of the new networking culture based on the World Wide Web.

As indicated above, another reason for the rapid and welcome adaptation of the technology and culture of social networking in this traditional society is also the conventionally positive attitude towards Western cultures from which the technology and "global" popular culture tend to originate. From the perspective of social development, Nepal has been dependent on international financial aid, revenue from "foreign" tourists, and diplomatic support from world powers like Britain and the U.S. Because Nepal is a small and landlocked country in between two giant Asian powers, there is also a political impulse to connect to the larger world, beyond the Indian subcontinent, among the Nepalese people. Thus, Nepalese society has historically derived ideas of education, technology, and progress from the Western world since its first contact with Britain around 1850. It continues to look to the West for the best of ideas and technologies even today. In short, as expressed in the adage "guests are gods," intellectuals, cultures, and ideas from other societies are generally held in high esteem by Nepalese society.

The openness and even attachment towards global cultures among Nepalese youth is also reinforced by their frustration towards the political situation in the country throughout their lifetimes. In other words, this generation has found that the new online social networks provide a platform for expressing its frustration about the political structures (or lack thereof), an activity in which they take pride. Moreover, the ways in which the traditional power structure—based on monarchy, feudalism, caste system, patriarchy, and hierarchical kinship/family relationships—have operated in the social and cultural life of the nation also make most young people resistant to the political, religious, and cultural values of the traditional society; and that frustration has accelerated their adoption and adaptation of the alternative value systems that they can easily access from global cultures via the Web. As opposed to the domination of discourse and culture by the feudal few in the past, the present generation embraces more democratic values of freedom and equality. Little can be found of the belief in a caste system among this generation. An increasing number of young women and younger adults are participating in the social network as a result of its being technologically mediated and influenced by other cultures. In short, these forces have created an increasing sense of global citizenship among these youth, motivating and enabling them to participate in cultural practices beyond their national and social borders.

While the younger generation draws on the positive practices of networking and sharing, it largely refutes the outmoded practices of traditional local culture, thereby creating new configurations of global and local cultures that are compatible with its intellectual and political awareness. This convergence of the elements of local and global cultures is giving rise to what Jenkins (2004) calls a "new pop cosmopolitanism," or a culture among young people who readily "embrace cultural difference, seeking to escape the gravitational pull of their local communities in order to enter a broader sphere of cultural experience" (p. 117). It must be noted at this point that we are using our idea of "the sense of global citizenship" in a sense similar to the cautious and unconventional sense in which Jenkins uses his term "cosmopolitanism" for referring to "the ways that the trans-cultural flows of popular culture inspire new forms of global consciousness and cultural competency," and not to indicate that Nepalese youth who are reshaping local cultures by drawing on global cultures have a "taste for international food, dance, music, art, or literature … [or] classical or high culture" (ibid.). The convergence and syntheses of local and global are motivated by the need to fulfill a lack in what the young generation needs from an otherwise absent local culture by using what it can get from the global, and vice versa. While these young people "use [Western] popular culture to express generational differences or to articulate fantasies of social, political and cultural transformation"(ibid.), they draw on local cultural resources whenever local cultural practices are compatible with their needs. "I think culture is nothing but the habits or things that everyone in a society loves to do and share," says Saurav, a freshman in Pharmacy Studies at Kathmandu University. "What a large group of people enjoy becomes their culture." This attitude about culture is in stark contrast with the traditional notion of culture in the Nepalese society: "culture" used to be generally understood as ancient practices that were usually generalized as national phenomena rather than specific to the diverse communities of Nepal, and it was also inextricably tied to the Hindu religion of the majority. The traditional understanding of culture was also limited to the values and practices of the dominant class, caste, ethnicity, and gender. In contrast to the traditional notion of "culture," most of the young generation has broad and flexible views about culture, as implied by Saurav's definition. Here is another striking illustration of what "culture" seems to mean to young people:

> For example, I have an uncle who lives in Canada and two sisters who live in the U.S. During festivals like Dashain and Tihar we share photos via Facebook

[and] … feel close to each other. There is an application named Dashain Gift in Facebook where you can give gifts like "Achheta" and "Jamara" [accessories for Dashain's ritual blessing of younger members of the family] and even "khasi" [lamb], "pakako mashu" [mutton], and "ashirbad" [blessings].

(Saurav, email interview 12 July 2010)

Access to popular culture practices on the Web and the possibility of connecting with friends and relatives around the world have helped the youth redefine traditional culture to suit their interests.

In the process of drawing on global cultures, local youth interpret those cultures in ways that fit their local needs and on the basis of their local political and cultural worldviews. For example, when our research participants were asked how concerned they were about privacy while sharing personal information and images on Facebook, less than 20 percent of respondents chose "concerned" or "very concerned." There was certainly a difference of concern among male and female users. Among the Facebook users who "friended" us in response to our research solicitation, male users had uploaded about 50 percent more images on Facebook. The observation of privacy settings by the same population also showed stricter settings on female users' accounts. However, while the increasing relaxation of default privacy settings by Facebook has become a matter of public furor in the U.S., few of our research participants considered privacy a serious issue. In a society that does not have either legal provisions or cultural norms about privacy of medical information, where academic grades are not completely private, and where family and social matters are highly public within local communities, new ideas of privacy might be evolving with the perceived needs of the young generation. Thus, the interaction of local and global cultural forces shapes the new forms of popular culture for these youth.

Remaking the Local: Evolution of Multiple Literacies

We have discussed how access to the platforms created by advanced information technologies have enabled Nepalese youth to create and practice new local cultures by learning from multiple cultures around the world, including the increasingly shared and understood "global" popular cultures. We will now discuss how this cultural platform created by information technologies plays an even more significant role in the evolution of multiple literacies, or forms and practices of learning, some of which remain isolated from and others that have some influence on school-based learning. Traditionally, Nepalese society defines "literacy" as the ability to sign a document ("signature literacy") and more recently to write and read letters. Even though the establishment of modern formal schooling in the last century, which replaced traditional formal education limited to the upper class and caste, significantly democratized learning, the recent advent of Web technologies has radically transformed the sphere of learning into an open space. In this new space, young people can not only learn from a much wider variety of sources, but also create and share new knowledge.

For example Mina, another participant, has a Facebook account with an application that automatically updates her daily "rashiphal" (horoscope). Created in the Nepali script by local users/developers, the horoscope tool on her status update is a literacy practice that draws on and transforms the important Nepalese tradition of fortune telling. Theoretically speaking, this cultural activity indicates a paradigm shift in the conception of knowledge among the young generation compared to even one generation ago. To this day, upon the birth of a new child, most Nepalese families visit the astrologer and ask him to create the newborn's "chinaa," or the astrological documentation of his or her nativity. This is used for determining the auspiciousness or otherwise of every rite of passage throughout life, as well as for "fixing" problems created by one's stars being in the wrong place, by consulting the astrologer, palm reader, or shaman. As in most societies, knowledge about the common individual's fate was strictly limited to the spiritual authorities, known as the "janne" (the knower) whose special knowledge was normally held in absolute reverence. For such a form of inaccessible, honorable, and unquestioned knowledge to become instantly accessible, publicly shared, and lightly taken is an example of a significant shift in the epistemological worldview in this society. Mina said during an interview that she activated the "rashiphal" application "just to share a joke" with her friends and family. She explained that the developer of the application "must have a hard time psychologically satisfying the 156 thousand users of the tool even if he or she was able to create or translate thousands of 'predictions' for at least 13 thousand individuals in each Zodiac sign." But the point about using this application, Mina added, is "to have something interesting to talk about with your friends and family." The sacred knowledge has been appropriated by far more people than the "jannes," it has become mediatized, and it reflects the radically changed view of literacy and learning. From a larger social perspective, this is also an example of how access to global popular culture of social networking online and the democratization of learning and literacy practices has broadened the overall outlook about social relationships. Thus, even while the knowledge of the traditional "janne" is still regarded by many as sacred, authentic, and superior, and against the society's continued admonishment, "don't be a janne, you kid," the kids have stolen the society's fire.

The access to networking technologies and exposure to "popular literacy" practices—or the popular culture activities of creating and sharing knowledge through new media—from around the world have subverted the hierarchy among different forms of literacy. For example, this access has blurred the boundary between sacred/ superior knowledge with which traditional society used to privilege a certain class, caste, and the male gender and vernacular literacies that are a part of the ordinary lives of the general masses. Moreover, in a society where, until very recently, literacy education was restricted within certain communities and where formal education has yet to become accessible to all classes, a radically new practice of multi-literacies—of different media, cultures, and forms of knowledge—is also beginning to characterize literacy practices among significant segments of the population. Through access to the global Web a generation of Nepalese youth has gained access to multiple media sites about cultures, media, entertainment, and social and political worldviews. Such access to knowledge resources, and the consequent political awareness about a globalized world, has been brought about in an unprecedented manner by the technologies and it would have been unimaginable before the recent political transformation of the society. In the words of Prasanna, a student of media studies at Kathmandu University:

> it is just amazing that in a matter of less than a decade, we suddenly have access to a whole new world technologies and knowledge. My brother, who studied his master's degree less than fifteen years ago in Kathmandu, wrote his thesis with a typewriter and used to send handwritten letters to us in the countryside. Today, I surf the net with my mobile, do video call to my brother who now lives in New Zealand, create videos and animation and share them online, learn more from the net than from books, participate in professional blogging communities, and things like that.

The sudden access to and influx of diverse texts on the Web have radically changed the landscape of knowledge, and how fast that has happened is just stunning.

Yet another site of literacy practices that have become popular among the young generation, perhaps like never before, is that of political discourse. In response to the political deadlocks that followed the political transformations in the last two decades, young people aspire to gain the freedom and progress that they perceive in other societies via the Web. They use that access and knowledge to share their frustrations, developing forms of expression that suit their taste, need, and convenience. As a result, political discourse has been dragged into "popular literacy practice" on the Web by young people. Recently, an increasing trend of doctoring and sharing of images of people in power received significant public attention, as a result of which legislative action has been proposed against such activities. While this simple example of freedom of expression exercised by young people would be extremely insignificant in some older democracies, the political furor about a teenager's act of photoshopping the Prime Minister's head on to a popular movie villain shows society's fear that such appropriation of political discourse by the young generation will corrupt and collapse the traditional value systems of knowledge and power. The emergence of political discourse outside party lines and in creative, satirical, and popular forms can be attributed to the advent of popular culture and literacy practices online.

Taking Learning In and Out of School: New Literacies, Media, and Education

The breaking of barriers and the convergence of multiple forms of literacy and discourses that have affected the social, cultural, and political domains have also similarly affected another area where knowledge and power is restricted, namely within the four walls of institutionalized education. The perception of the Web as a "fun place for learning about the whole world," in the words of an English major, has provided not only the space for learning/creating and sharing entertaining discourses but also a great source for enhancing the learning done in school. Our case studies illustrated that the Nepalese youth seem to find the virtual space on the net both an escape and a better substitute for a frustratingly outmoded educational system, hopeless political crisis, and a conservative society. This perception of the Web is not likely to be unique to Nepalese society.

One of those cases was that of Pratik, a bachelor's degree student of English literature and journalism, who has a significant number of subscribers on his blog where he writes poetry, multimodal stories, and semi-fictional love letters to his girlfriend. "Because I never get a chance to share my works with my classmates in college—forget about the creative writing teacher—my blogs are a blessing to me," Pratik wrote in his email to us. Compared to his learning and practice of creative writing in college, Pratik's creative writing activities online provide what Gee (2004) calls "situated learning": "people learn best when their learning is part of a highly motivated engagement with social practices which they value" (p. 77). Moreover, Pratik's case also exemplifies a new type of learning space, which Gee calls an "affinity space," where education is learner driven, collaborative, non-hierarchical and not imposed from outside, as well as practical and based on problem-solving.

The seeds of the sense of global citizenship, as well as democratic values, were sown in Nepalese society along with the very establishment of formal and modern education (i.e., with the first attempt at adopting democracy in 1950). However, democratic movements have been repeatedly hijacked by the feudal system and still continue to fail due to the same traditional anti-democratic value systems, and as a result formal education has become increasingly difficult for the general public to access. It must be noted that literacy has increased from 5 percent to almost 50 percent in this country in the last six decades (Montgomery, 2002), but social class division based on feudalism, caste system, and patriarchy have reinforced a similar division in the access to quality education, which also makes technology and the new world of information only available to the traditional ruling class and a small minority of rising middle class that evolved from "democratic" movements and a new remittance economy. That is to say, we are not telling the story of a general social and cultural transformation brought about by education, technology, global popular culture, or media and information. Nonetheless, even if education and other privileges are limited to upper and middle class populations mainly in urban areas, globalization, technologies and information, multi-media, and multi-literacies have made a remarkable impact on formal education, local culture, and the socio-political life of Nepal.

Compared with societies like the United States—where mass literacy is not new, democratic values are long established, and technology gradually evolved from the ground up alongside popular culture—the case of Nepal is striking because literacy, and multiple forms of it, have suddenly made a tremendous top-down impact on society. As the younger generation exercises unprecedented amounts of freedom as well as radically redefines social and cultural values, highly advanced technologies have exploded onto the scene before even the basic technologies became available. Even though these developments are still limited to small segments of society, they have already shown signs of transforming local cultures (especially in communication and networking), education, and the political and social lives of the nation at large. A striking example of this technological, literacy, and cultural leap is that of a "school" based on one solar-powered laptop with which students in a remote village in western Nepal are taught by a volunteer teacher in the city (which is two days' walk away) using Skype audio and video calls. These students, who have never seen motor vehicles or traditional telephone lines, have exposure to educational and cultural resources from around the world via the Web. Such stories, while not representative of the whole of Nepalese society's educational reality, illustrate how the sudden access to technology and global archives of information and knowledge has threatened the social mechanisms that continue to keep formal education class-based, undemocratic, and impervious to the influence of what we have called popular literacy. This is another powerful case of how the boundary between "authentic" education that schools provide and learning activities outside school is being radically blurred. Gee's contention that "children are having more and more learning experiences outside school that are more important for their futures than is much of the learning they do at school" (2004, p. 5) is particularly true for a society like Nepal, which is being thrown headlong into a global space, even while that "globalization" is quite uneven.

Non-traditional literacy practices are not only found in relatively rare cases like that of students in faraway places who get their education through solar-powered laptops, Skype communication, and Facebook updates: they have an equally heavy influence on the academic learning of large majorities of school and college students in urban and suburban areas. Due to the lack of educational resources in academic institutions, the outmoded nature of curricula, and an extremely teacher-centered pedagogic culture in general, students turn to resources and popular literacy practices online by which they make their school education more motivating and productive. For example, in the anecdotes with which we began this essay, the students who used Facebook updates to instantly inform their peers about traffic jams, the project group that used spaces and resources online for accomplishing what their teacher might not even know, or the young woman who opted to engage in popular culture and literacy practices that are not generally recognized as such by the society are all evidence of how informal learning and popular cultural practices are transforming what the Nepalese society understands as "education."

Implications: Contextualizing the Meanings of Literacy

The larger implication of this interplay between formal and informal learning practices and spaces could be that education, for large numbers of Nepalese students, could be redefined as a multifaceted practice even before traditional text-based literacy becomes widespread. Such changes could break the traditional barriers before they are even erected. Nepalese youth may also be exposed to and become competent in learning and using multiple forms of literacy, including knowledge about other cultures and societies, technological skills in different modes and media, and information of as well as participation in local and global popular culture. For example, for students who start learning through audio/video channels and using multimedia resources on the Web, the very notion of being literate could mean being multiliterate. Similarly, the traditional distinction between popular culture and literacy practices—the latter of which are traditionally aligned more closely to school learning—is also subverted by students who participate in (global) popular culture as literacy practices, as in the case of the "distance learners" in the upper Himalayas. Others who use social networking for doing schoolwork similarly hybridize popular culture and literacy practices, whether global or local. And, finally, learners who define school learning against what we have called popular literacy practices might find an escape from the former into the latter for motivation and better learning. Nonetheless, all these interactions between school learning and out-of-school learning redefine what it means to be literate, especially in terms of diversifying the forms and practices of literacy.

This study suggests that the interaction between local and global forces in both popular culture and literacy practices must be understood in terms of how those phenomena are perceived and defined within the Nepalese socio-cultural world-views. Literacy is a social phenomenon, and therefore "[g]rasping what literacy 'is' inevitably involves social analysis: What activities are carried out with written symbols? What significance is attached to them, and what status is conferred on those who engage in them? Is literacy a social right or a private power?" (Scribner, 1984, p. 8). In the case of Nepal, the extremely hierarchical structure of its traditional society has been a powerful determining factor of what it means to be literate. Similar to the tripartite division of literacy types in Scribner's article "Literacy in Three Metaphors," it can be argued that three major views about literacy are prevalent in Nepalese society. First, there is literacy as social and spiritual authority, or the authority of the secret or sacred knowledge of the "janne" (the knower, including the priest, fortune-teller, and the shaman) which was not only an important means of survival for the community but also a means for maintaining the social structure. There is also the perception of school literacy which has been available for about half a century to the general masses, many of whom are still prevented from achieving it due to economic deprivation and social barriers. Third, there are the new multi-literacies: the knowledge and skills derived by middle and upper middle classes especially in the few urban areas of the country as a result of their exposure to advanced media and information technologies, local and global popular cultures, and the new culture of participatory epistemology. Theoretically, the growing mass of literate citizens in general and the appropriation of traditional literacy by the young generation have significantly marginalized the protected forms of knowledge owned by social and spiritual leaders of the traditional society. The disruption of the barrier to knowledge has also impacted society's power structure. Nonetheless, in spite of the relatively democratized landscape of knowledge/literacy outside of school, formal education continues to perpetuate the view that only it can provide authentic "knowledge"; the society in general and formal education in particular absolutely refuses to recognize the value of literacy practices outside school. The traditional worldviews about learning still greatly influence who can own and exercise knowledge as power, and indeed who can gain access to formal schooling and increase their socio-economic opportunities. "Just as social relations reproduce class distinctions and often reinforce class status, literacy practices and the qualities ascribed to the people enacting those literacy practices often work in the same way. What one reads or writes, in what context, and for what audience, is frequently a subtle way of revealing social bonds and affiliations" (Williams & Zenger, 2007, p. 43). In countries like the United States, the fact that everyone has access to a certain level of education gives rise to a worldview (or "myths," as Williams and Zenger call it in their book *Popular Culture and Representations of Literacy*) about education as an equalizing force; but where economic division sharply divides the access to quality education, and to any opportunity for literacy at all, the traditional view of education as a privilege reinforces and is also reinforced by insurmountable class divisions.

Multiliteracies and literacies for global citizenship are still the somewhat exclusive domain of a relatively small upper class and urban population. However, the sudden and pervasive adoption of new information technologies among the urban and upper middle class, and a limited but powerful penetration of technologies and literacies across geographic and economic social strata, seems to be a harbinger of a significant transformation in the worldview about what it means to gain, own, and create knowledge. That is, while it may take a long time for everyone to have easy access to multiliteracies and global popular cultures, as well as equitable opportunities for formal schooling, the genie of those literacies is out of the bottle. The diversification of literacies, the advent of new media, and the access to the global Web of information are helping to radically redefine traditional notions of literacy. Authority is subverted because the learner participates and produces knowledge; far fewer people perceive knowledge for social survival as the domain of the few "janne"; and even school literacy is now no longer galvanized within the four walls of schools, even while formal education does the gatekeeping for economic and social opportunities. And even though academic and social institutions still adamantly hold on to hierarchical value systems, it is remarkable that in such a society young people's literacy practices reflect the best of the changes that are taking place due to increasing access to information technology and global popular culture online. In the words of Hagood (2008), this global trend, which is striking in the case of Nepal, goes beyond traditional modes of reading and writing, encompassing all aspects of semiotic meaning-making. Young people are participating in shared cultural activities across national and cultural borders by using a variety of devices and alternative technologies; and literacy has been redefined not just as an individual cognitive process of meaning-making but also as a social practice whereby its practitioners collaboratively participate in multimodal practices.

Another issue that must be highlighted here regards the supposed "tension" between global and local cultures. While Nepalese youth are open and accepting of "foreign" influence on their local cultures, they do not seem to adopt "global" cultures wholesale; they are not only conscious about the importance of their local popular cultures, they also define "global" in a broader sense than it is conceived of in Europe and North America. For example, they are as engaged in celebrating the FIFA World Cup as they were in paying tribute to Michael Jackson when he died, in sharing Japanese manga, listening to music from Bollywood movies, or watching Brazilian Samba dance videos on YouTube. An overwhelming majority of respondents to our survey explicitly or implicitly stated that they are able to appreciate and learn from different cultures as citizens of a new "global village."

Listening to Stories: How Youth Cultures Defy Conventional Wisdom

This research is not meant to be representative of the country or region. We instead wanted to present stories of individuals and groups in order to discuss certain sociocultural trends and phenomena. While this sample population was unique, the cultural and literacy practices that these people are involved in seemed to indicate dramatically new and interesting developments in the sphere of popular culture and literacy practices. From the perspective of a global audience, this is seen as a case study about the global–local contact of those practices.

It is hard to say whether the extremely volatile political situation of a country like Nepal will allow the fascinating developments that we have described in this essay to continue, or what shape this progress will take in the future. What is striking, however, is the series of contrasts that seem to emerge from how young people participate in global popular cultures and develop "glocal" cultures through the use of information technologies. Even where there are starkly adverse material and political conditions, there have already been striking developments in literacy practices and popular culture online. In spite of sheer lack of resources, highly advanced technologies are becoming more common as a result of people trying to find alternatives. Similarly, in an otherwise extremely traditional society, cultures from outside are greatly appreciated and meshed with local cultures. Perhaps as a result of having to live through difficulties and radical changes, Nepalese youth seem to recognize and adopt/adapt cultural and literacy resources from any and every source to perform their new identity as global citizens. In sum, these apparent paradoxes seem to be contrary to conventional beliefs about cultural clashes, social and technological advancements, political conditions and globalization, and the very meaning of literacy, because those beliefs fail to consider how people overcome those limitations. In particular, one might assume that in global peripheries with severe material and socio-political limitations, as in contemporary Nepal, the dramatic developments that this chapter demonstrated would not be possible. We suggest that it is time to question these assumptions. Only stories can tell us how much motivated young people can achieve with so little.

References

Gabardi, W. (2000). *Negotiating postmodernism*. Minneapolis, MN: University of Minnesota Press.

Gee, J. P. (2004). *Situated language and learning: A critique of traditional schooling*. New York: Routledge.

Hagood, M. C. (2008). Intersections of popular cultures, identities and new literacies research. In J. Coiro, M. Knobel, C. Lankshear, & D. J. Leu (Eds.), *The handbook of research on new literacies*. New York: Lawrence Erlbaum Associates/Taylor & Francis Group.

Jenkins, H. (2004). Pop cosmopolitanism: Mapping cultural flows in an age of media convergence. In M. M. Suarez-Orozco & D. B. Qin-Hilliard (Eds.), *Globalization: Culture and education in the new millennium*. Berkeley, CA: University of California Press.

Montgomery, L. (2002). NGOs and the internet in Nepal. *Journal of Computer Mediated Communication, 7*.

Nepal Telecommunications Authority (NTA). (2003, 2010). MIS archive. Retrieved 12 August 2010 from www.nta.gov.np/en/content/index.php?task=articles&option=view&id=36

Pandey, I. P. (2006). Literate lives across the digital divide. *Computers and Composition, 23*, 246–257.

Savada, A. M. (Ed.). (1991). *Nepal: A country study*. Washington, DC: GPO for the Library of Congress.

Scribner, S. (1984). Literacy in three metaphors. *American Journal of Education, 93*, 6–21.

Williams, B. T., & Zenger, A. A. (2007). *Popular culture and representations of literacy*. New York: Routledge.

12

QUEERING THE TEXT

Online Literacy Practices, Identities, and Popular Culture

Mark Vicars

When we look at the practices of such [social] groups, it is next to impossible to separate anything that stands apart as a literacy practice from other practices. … You can no more cut the literacy out of the overall social practice, or cut away the non-literacy parts from the literacy parts of the overall practice, than you can subtract the white squares from a chess board and still have a chess board (Gee, 1990, p. 43).

Growing up queer in a small northern town in the UK, I discovered considerably early on in life what fun could be had with popular cultural texts. I first fell in love watching *Seven Brides for Seven Brothers*. I couldn't for the life of me understand why June Allyson as "Little Jo" in Mervyn LeRoy's (1949) MGM film of *Little Women* wouldn't want to marry her handsome neighbor; I would have snapped him up in an instant. My dyke friends tell me the character "Little Jo" was something of an inspiration growing up and it has been remarked how:

> Even though *Little Women* brings its tomboy heroine to the expected end of marriage, this conclusion is so unsatisfying and incoherent that most readers reject it in favor of the far more queer middle of Jo's plot, where meanings do not line up into a seamless univocal whole. In this way Alcott perhaps unknowingly presented all readers with an epistemological occasion to develop a queer reading praxis.
>
> *(Quimby, 2004, p. 8)*

Popular culture provided a fold in which to re-think the complexity of who "I" was; and that fold became a refuge from a domination of heteronorming logic; it provided a location from which I began to start to question the social and cultural practices that policed my everyday life. The enchantments I found in popular culture often resulted in intense episodes of living. I would read and re-read the same book or repeatedly watch the same film, as I could not bear not to have contact with a world of which I needed to be a part. It has been suggested how:

> for many of us in childhood, the ability to attach intently to a few cultural objects, objects of high or popular culture or both, objects whose meaning seemed mysterious, excessive, or oblique in relation to the codes most readily available to us, became a prime resource for survival.
>
> *(Sedgwick, 1994, p. 3)*

My queer reading praxis eventually led me to pursue Doctoral study during which I investigated how print and multimodal texts had been used by gay men during adolescence to perform identity work. In *Dissenting Fictions: Investigating the Literacy Practices of Gay Men* (Vicars, 2009), I explored how literacy was constructed within socio-sexual worlds and how texts ceased to be merely words on the page but connected with the wider landscapes of class, gender, race, and sexuality. Moving beyond the surface of printed symbols, I was able to investigate the flows between textual practice and sexual identity and I considered the ways in which literacy provided my participants with plateaus to engage in imaginary dialogues with the future (Eagleton, 2000). My informants commented how:

> I remember when I was six having a conversation with some sissy boy in the neighbourhood about who was the nicest looking out of all the dolls in *Thunderbirds*. It was in the different way I talked about comics, cartoons and played with my toys that was so unlike other boys, that is how I knew. Both my brother and I had Action Men, my brother's had bits missing 'cos he had chucked him out of the window with a home made parachute or had sent him down the death slide but my Action Man was shop perfect. I had chosen [him] especially because I had wanted the one with the beard and he had come dressed up as an Arc Royal sailor. We got them at the same time but there wasn't a blemish to be found anywhere on mine. In my mind, playing Action Man consisted of taking him off the shelf, getting him out of his box, putting him on the floor and taking all his clothes off. (R)

> Texts got me through. I constructed a whole world around them, and they became my whole life: my purpose, my way out, my means of constructing patterns of behavior that would ultimately lead to success. I have sort of started to live in a secret world of textual dalliances because there is no other way of convincingly resisting the forces that have shaped who I have become. Undercover of text, I was able to worm my way beneath the surface of culture and safely accrue knowledge of my particular way of being in the world.

The first time I heard "The Only Living Boy in New York," I was lying on my bed doing nothing, going nowhere. Listening to those words I fantasized about living the kind of life in which I was free of all the constraints. I started to put up pictures of TV characters I fancied on my bedroom wall and I suppose those images were significant in terms of marking a different kind of space within that shared room. The pictures, books and music, were an attempt at saying I am not the same, I was constructing an identity for myself in relation to what I had read or watched and on some veiled level they signified a narrative of suppressed sexuality. (D)

Growing up where and when I did, I was easily marked as Other, or as the kids on the estate put it, a fat poof! I always knew I was queer but it took some time to say to myself this is what I am in my head. I remember when I was six having a conversation with some sissy boy in the neighbourhood about who was the nicest looking out of all the dolls in *Thunderbirds*. It was in the different way I talked about comics, cartoons and played with my toys that was so unlike other boys, that is how I knew. Being a poof wasn't a good thing I learnt that incredibly early on from watching film. When *Star Wars* the movie came out there was this bit where Harrison Ford get frozen and it was like 'Ooooo!'. I made a decision there and then that I wanted a Han Solo *Star Wars* pencil case. All the boys in my class had one with that horrible hairy gorilla thing on it but I was into Han Solo, looking at him made me feel funny. Strange how one's taste changes!

I can remember the first time I saw the film *Seven Brides for Seven Brothers*, I was allowed to stay up to watch it 'cos it was Christmas, and it was my dad's favourite film. I loved the romanticism and I loved the kidnapping idea. I wanted to be one of the kidnapped girls 'cos I knew I would get to be banged senseless in a log cabin by Howard Keel ... Is it that we were ever taught the gay subtexts? I mean there were all these queens in Hollywood in the 1940s and 1950s writing these movies and I was sooo getting it sat in my bedroom years later. Is it only when we know what to look for that we are able to identify with those things? I don't think so. Texts leave an indelible print and I knew there was a difference, I saw it in film and I saw it on TV. (R)

In my continued quest of "making the familiar strange," my focus in this chapter is to apply a queer lens to participatory cultural practices. I view Queering as a deconstructive disruptive way of knowing that has the potential to be "a messy, anarchic affair ... It transgresses and subverts" (Plummer, 2001, p. 359). Queering, as a critical hermeneutical approach, is productive for re/textualizing identity as a source of knowledge in communities, practices, and social relations. Queering affords the tacit technology of fugitive knowing to become materialized by:

A willingness to interrogate areas which normally would not be seen as the terrain of sexuality, and to conduct "queer" readings of ostensibly heterosexual or non-sexualized texts ... Turning the queer lens on texts, subjectivities, social practices.

(Green, 2002, p. 522)

My exploration of participatory culture is located within gay "affinity groups," i.e. groups of people who share norms, values, and knowledge allied with a given semiotic domain (Gee, 2004) and is framed by my ongoing concern to understand how textual practices are socially embedded in larger life practices and discourses (Barton & Hamilton, 1998; Gee, 1996).

My interest in how identities can be constituted through literacy and participatory practices was provoked some years back as I attended a gay pride march whilst working overseas in Asia. As the floats passed by the biggest cheers went up for a group of Asian trannies doing Dorothy and her friends (*Wizard of Oz*), a coterie of Thai drag queens doing Patsie (*Absolutely Fabulous*, a UK situation comedy), and a bunch of Thai muscle Marys dolled up as the family Von Trap (*Sound of Music*). The visible presence of Western cultural iconography in a non-Western setting struck me at the time as somewhat being out of place and at odds with local socio-cultural narratives of homosexuality. The dissonant and carnivalesque play started me thinking about the interconnectivities between participatory popular culture; the performativity of identity in gay culture and how the diaspora of queering is:

Providing new ways of contesting traditional family and kinship structures—of reorganizing national and transnational communities based not on origin, filiation, and genetics but on destination, affiliation, and the assumption of a common set of social practices or political commitments.

(Eng, 2003, p. 4)

Speaking from the tacit knowledges and pleasures of what queer bodies are and what they do, I locate queer literacy as an event and behavior of subaltern cultural participation and practice. Blending the critical tools of cultural literacy, critical literacy, and Multiple Literacies Theory to trace participatory cultural practices' ever increasing protean quality, shape-shifting excesses, self-reflexivity, and performativity, I consider how:

Literacies as texts ... take on multiple meanings conveyed through words, gestures, attitudes, ways of speaking, writing, valuing and are taken up as visual, oral, written and tactile [and how] ... These contexts are not static. They are fluid and transform literacies that produce speakers, writers, artists, communities.

(Mansy, 2009, p. 13)

Reframing how "literacies as texts" are produced in and consumed by gay male communities of practice, I draw on the rhizome, the tubular assemblage of multiple connections, to map how participatory cultural practices can be conceived as a constant becoming; a generative relation to others.

Towards a Rhizomatic Reading: How Queer!

Dreyfus and Rabinow (1982) noted how, "The more one interprets the more one finds not the fixed meaning of a text, or of the world, but only other interpretations" (p. 107) and considering how participatory cultural practices are articulating new discursive configurations of identity (Haraway,1994), I have chosen to locate a rhizomatic route through participatory cultural practices and do so because:

> Unlike a structure, which is defined by a set of points and positions, with binary relations between the points and biunivocal relationships between the positions, the rhizome is made only of lines: lines of segmentarity and stratification as its dimensions, and the line of flight or deterritorialization as the maximum dimension after which the multiplicity undergoes metamorphosis, changes in nature.
>
> *(Deleuze & Guattari, 1987, p. 21)*

A rhizomatic approach is, I suggest, productive for tracing how queer popular cultural practices constitute spaces of self-representation that are simultaneously connected to and free from social norms. I am employing the figurative device of the rhizome to trace and map how socio-cultural participatory practices connect with ways of becoming. Becoming that is disconnected from grand teleological narratives of self is, in late modernity, situating the practices and performances of identity in: "a wide range of desiring, identifying, representing, repelling, paralleling, differentiating, rivaling, leaning, twisting, mimicking, withdrawing, attracting, aggressing, warping and other relations" (Sedgwick, 2004, p. 8). See Figure 12.1.

Locating the articulation and negotiation of possible ways of being within participatory cultures of meaning-making is a shaping relation to self and others. Kincheloe (2011), in considering critical ontology, notes how becoming is:

> A conversation between diverse parts of a system ... Autopoesis as the process of self-production is the way living things operate. Self construction emerges out of a set of relationships ... Thus, in an ontological context meaning emerges not from the thing-in-itself but from its relationships to an infinite number of things. In this complexity we understand from another angle that there is no final meaning of anything; meanings are always evolving in light of new relationships, new horizons.
>
> *(p. 214)*

If, therefore: "Meanings do not exist in objects or activities; they are assigned to events by people who perceive and interpret their context" (Smircich, 1983, p. 165),

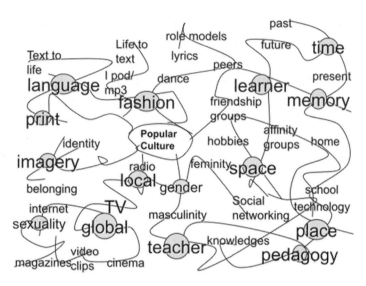

FIGURE 12.1 Location is an Itinerary

FIGURE 12.2 Queers Read This

I now turn my gaze to the ways that participatory popular culture has the potential to discursively constitute queer connections within the everyday.

Analysis of texts has been considered as one form of doing ethnography of culture (Badley, 2004) and situating dissident and non-normative readings as a way of world-making and self-making. I consider how "desire, subjectivity, difference, investment, reading and deterritorialization" (Masny, 2009, p. 13) are located in participatory textual practices and how they become the scene and setting for identity work (see Figure 12.2).

As an illustration of "acts of activism ... within 'everyday' places" (Hickey-Moody & Haworth, 2009, p. 80) this re-texualization of a street signage is an invitation to read the self in the world as offered by the world of the text (Freire, 1970). It affords and makes visible the lines of appearance and disappearance of sexual subjectivities, practices, and cultures in public domains. The palimpsest disruption of the doxa of sexual difference (Felski, 1997; Braidotti, 1997), as the interior world of sexuality is made visible, unfolds a textual occupancy that queers the disciplined spaces of everyday life. As a participatory "text [it] invites the reader to think of the implications between: reading and becoming; imagination and everyday; presence and absence; public and private; vulnerability and defence, conceptualization and desire" (Sumara, 1996, p. 68). In re/textualizing as a form of participatory presence, it is re/ making place queer and in doing so provides a new context for interpretation that makes "it possible to see the world differently ... it [provides] the space to ... be different" (Schratz & Walker, 1995, p. 125).

The signage is "real" enough in terms of an actual place within the city of Manchester, UK. It is also referential to a fictitious place in the UK cult drama serial *Queer as Folk* set in Manchester's gay village. Re/textualized the obliterated "C" remakes Canal Street into Anal Street. The signage becomes a provocative making visible of dissident sexuality and as a narrativizing sexual/textual practice, it is a challenge to tacit hetero-norming social and cultural practices of place making. It performatively re/inscribes a queer way of reading the word/world and in doing so it is making "a vigorous challenge to that which has constrained what may be known, who may be the knower, and how knowledge has come to be generated and circulated" (Honeychurch, 1996, p. 342). Queering the dominant idiom, the silent, the unspoken and the normalized "presumption of heterosexuality which is encoded in language ... and the encounters of everyday life" (Epstein & Johnson, 1998, p. 198), the re/textualization is pedagogical. As a resistant cultural location in everyday constructions of social reality, it interpolates queer within the quotidian, resituating "Texts [as] traces and tracings of otherness" (Frow, 1990, p. 45).

Considering how, as a textual practice, identity becomes *materialized and inscribed* within texts and how textual practices can become a way of acting visible within intricate relations with others, I posit the idea that homo-textual representations of lives are sites of identity formation, self-definition, and affiliation (King, 1999). As a social practice, participatory literacy is a critical space for queerly becoming, and I will now consider how involvement with participatory culture texts facilitates an essential part of one's narrative construction of self-making. I suggest how narrative acts of reinvention are interpolating subaltern voices to multiply discourses and proliferate folk taxonomies of contemporary sexual identities.

Connections to participatory cultural practices and texts can be examined to better understand the rituals through which identities are being formed. As literacy practices and behaviors are increasingly contoured away from one of individual expression to one of community participation, the folds and pleats held tight by the highly conventional stories of interpersonal relationships and social networks can show something of how "literate behaviours come together through becoming with the world" (Masny & Cole, 2009, p. 6).

Thinking about how contemporary identities cease to be restricted to the places or the communities in which they are initially formed has meant recognizing how cultural communities increasingly connect via cultural instruments and products. One only has to think of how popular culture has historically positioned Queer in ways that contest dominant constructions of normativity: *Shrek*—the abjected/cross species desire; *X-Men*—abjected Other/Hybridity; *Finding Nemo*—Dory short-term memory loss; Laurel and Hardy—same sex intimacy; *I Love Lucy*—subverted gender roles; *Bewitched*—camp as everyday; the list goes on and on. These texts offer playful interruptions to traditional normative representations of gender, the body, and the family, and textually situate Otherness as a ludic construction, one in which the boundaries between what is real and unreal, time-present, past and future; the normative body and gendered identities are contested and reworked. Considering how popular cultural textual practice provides a context and a framework for re-scripting self, I now consider how technology has transformed the social rituals and practices within online gay affinity groups.

Sexting the Text: Virtually Queer!

During a recent visit to a gay club in Melbourne, a friend remarked how the young gay men were cruising each other not on the dance floor but online on their mobile phones. From my vantage point of the balcony, I started to observe how the men in their late teens and early twenties were Tweeting messages to the club that were being displayed on a very large screen and were *Grinding* images of other men in the club prior to making a physical approach (Grinder is an iPhone app that enables the user to check out, text, and arrange a hook up with potential partners for dates, hook-ups, or sex). The young men were textualizing the spaces of the nightclub in ways that for gay men of my generation (40 plus) were unimaginable. Their behaviors started me thinking about the ways in which the online practice and performance of sexual identity is experienced in a very different relationship to other identities.

The more I watched the Grinding, Tweeting, texting behavior, the more I started to mentally interrogate the online constructions of sexuality and sexual identities. As my eyes followed the ongoing performance and rituals of twenty-first century cruising, I texted a memo to myself to look up the research on how new technologies and multi-modal texts are an increasingly salient aspect of how young people are engaged with and experience cultural literacy.

Discussing, with friends, the demise of real time cruising and the rapid increase of online chat sites, websites, blogs, and other forums, I started to think about how online communicative practices had become the main source for meeting sexual partners or making social contacts. The majority of my gay friends and acquaintances had abandoned the clubs and bars in favor of the computer screen or the smart phone. Increasingly our social and sexual lives were being conducted in online chat rooms, cam chats, and other "bodily economies of reading and transacting with texts" (Amsler, 2004, p. 3) and it has been remarked on how:

> For gay men the emergence and increasing dominance of on-line gay chat rooms and web-sites offering social and sexual contact has created behaviors that are "both physical and 'virtual' [and] … these two concepts are not discrete but pervade one another, with digital communication often structuring physical practices, identities and experiences."
>
> *(Mowlabocus, 2010, p. 2)*

During a recent conversation about gay male online behaviors, a friend remarked:

> I was particularly a *Gaydar* user. … And when it first started in about 2000 there was the option of paying for a profile and getting an unlimited number of viewings of profiles and messages or having a free profile with restricted access to the site. Most people I knew had two profiles, a free one and a paid one in order to double the amount of space that you got for messages but also … so you could have a fetish profile and a regular profile. … And of course you had different pictures on each profile depending on what you wanted to display and portray: top, bottom, safe, not safe, group, water sports, voyeur etc.
>
> Now smart phones are the big thing and they have location services and GPS so apps are basically modern versions of *Gaydar* and *Grinder* and *Crusher* show you how far away the nearest man on line is so rather [than] having to go in to a *Gaydar* room, and you wouldn't know how far people were away, they would give you a postcode so you had an idea but generally you could be talking to someone, especially in one of the specialist rooms, that were miles away. With *Grinder* you don't have to be sat at home on a computer every night, now u can be out in public and cruise who is nearby and look at their profile and chat and then decide if you want to meet.
>
> Facebook and Twitter ways have led to geoscoping and people have become used to locating themselves as they are travelling around and they are doing events and places as they are at a club and are saying look at me I am fabulous. It is all about the profile now, doing it and keeping it up to date … the pressure is in creating interesting profiles. When I was younger, 10 and a half stone, with a washboard stomach and massive erection, I thought I had a fab profile. I spent a lot of time writing what I thought was a fab profile. All the text was lovely but when it didn't get masses of hits and a new boyfriend immediately, I started to think well what is wrong with that profile and then it would be changed. (Justin)

It would be not too far wide of the mark to suggest how online participatory practices are evoking and engaging bodily sensations that can be read as signifying textual practices of the self (Vicars, 2009). In scripting emblematic indicators of self, those features or practices of personhood "that serve an identity function or otherwise mark and maintain social boundaries" (Kochner, 1987, p. 220), I have become adept at virtually signifying my psychic, sensual, and intimate passions and preferences. As I let it be known who I am and to what I aspire, I constantly evaluate whether I am making too much of my particular claims of self. I purposefully am engaging with identity as masquerade, in a reworking of the body and identity, I become a ludic construction formed "through the ambivalent articulations of the realm of the aesthetic, the fantasmatic … the body political" (Bhabha, 1994, p. 230). At times decidedly sleazy, I drag myself up in leather talk:

Bottom seeks tops for NSA dirty (no w/s fun)

Alternatively, "I" in my online narrativizing becomes:

DTE Prof guy, seeks SA S&S for dates and mates

And in more taciturn moments:

No face pic, no reply: No time-wasters, No married men, partnered, No fat, NO fems, No Kink

Tracing the performances of sexual identities through online landscapes of textual practice, I am increasingly conscious of the ways in which my body is in a constant space of re/textualization and my online self has me constantly re-questioning my: "imaginary relationship [to my] real conditions of existence" (Althusser, 1971, p. 162). I regularly change my profile image and accompanying text depending on what I am looking for online. Treating these narratives as "readable moments as modes of shaping … and ways of becoming subjects" (Hickey-Moody & Haworth, 2009, p. 79), I am able to map how, in online semiotic domains, participatory culture does identity work by "using texts strategically … [as] an enactment of subjectivity" (Hagood, 2004, p. 158).

Online, as I am cruised and I cruise, I participate in the "collective [cultural] imageries, vocabularies and mythologies" (Strauss, 1995, p. 10) of gay sexuality. The virtually queer cultural habitats of queer corporeality—the Nautilized torso, the washboard stomach—are signification of how online words alone fail to convey the nervous excitement, anxious moments, and joy of playing with the visually textual narrations of desire. I flick through the profiles, and my gaze evaluates: the intended readership of the text, the genre of the words and images, and the referents they evoke; the language; the construction and representation of character; the absences and omissions and the possible interpretations that could be made, I am selecting who I will "flame" or send a wink or start a chat with, and who I want to meet and how we might kiss, suck, fuck, or not as the case may be. It has been noted how "online communication does not replace face to face communication, rather, it germinates modes of relation that are taken in to face to face relationships" (Hickey-Moody & Haworth, 2009, p. 81) and in many ways my relationship with texts has become my undoing. It has, and continues to, destabilize my sense of how participatory:

> Culture ... designate[s] not merely something to which one belongs but something that one possesses and, along with that proprietary process, [participatory] culture also designates a boundary by which the concepts of what is extrinsic or intrinsic to the culture come into forceful play.
>
> *(Said, 1991, p. 9)*

Concluding Traces

Throughout this chapter, I have sought to trace the emergent rhizomatic flows of literacy and identity across cultural practices. Drawing on my own interpretative location, I am aware of the partiality of my "reflection, interpretation confrontation and discussion" (Dahlberg & Moss, 2005, p. 13). However, having the experience of not belonging to "straight" communities of meaning, I am mindful of how gay online social networks are increasingly orientated around re/textualizing the practices of becoming. Queering identity in participatory cultures increasingly consists of negotiating the meanings of: "membership in social communities. [therefore] The concept of identity serves as a pivot between the social and the individual, so that each can be talked about in terms of the other" (Wenger, 1998, p. 145).

As I have become accustomed and attuned to quickly surveying the conventions, cultural understandings, and assumptions of the re/textualization of what it means to be "gay" in the domains in which I live and play, I am constantly becoming implicated in the "complex and partial, contradictory and supplemental, intractable and mutually constitutive" relations (Bravmann, 1997, p. 22) of re/textualizing my identity. In my professional life this has provoked and involved me in:

> Writing about my own experiences rather than an act of self indulgence, becomes a form of social analysis. This is because culture circulates through all of us, the self is a social phenomena, all identity is relational and my subjective experience is part of the world I/we inhabit.
>
> *(Sparkes, 2003, p. 158)*

I have chosen to write from and out of this relation to textualize the shifting re/ locations in which the social and individual identities emerge beside and between participatory textual practices. Participatory popular culture has become a plateau in which self-making and world making are intertwined and as it has been suggested "Writing has nothing to do with signifying. It has to do with surveying, mapping, even realms that are yet to come" (Deleuze & Guattari, 1987, p. 4–5). It remains to be seen in what form participatory popular cultural practices will continue to re-invent the practices and performances of "I" and what we will become as readers and writers.

References

Althusser, L. (1971). Ideology and ideological state apparatuses. In *Lenin and philosophy and other essays* (translated by B. Brewster). London: New Left Books.

Amsler, M. (2004). Affective literacy: Gestures of reading in the Later Middle Ages. University of Wisconsin-Milwaukee, retrieved October 11, 2005, from http://muse.jhu.edu/journals/essays_in_medieval_studies/v018/18.1amsler.html

Badley, G. (2004). Reading an academic journal is like doing ethnography. *Qualitative Social Research*, 5(1), Art. 40, http://nbn-resolving.de/urn:nbn:de:0114-fqs0401408

Barton D. & Hamilton, M. (1998). *Local literacies: Reading and writing in one community*. London: Routledge.

Bhabha, H. (1994). *The location of culture*. London: Routledge.

Brady, I. (2000). Anthropological poetics. In N. K. Denzin & Y. S. Lincoln (Eds.), *The handbook of qualitative research* (2nd ed.). Thousand Oaks, CA: Sage.

Braidotti, R. (1997). Comment on Felski's "doxa of difference": Working through sexual difference. *Signs 23*(1), 23–40.

Bravmann, S. (1997). *Queer fictions of the past*. Cambridge: Cambridge University Press.

Dahlberg, G. & Moss, P. (2005). *Ethics and politics in early childhood education*. London & New York: Routledge Falmer.

Deleuze, G. & Guattari, F. (1987). *A thousand plateaus. Capitalism and schizophrenia*. London: Continuum.

Dreyfus, H. & Rabinow, P. (1982). *Michel Foucault: Beyond structuralism and hermeneutics*. Chicago, IL: University of Chicago Press.

Eagleton, T. (2000). *The idea of culture*. Oxford: Blackwell.

Eng, D. L. (2003). Transnational adoption and queer diasporas. *Social Text 21*, 31–37.

Epstein, D. & Johnson, R. (1998). *Schooling sexualities*. Buckingham: Open University Press.

Felski, R. (1997). The doxa of difference. *Signs 23*(1), 1–21.

Freire, P. (1970). *Pedagogy of the oppressed*. New York: Continuum.

Frow, J. (1990). Intertextuality and ontology. In M. Worton & J. Still (Eds.), *Intertextuality: Theories and practices*. Manchester: Manchester University Press.

Gee. J. P. (1990). *Social linguistics and literacies: Ideology in discourses. Critical perspectives on literacy and education*. London: Falmer Press.

Gee, J. P. (1996). *Social linguistics and literacies: Ideology in discourses*. London: Routledge.

Gee, J. P. (2003). *What video games have to teach us about learning and literacy*. New York & London: Palgrave Macmillan.

Gee. J. P. (2004). *Situated language and learning: A critique of traditional schooling*. London: Routledge.

Green, A. I. (2002). Gay but not queer: Toward a post-queer study of sexuality. *Theory and Society 31*, 521–545.

Hagood, M. C. (2004). A rhizomatic cartography of adolescents, popular culture, and constructions of self. In K. Leander & M. Sheehy (Eds.), *Spatialising literacy research and practice*. New York: Peter Lang.

Haraway, D. (1994). The promises of monsters: A regenerative politics for inappropriate/d others. In L. Grossberg, C. Nelson & P. Treichler (Eds.), *Cultural studies*. London: Routledge.

Hickey-Moody, A. & Haworth, R. (2009). Affective literacy. In D. Masny & D. Cole (Eds.), *Multiple literacies theory: A Deleuzian perspective*. Rotterdam: Sense.

Honeychurch, K. (1996). Researching dissident subjectivities: Queering the grounds of theory and practice. *Harvard Educational Review 66*(2), 339–355.

Kincheloe, J. (2011). Critical ontology: Visions of selfhood and curriculum. In K. Hayes, S. Steinberg, & K. Tobin (Eds.), *Key works in critical pedagogy*. Rotterdam: Sense.

King, J. R. (1999). Am not! Are too! Using queer standpoint in postmodern critical ethnography. *Qualitative Studies in Education 12*(5), 473–490.

Kochner, T. (1987). The ethnic component in black language and culture. In J. S. Phinney & M. J. Rotherham (Eds.), *Children's ethnic socialisation: Pluralism and development*. Newbury Park, CA: Sage.

Masny, D. (2006). Learning and creative processes: A poststructuralist perspective on language and multiple literacies. *International Journal of Learning 12*(5), 149–155.

Masny, D. (2009). Literacies as becoming: A child's conceptualizations of writing systems. In D. Masny & D. R. Cole (Eds.), *Multiple Literacies Theory: A Deleuzian perspective* (p. 13–30). Rotterdam: Sense Publishers.

Masny, D. & Cole, D. (2009). Introduction to multiple literacies theory: A Deleuzian perspective. In D. Masny & D. Cole (Eds.), *Multiple literacies theory: A Deleuzian perspective*. Rotterdam: Sense.

McLaren, P. (1994) Border disputes: Multicultural narrative, critical pedagogy and identity formation in post-modern America. In J. Mcaughlin & William G. Tierney (Eds.), *Naming silenced lives*. New York: Routledge.

Mowlabocus, S. (2010). *Gaydar culture: Gay men, technology and embodiment in the digital age*. Abingdon: Ashgate.

Plummer, K. (2001). *Documents of life 2: An invitation to critical humanism*. London: Sage.

Quimby, K. (2004). The story of Jo: Literacy tomboys, *Little Women* and the sexual-textual politics of narrative desire. *Journal of Lesbian and Gay Studies 10*(1), 1–22.

Said, E. W. (1991). *The world, the text, and the critic*. New York: Vintage.

Schratz, M. & Walker, R. (1995). *Research as social change*. London: Routledge.

Sedgwick, E. K. (1994). *Tendencies*. London: Routledge.

Sedgwick, E. K. (2004). *Touching feeling: Affect, pedagogy, performativity*. London: Duke University Press.

Smircich, L. (1983). Studying organizations as cultures. In G. Morgan (Ed.), *Beyond Method: Strategies for social research*. London: Sage.

Sparkes, A. (2003). From performance to impairment: A patchwork of embodied memories. In J. Evans, B. Davies, & J. Wright (Eds.), *Body knowledge and control*. London: Routledge.

Strauss, A. (1995). Identity, biography, history and symbolic representations. *Social Psychology Quarterly 58*(1), 4–12.

Sumara, D. (1996). *Private readings in public: Schooling the literary imagination*. New York: Peter Lang.

Vicars, M. (2009). *Dissenting fictions: Investigating the literacy practices of gay men*. Saarbrücken: VDM Verlag.

Wenger, E. (1998). *Communities of practice: Learning, meaning, and identity*. Cambridge: Cambridge University Press.

13

CREATING A FANDOM VIA YOUTUBE

Verbotene Liebe and Fansubbing

Karen Hellekson

The sweet, angsty love story between Oliver "Olli" Sabel and Christian Mann began in 2007 on the German-language soap opera *Verbotene Liebe* (*VL: Forbidden Love*, 1995–). Openly bisexual Olli's love for a conflicted (straight… or is he?) Christian unfolded in typical soap opera fashion, with misunderstandings, girls used as beards, denial of homosexuality, panic about outing to relatives, overheard outpourings of romantic angst to sympathetic roommates, and anonymous online chatting. Once Christian and Oliver had gotten together, their love was tested by Christian's illness, Olli's too familiar relationship with a business associate, and an AIDS scare. True love won out: Christian and Oliver married in a grand church wedding—the first broadcast church wedding of a gay couple—in September 2009 (Langford, 2010). The couple then tried to start a family, only to be thwarted in their attempts to adopt, then to create a family with a lesbian couple. They took in, and promptly fell in love with, a foster daughter whose return with her father to Cameroon so devastated the couple that they split up. As of late 2011 they remain married but separated and Christian has begun dating a woman.

This wasn't the first time *VL* had addressed the topic of homosexuality. Olli had previously dated Tom in a 1999–2001 plot, and other gay and lesbian characters, both major and minor, have made appearances (Wikipedia, 2011b). Nor is *VL* unique in spending time on a drawn out homosexual romantic plot: the first such plot in the United States with a regular cast character was Bianca in *All My Children* (1970–2011) in 2000. *As the World Turns* (USA, 1956–2010) paired the teen characters of Luke Snyder and Noah Mayer in 2007. British and German soap operas have recently aired similar long-form stories, such as John Paul and Craig from *Hollyoaks* (UK, 1995–) and Deniz and Roman from *Alles Was Zählt* (Germany, 2006–). But the Christian/Oliver love affair caught on thanks to subtitled YouTube uploads of their *VL* plotlines, and the characters are now internationally known. In fact, so resonant is their story that a former HBO executive purchased an option to the story, to be turned into an American commodity should the project go forward (Hector, 2010).

The worldwide popularity of Chrolli—the pairing has been shorthanded, in the obligatory pop-culture portmanteau style, as "Chrolli" or "Ollian," with the former preferred by German speakers and the latter by English speakers—garnered by the YouTube videos caught the actors by surprise. In a 2008 interview, Thore Schölermann, who plays Christian Mann, notes, "The first letters came from Switzerland, then from England and suddenly from Canada and the USA! One day Jo [Weil] showed me a video of us on YouTube, with subtitles in English and 100,000 views, and I thought, 'Awesome! Unbelievable!'" (Bhattacharjee, 2008). The page view numbers are indeed stunning: as of late 2011 the 4 April 2008 episode, where the two first consummate their love, had over 981,000 viewings. Costar Jo Weil (Olli) remarks in an e-mail interview with AfterElton.com on 18 August 2008, "we get awesome feedback to our story from Germany. But the English-language fans, in a very positive manner, seem to be more 'extreme'" (Jensen, 2008b, p. 2).

These extreme fans are a manifestation of the way fans have constructed their modes of engagement: they are using public and private spaces on the Internet to disseminate the source media, create artworks around it, and discuss it. The rhetoric of television viewing has greatly altered now that fans can speak to each other freely, in real time, almost instantaneously after the show has aired. Further, ancillary Web content provided by the producers and fan forums such as Television Without Pity, which TV producers keep an eye on, have changed the landscape of broadcasting: fans no longer simply consume what is provided to them—if in fact they ever did. Fans still write letters to actors and producers and attend conventions. But producers can now hear and respond to fan preferences; sometimes they even choose to respond to fan feedback. One famous example occurred in 2007 with *Lost* (2004–2010), when the producers spectacularly killed off two characters, Nikki and Paulo, whom fans vocally despised. "We listened to the fans and decided to bury them alive," show runner Carlton Cuse noted (ShinyMedia, 2007). This kind of response has complicated the creator–consumer model: it is now possible for fans to make their voices publicly heard, and for producers to react to please fans. Before near-instantaneous communication and feedback to the producers was possible, the rhetorical situation was static and flowed mostly one way: from the producer to the consumer. Now the rhetorical situation is more fluid and complex, with producer, consumer, and artwork interacting with one another at an unprecedented level.

In the case of *VL*, fans are responding not to the original half-hour German-language episodes as they air, but to the modified, English-language fan-subtitled (fansubbed) cut versions posted on YouTube, which greatly expanded the soap's audience. The *VL* phenomenon owes its success to fan labor, and fans from all over the world have continued to engage with the program in a number of venues, including YouTube, *VL*'s official site, fan-run wikis, and fan-based Internet communities. By pulling out a compressed-plot narrative focusing exclusively on the Chrolli story line, fans have engaged in a form of alternative textual productivity centered around homosexuality, an alternative sexuality, to create a queer space as a form of advocacy, but none of this would have been possible without the Internet, highly engaged fans, and an active producer. Although similar gay-themed, plot-removed, and fansubbed shows are available on YouTube, notably *Alles Was Zählt*, *VL*'s popularity far exceeds it due to the combination of a compelling story line, beautiful actors, accessibility in English, and a producer, Das Erste, willing to provide a site for fan engagement.

Fansubs and Vlogs

Although the Chrolli plot has been mentioned in mainstream magazines, such as *Soap Opera Digest*, and several gay-themed blog sites devoted to expressions of homosexuality in popular culture and soap operas, like AfterElton.com and the Gays of Daytime (www.gaydaytime.blogspot.com), it's safe to say that the broad popularity of Chrolli is a result of fan labor, coupled with the broad dissemination made possible by YouTube—as well as copyright holder Das Erste's seeming lack of interest in pursuing clip takedowns. Episodes are occasionally muted as a result of music copyright concerns and are promptly re-uploaded; sometimes the fansubber replaces music that she knows will prompt a takedown with music less likely to cause problems, which she notes in remarks attached to the entry. Yet even this sort of proactive action is in keeping with the complex creation of a derivative artwork, as she chooses music meant to evoke a similar mood.

The activity of subtitling a foreign-language video is known as *fansubbing* or *digisubbing*, a term mostly associated with Japanese-language anime being dubbed into English (Anime News Network, n.d.). The term *fansub* emphasizes the fan part of the activity: unpaid volunteer fans, working with unofficial, recorded copies of the primary source, create these artworks, sometimes working in teams (chrno, 2003; Diaz Cintas & Munoz Sanchez, 2006). In the case of Chrolli, the fansubber cuts together a day's or a week's worth of soap opera plot, focusing only on Christian and Oliver and usually excising all else. The Chrolli fansubs show every scene that Christian and Oliver are in, even if they are literally just standing around in the background, so viewers see inexplicable segments unrelated to Chrolli's struggle toward romantic closure: Why is Rebecca acting so weird? Who is the woman that Christian's brother, Gregor, seems to be obsessed with? What hideous revelation managed to utterly destroy Lydia and Sebastian's wedding? The fansubber will use the YouTube interface to gloss a clip to provide some context, but these text snippets are separate from the clip itself. Those following the Chrolli story see a chopped-up version that compresses and accelerates the usual drawn-out storytelling pace of a soap. Some five-minute fansubbed clips contain literally a week's worth of appearances.

The condensed plots, which are usually three to nine minutes long and which are sorted by air date, are available two ways: in the original German (www.youtube.

com/user/ichglotzgerman), and subtitled in English (www.youtube.com/user/ich glotzutube and www.youtube.com/user/MercuryMay02). Full-length half-hour German-language episodes of *VL* are available too (older episodes are available via YouTube at http://de.youtube.com/user/VerboteneLiebesoap [no longer updated]; official episodes are available at http://mediathek.daserste.de/sendungen_a-z/439104_verbotene-liebe). Each of these sites contains spaces for comments, and fans take advantage of this, writing notes, mostly in German and English, with their thoughts about the episode. Often posters will include their location, so it's possible to see how truly far flung the audience is.

Presumably the free publicity and international audience garnered by the YouTube videos are worth any copyright-related annoyance for Das Erste. After all, the show is being widely distributed, with high-quality translations appended, without them having to pay a thing. This realization is shared by many copyright holders, who are willing to relinquish total control of their property in exchange for free advertising and the promise of a vocal, active fan base to help spread the word (Kirkpatrick, 2003; Jenkins, 2006; von Riedemann, 2006a, 2006b). Das Erste seem to have thrown themselves into marketing to the Internet-driven Chrolli fan base: in addition to officially using the term Chrolli, they have made official Chrolli content available on their *VL* website (www.daserste.de/verbote neliebe/). Fans can download Chrolli computer desktop wallpaper showing the men gazing into each other's eyes. Images of various actors and actresses presented singly are also available for download, including, of course, Weil and Schölermann, although the montage that makes up the desktop image shows them together as well (www.daserste.de/verboteneliebe/desktops.asp).

Perhaps more significantly than providing sanctioned Chrolli images, Das Erste created an official Chrolli blog as an adjunct to the Chrolli plot on *VL*, advertised via a German-language Twitter feed (http://Twitter.com/chrolli/). For about a year, Christian and Oliver recorded short two- or three-minute vlogs that they posted publicly. Through the fiction of the vlog, Christian and Oliver—never Jo Weil and Thore Schölermann—interacted directly with their fans. The characters discuss current events that take place in the soap opera. The early vlogs began as status reports to Olli's friends in Ibiza, but the tone soon shifted to a more inclusive audience: whoever was following them online. In several clips, Christian or Olli ask viewers what they think of a particular topic and urge them to write comments. They even refer to themselves as "Chrolli." In other clips, the characters give monologues, staring directly into the camera, providing extra insight into their feelings. In *VL* itself, Olli can sometimes be seen vlogging or uploading a video, adding a further layer of intertextuality.

These clips appear to be informally created. Olli ostentatiously sets up the handheld camera; Christian plays with the remote control so the camera randomly zooms in and out; the camera moves crazily while recording, resulting in images of a blurry floor or the side of a face. They mimic amateur videos, although they were scripted and produced by the studio. The fiction that the vlogs are totally spontaneous and completely the work of Christian and Olli was broken with the posting of "Best-of und Outtakes" on 7 July 2010, in an entry available only on the German-language version of the site, signed "Das gesamte Vlog-Team." The blog content is provided twice, once in German and once in English. In the English-language version, the brief single-sentence blog text is in English and the videos are subtitled. The vlogs were put up on Fridays at 6:30 p.m. after the show aired, from July 2009 until June 2010, when the vlogs ended altogether with a formal sign-off from Christian and Oliver while they vacationed in New York City: they wanted to spend more time together and work on their relationship, so they decided to stop recording:

> In a July 27, 2009, interview with AfterElton.com, Jo Weil said of the vlogs, [They decided to do this] because of our amazing fans. Our producers have already known for a long time that we get an exceptionally huge and especially emotional support from all over the world. And certainly in our special case the Internet plays an important role, because so many of our fans from every-where can watch *Forbidden Love* although it is originally broadcasted only in German-speaking regions. Everybody thought that is something very special and we have to say thank you. Chrolli.de is the result.
>
> *(Langford, 2009, p. 2)*

The official Chrolli.de blog (now taken down) thus tacitly acknowledges the Internet community that made the Chrolli pairing a worldwide sensation: those who follow the story via English-language subtitled YouTube fansubs. When asked where feedback about Chrolli.de was coming from, Germany or English-speaking areas, Weil noted, "As always, the emails I got are from all over the world. It's great to see that people all over the world are happy about chrolli.de. The subtitles are a credit and thank you from us for our international fans" (Langford, 2009, p. 2),

The blogs' comments, written mostly in German and English, are combined together, so it doesn't matter if they are accessed from the German- or English-language portion of the site. This helps fuse the readership into a single community, united in their love of Chrolli rather than separated by a language barrier. The presentation of subtitles is inspired: it hearkens to the fansubbed YouTube videos, thus alluding to the original source that many fans use to access the story line. More than 200 comments written by fans all over the world have been appended to the final vlog entry, posted on 28 June 2010. The comments and locations show the fans to be similar to the ones who post at the fansub YouTube site: "thousand kisses from FRANCE" (MALOU65 FRANCE), "greetings from Sonora Mexico" (albertho rivera), "Regard from Chile" (Luis and Patricio), "Big shout out from Jamaica!!!" (Kingston), "XOXO from Hungary" (Alexeee), "Thousands of kisses from his countless admirers Brazilians!" (George), "LIEBE GRÜSSE AUS WIEN" (WM—Walter & Michael).

In addition to marking the audience as truly wide ranging and international, the comments to this Chrolli vlog entry, which I'm treating as representational of comments to any Chrolli site, demonstrate a few other things. One is the conflation of the fictional characters of Christian and Oliver with the actors who play them, as this representative remark from Tigger12 shows: "Hi Thore @ Jo; You guys are amazing I really liked this Vlog it was wonderful to see you together and loving each other again, may it be this way always for you. Sad yes I am that the Vlogs are ending but happy also that you guys are concentrating on each other." Related to this is a relatively common fan query: "I have a question to Jo or Thore, Do you have in the real life a relationship? because my opinion is the impression given," Luis and Patricio write from Chile. Erik, Canada, writes, "Jo & Thore: thanks for the improvisations in the vlogs—it made them so real." I'm not sure whether Erik, Canada, is talking about the business the actors do that adds so much to their performance—gestures, glances, touching one another—or whether he thinks the actors are actually improvising, but the latter is a common fan remark. In his 27 July 2009 AfterElton.com interview, Weil notes, "The blog is completely scripted and produced by a special team. We have scripts, make-up, costume and so on. But it's our aim to make it seem like a real, spontaneous blog. In this respect, it's a very nice compliment when viewers puzzle over the fact if it's all improvised or not" (Langford, 2009, p. 2).

In addition to hosting the vlogs and providing a place for fans to write notes, Das Erste also provided a guest book for fans to sign to congratulate Christian and Olli on their wedding, which aired on 3 and 6 September 2010 (www.daserste.de/verboteneliebe/gaestebuch.asp). The sixty-one pages of comments appended here run the gamut from simple congratulations to the newlyweds to thank-yous to the actors and to Das Erste. One theme is the transcendence of love: as gelybi writes on 12 September 2010, "This amazing love-story have already changed many lives and given hope to many others showing that LOVE is all that matters beyond barriers of gender and language."

Das Erste's willingness to provide a forum for fan voices to be heard indicates that the conceptions of text and audience are changing: the show is no longer perceived as being German but as transcending national boundaries, thanks to the audience generated by the YouTube fansubs. The vlogs and wedding guest book invite fans to respond. Fans have always done more than consume, but producers often fail to recognize this. Not so in the case of *VL*, where the producers provide a site for engagement. The mode of response is directed and limited to text, but this seems appropriate for an artwork that so many consumers discover via the fansubs. The producers do not engage directly with the fans by posting publicly or responding to comments, although the comments are probably silently moderated and inappropriate ones taken down. Further, the text-only mode doesn't permit threaded commenting, and fans aren't invited to engage with one another. Despite its limitations, the mere existence of a producer-run text-only commenting system acknowledges the producers' indebtedness to the fans who have made the Chrolli story line a sensation. These fan-specific sites signal the permeability of the producer–consumer relationship. Interestingly, Das Erste maintains the fiction that Christian and Oliver are real people; the fans sometimes follow along, but just as often, they acknowledge Thore Schölermann and Jo Weil, as well as Das Erste for airing the show and being so supportive of the Chrolli story line.

Soap Operas and Homosexuality

Soap operas have long walked a fine line: to generate dramatic stories, soaps tend to address controversial topics. Yet soaps also seek to reaffirm family, place, and harmony (Gitlin, 1986, p. 48), although this is endlessly deferred because soap operas are a "serial form which resists narrative closure" (Fiske, 1987, p. 179). On soap operas, treatments of homosexuality—usually the gay experience rather than the lesbian experience (Geraghty, 1991, p. 158)—are generally treated not as normative occurrences but as a social issue (Fiske, 1987; Liebes & Livingstone, 1998; Newcomb, 1974; Rapping, 2002; Wittebols, 2004). C. Lee Harrington (2003a) spells out the unspoken rules for treatment of gay characters on daytime American TV:

> (1) Gay or lesbian characters must be restricted to one-time appearances in television series or one-shot television movies; (2) Gay and lesbian characters can never be "incidentally" gay—instead, their sexuality must be the "problem" to be "solved"; (3) Their problem should be explored in terms of its effects on heterosexuals; and (4) Gay and lesbian erotic desire must be completely absent.
>
> *(p. 218)*

Even today, in what many would hope would be a more progressive, left-leaning, post-*Will and Grace* landscape (Becker, 2006), American soap operas tend to treat the issue of homosexuality with kid gloves. The first attempt to integrate a long-term character as homosexual, as opposed to having transient gay characters who left when their story line was finished, occurred in 2000, when *All My Children*'s sixteen-year-old Bianca came out as a lesbian (Harrington, 2003a, 2003b).

Not much has changed in the American soap scene since Bianca's coming out. Ten years later, several other long-term gay story lines have been attempted, with varying success, and usually hewing to Harrington's fourth dictum: "gay and lesbian erotic desire must be completely absent." In practice, this means that viewers see little, other than longing glances, even as straight characters hop from bed to bed. In terms of homosexual-themed plots that recently aired on American daytime television, Luke and Noah ("Nuke") kissed so infrequently on *As the World Turns* that AfterElton.com started a Nuke Liplock Clock as fans agitated behind the scenes to get a kissing ban lifted. It reached 211 days, 14 hours, 45 minutes, and 45 seconds before it could be reset. AfterElton.com eventually converted it to a Nuke Consummation Clock, which counted down the days between courtship and consummation (Jensen, 2008a). The Nuke plot ended with the abrupt cancellation of *As the World Turns*, which ended in September 2010. *One Life to Live* (USA, 1968–2012) paired Kyle Lewis and Oliver Fish ("Kish") in 2009–2010, even going so far as to air the very first gay love scene, in a bed, ever shown in the United States on daytime TV (Huffington Post, 2009; St. James, 2010), on 30 December 2009—and then quickly dissolved the story line and released the actors. Dwindling ratings and audience backlash to the gay-themed story were cited as reasons for the characters' removal (Waldman, 2010).

In this landscape it is therefore no surprise that Americans in particular view *VL* with such joy. The program's take on queer characters is markedly different than that of American soaps. American soap producers are quick to respond to audience protests, and slow to show in gay characters what they regularly show in straight characters. In *VL*, it's clear that Christian and Oliver love each other. In addition to saying this aloud, they gesture toward it in a myriad of ways. They are always touching; in fact, they tend toward public displays of affection. They kiss each other hello and goodbye. They catch each other's eye and share a wordless moment. They sit shirtless in bed together and talk. Sometimes there are sex scenes—pretty hot sex scenes, although the camera is careful to never reveal too much. The steamiest love scenes have been flagged in YouTube as requiring an age statement click-through to view, much to fans' disgust, even though the clips show nothing more than kissing and bare chests. The requirement for a click-through implies that something is seedy and wrong, because the clips are not explicit. Christian and Oliver are treated, in short, like a committed, happy, relaxed couple in love. To American soap opera viewers, this can seem like real life or it can seem like titillation; to viewers in parts of the world where homosexuality would never be publicly acknowledged, this is a life-changing revelation.

The fansubs' determined focus on Chrolli, their removal to an exterior site, their excision from a larger narrative, their lack of an attempt to provide context for other story lines, and their subtitling reflect an alternate textual productivity related to alternate sexuality. The fansubs create a queer space, removed to a site outside the larger hegemonic world. Even if *VL* isn't prioritizing the Chrolli plot, or if the fansubber is busy and a few days behind in translating and posting new material, YouTube has all the clips one might wish for, to view and view again; or a viewer who just can't wait might choose to watch the unsubtitled version, just to watch the characters engage with each other. The endless repetition inherent in soap opera plots, with their flashbacks and explicating remarks (Cantor & Pingree, 1983, p. 23), is here substituted for by YouTube's invitation: Play again?

More than one comment reflects a common theme in Chrolli fan response: the importance of the gay-themed plot to watchers. "I am touched by those who are writing to you from countries w[h]ere being gay is still illegal," Nalunelly writes. "You have had a great opportunity to both take on some fun acting challenges and make a difference in the world. It doesn't get better than that." "Making a difference in the world" is an important part of the Chrolli text as constructed by fans: the Chrolli text, merely by existing, presents a form of advocacy by failing to remark on the progressiveness of the advancement of a homosexual romance plot. John Fiske notes, "Soaps constitute a particular discourse through which change in a society is spoken and the way in which this process occurs sets up a range of invitations to the audience. How far social concerns can be pursued in soaps involves a myriad of factors, including overt censorship and professional conventions within television about what is possible" (Fiske, 1987, pp. 134–135). *VL* has long presented gay- and lesbian-friendly plotlines, and German soap operas' willingness to show same-sex sensuality contrasts markedly with that of American soaps.

Although *VL* has an international audience, it's an international audience with access to YouTube and the ability to speak German and/or read English, so the fansubs' accessibility is not truly worldwide. Further, fan reaction tends to be policed by fans themselves, with remarks perceived as inappropriate, often spoilers but also homophobic remarks, deleted by the YouTube account holder. It is thus hard to discover whether audience response differs from culture to culture, particularly because many posters do not indicate their country of origin. In areas of the world where YouTube is blocked altogether, such as China and Libya (Wikipedia, 2011a), fans would have to be both dedicated and tech savvy to view the fansubs. The result is a fairly homogenous type of post, with most falling into one of five categories: general appreciation, thank-yous, and good wishes; requests for information, such as song titles, insight into whether the actors are really dating, or the availability of the show on DVD; remarks about the show's current plot, in social terms (gay marriage, gay adoption/fostering, AIDS) or otherwise; affirmations of the desirability of a love that transcends gender; and remarks indicating personal engagement with the show, perhaps spurring the viewer to action.

Some of the international postings—and here I cite remarks appended to YouTube user ichglotzutube's general comments page as representative—indicate that the Chrolli story has given gay viewers comfort by providing an accepting worldview at odds with their culture's disapproval of homosexuality: "Being Asian, gay couples are still a taboo. I hope one day we can enjoy the same kind of open love and affection that Christian and Oliver shares without having others around us judge us with weird eyes," plutozon (country not specified) writes. Similarly, "Watching the episodes of Christian and Oliver, I have decided to come out after so many years of self-denial. I'm 38 years old and I hope that I can finally be free and happy for the first time in my life," Brazilian poster darcidesouza says. But the Chrolli plot does more than validate gay viewers' feelings and experiences; it may also promote tolerance. Kzzrd from Malaysia writes, "I used to have bad opinions about people who I came to know as gays and lesbians but after seeing stories like these including QAF [*Queer as Folk*], my perception changed to 'this is about genuine love and care one feels between 2 individuals regardless which sex they are'... and GOD... if HE is a loving GOD ... HE will not punish 2 same sex people for having loved each other."

Although fan interest resulted in a response from Das Erste in terms of providing a forum for fan voices to be heard and in terms of creating ancillary Web content, such as the vlogs and downloadable computer wallpapers, the always-progressive show itself has not really changed. Fans were puzzled when, after the huge drama of Christian and Oliver finally getting together was over, the Chrolli story line was not prioritized and they had very little to do. Some fans worried that the characters would be written out altogether, as often happens with *VL* when a plot closes down; the soap opera has a revolving door for young, attractive twentysomethings, who move in and out of Christian and Oliver's flatshare with some regularity. The program ramped up the Chrolli plot again by moving their relationship toward a blended family when they sought to adopt as a gay couple, in a social justice plot that paralleled the other timely social topics that *VL* has already covered through the Chrolli story line, such as AIDS and gay marriage. The Chrolli plot provides a pretext for Das Erste to air episodes that make a difference, but this is done within the context of a soap opera airing social-justice plotlines. In 2011 the characters broke up, although they remain married and subtext indicates that they still care deeply for one another. Fans see this as a hopeful sign: the next major drama for the couple will be their inevitable reunion.

Fans and the Metatext

One hallmark of soap opera fans is their often passionate engagement with the source material: fans read soap magazines, write letters to the actors or the network, obtain autographs, join fan clubs, exchange photos and videotapes, and engage in online posting on bulletin boards (Harrington & Bielby, 1995) or Usenet posts (Baym, 2000). Soap fans have been on the Internet for years. Fans of the Chrolli text engage online in a variety of ways: they watch the videos at YouTube and the vlogs at Chrolli.de and leave comments; they sign the wedding guest book; they join a wiki; they write e-mails and letters to the actors and thank-you notes to Das Erste; they read various blogs and comment; they write and post fan fiction; they create music videos from clips from the originary source and post them on YouTube and elsewhere.

As I noted above, fans are attuned to the advocacy and norming of alterity inherent in a gay-themed story line. *VL* treats the Chrolli plot like any other romance/love plot, although there are trappings specific to homosexuality, including closeting, self-delusion, gay/straight confusion, surprise on the part of friends and ex-lovers (who quickly get over it and seem fine with the revelation), and even some gay bashing that gets physical such as when Olli is beaten up by a homophobic boxer. Fans regularly comment on the meaningfulness of Christian and Oliver's struggle to be true to themselves and each other, even as they constantly get into situations where that trueness is tested, such as when Christian must remain closeted to maintain his boxing career, or Olli must go clubbing with the evil, manipulative Rob because Rob has connections that Olli needs for his business. In the end, they reject these impediments to their hearts: Christian dramatically comes out after a winning a boxing match by publicly kissing Olli, to their friends' wild applause, and Olli rejects Rob.

"Be true to yourself" is certainly a die-hard soap opera message. Similarly, the support and help of the community and friends is integral to soaps' worldview (Gitlin, 1986, p. 66). The Chrolli story line presents love as human, inevitable, and special. Their friends are supportive and their enemies despicable. Even Olli's homophobic mother is converted, and she attends their wedding after a threatened boycott. Christian and Oliver's message is further boosted by Schölermann and Weil, who have themselves become advocates: they have been invited to appear at several gay pride events, including an event in Canada in 2009 (AfterElton.com Staff, 2009; Jensen, 2009) and another in New York City in 2010, where events were held at the iconic Stonewall Inn (Bhattacharjee, 2010). In a move that blurred the boundaries between character and actor, the actors' absence from *VL* to make the 2010 appearance was explained as the characters' romantic trip—to New York City. There, Christian and Oliver planned to check out clubs (so Olli could get some ideas for his business) and shop. They taped several vlogs, including one shot atop the Empire State Building. From the rooftop, they pointed out the probable location of the Stonewall Inn.

The audience participation invited by the producer and the forums that the fans create for themselves work together synergistically, creating a complex rhetorical interaction between producer, viewer, and the two artworks at stake here: the original German-language *VL*, shown in its entirety, and the cut-out subtitled Chrolli plots. The producer never directly acknowledges or links to the YouTube fansubs, but the existence of the vlogs and wedding guest book tacitly acknowledges the work of the fansubber, and the fansubber links to Das Erste's official fan spaces in her upload comments, thus inviting fans to cross from fan space to official producer space. The combination of all the Chrolli texts, including the fansubs, the official vlogs, the comments, and the various forums where fans engage, extends the normativity presented in *VL* into advocacy. In the soap world, normative treatment of homosexuality is indeed a form of advocacy, and one that the actors take seriously and choose to extend by lending their presence to events, by granting interviews to gay-specific media outlets, and by wholeheartedly encouraging and embracing their fans. The alternate textual productivity creates a space that permits the narrative to be extended and a multiplicity of points of view to be presented, resonating around the common theme of a successful, normative, everyday romance.

Note

Fan quotations have been slightly edited to normalize spelling.

References

AfterElton.com Staff, B. (2009, March). Exclusive video interview with Thore and Jo from *Forbidden Love*. *AfterElton.com*. Retrieved from www.afterelton.com/blog/brianjuer gens/exclusive-video-blog-vlog-interview-thore-scholermann-jo-weil-forbidden-love

Anime News Network. (n.d.). Fansub. *Anime News Network*. Retrieved from www.anime newsnetwork.com/encyclopedia/lexicon.php?id=63

Baym, N. K. (2000). *Tune in, log on: Soaps, fandom, and online community.* Thousand Oaks, CA: Sage.

Becker, R. (2006). *Gay TV and straight America.* New Brunswick, NJ: Rutgers University Press.

Bhattacharjee, M. (2008). Like ATWT's Nuke? Meet VL's Ollian! *Soap Opera Digest and Soap Opera Weekly.* Retrieved from www.soapoperadigest.com/content/atwts-nuke-meet-vls-ollian-0

Bhattacharjee, M. (2010). GOOL ties: A gay soap-palooza! *Soap Opera Digest and Soap Opera Weekly.* Retrieved from www.soapoperadigest.com/features/gool_ties_a_gay_soap-palooza/

Cantor, M. G., & Pingree, S. (1983). *The soap opera.* Beverly Hills, CA: Sage.

chrno. (2003, November). How are fansubs created? *AnimeSuki Forum.* Retrieved from http://forums.animesuki.com/archive/index.php/t-1296.html

Diaz Cintas, J., & Munoz Sanchez, P. (2006). Fansubs: Audiovisual translation in an amateur environment. *Journal of Specialised Translation, 6,* 37–52.

Fiske, J. (1987). *Television culture* (pp. 179–197). New York: Methuen.

Geraghty, C. (1991). *Women and soap opera: A study of prime time soaps.* Cambridge: Polity Press.

Gitlin, T. (1986). Search for yesterday. In T. Gitlin (Ed.), *Watching television* (pp. 42–67). New York: Pantheon Books.

Harrington, C. L. (2003a). Homosexuality on *All My Children*: Transforming the daytime landscape. *Journal of Broadcasting and Electronic Media, 47,* 216–235.

Harrington, C. L. (2003b). Lesbian(s) on daytime television: The Bianca narrative on *All My Children. Feminist Media Studies, 3,* 207–228.

Harrington, C. L., & Bielby, D. D. (1995). *Soap fans: Pursuing pleasure and making meaning in everyday life.* Philadelphia, PN: Temple University Press.

Hector, A. (2010, February). American remake of German gay soap opera to be set in Portland. *qPDX.com.* Retrieved from http://qpdx.com/2010/02/american-remake-of-german-gay-soap-opera-to-be-set-in-portland/

Huffington Post. (2009, December). *One Life to Live* gay sex scene is first ever on daytime TV. *Huffington Post.* Retrieved from www.huffingtonpost.com/2009/12/31/first-ever-daytime-gay-se_n_408349.html

Jenkins, H. (2006, December). When piracy becomes promotion: How unauthorized copying made Japanese animation profitable in the United States. *Reason.com.* Retrieved from http://reason.com/archives/2006/11/17/when-piracy-becomes-promotion

Jensen, M. (2008a, April). Gay teens finally kiss again on *As the World Turns. AfterElton.com.* Retrieved from www.afterelton.com/TV/2008/4/lukeandnoahkiss

Jensen, M. (2008b, August). Interview with *Forbidden Love*'s Jo Weil. *AfterElton.com.* Retrieved from www.afterelton.com/people/2008/8/joweil

Jensen, M. (2009, January). Meet *Forbidden Love*'s Ollian at Whistler's Winter Pride! *AfterElton.com.* Retrieved from www.afterelton.com/blog/michaeljensen/meet-forbidden-loves-ollian-whistler-winterpride

Kirkpatrick, S. (2003). Like holding a bird: What the prevalence of fansubbing can teach us about the use of strategic selective copyright enforcement. *Temple Environmental Law and Technology Journal, 21,* 131–153.

Langford, A. D. (2009, July). *Interview with Jo Weil. AfterElton.com.* Retrieved from www.afterelton.com/TV/gayslives/07–27–09

Langford, A. D. (2010, September). Marital bliss: Jo and Thore talk about the *Forbidden Love* wedding! *AfterElton.com.* Retrieved from www.afterelton.com/tv/gayslives/09–08–2010

Liebes, T., & Livingstone, S. (1998). European soap operas: The diversification of a genre. *European Journal of Communication*, *13*, 147–180.

Newcomb, H. (1974). Soap opera: Approaching the real world. In H. Newcomb (Ed.), *TV: The most popular art* (pp. 161–182). Garden City, NY: Anchor/Doubleday.

Rapping, E. (2002). Daytime utopias: If you lived in Pine Valley, you'd be home. In H. Jenkins, T. McPherson, & J. Shattuc (Eds.), *Hop on pop: The politics and pleasure of popular culture* (pp. 47–66). Durham, NC: Duke University Press.

ShinyMedia. (2007, October). *Lost* producer blames fans for the failed Nikki/Paulo plot. *TV Scoop*. Retrieved from www.tvscoop.tv/2007/10/lost_producer_b.html

St. James, J. (2010, March). Farewell Kish. *WOW Report*. Retrieved from http://worldof wonder.net/2010/03/11/KISH_kibosh/?utm_source=wow&utm_medium=perma link&utm_campaign=related

von Riedemann, D. (2006a, October). Fansubs 3: What cost piracy? How badly does illegal downloading hurt movie studios? *suite101.com*. Retrieved from www.suite101.com/content/fansubs-3--what-cost-piracy--a7440

von Riedemann, D. (2006b, September). Fansubs: Publicity or piracy? *suite101.com*. Retrieved from www.suite101.com/content/fansubs--publicity-or-piracy--a6055

Waldman, A. (2010, March). *One Life to Live* dumps the gay love story. *TV Squad*. Retrieved from www.tvsquad.com/2010/03/13/one-life-to-live-dumps-the-gay-love-story/

Wikipedia. (2011a, September). Censorship of YouTube. *Wikipedia*. Retrieved from http://en.wikipedia.org/w/index.php?title=Censorship_of_YouTube&oldid=447988796

Wikipedia. (2011b, August). List of soap operas with LGBT characters. *Wikipedia*. Retrieved from http://en.wikipedia.org/w/index.php?title=List_of_soap_operas_with_LGBT_characters&oldid=446988189

Wittebols, J. H. (2004). *The soap opera paradigm: Television programming and corporate priorities*. Lanham, MA: Rowman & Littlefield.

14

VIRTUAL PLACES IN THE PHYSICAL WORLD

Geographies of Literacy and (National) Identity

Rick Carpenter

On 1 May 2010, Faisal Shahzad attempted to detonate a car bomb in the middle of New York City's bustling Times Square. Fortunately, the makeshift fertilizer-fueled bomb malfunctioned and failed to detonate, and Shahzad was arrested two days later. In the days that followed, as more and more information surfaced, media accounts as well as the street conversations and online discussions of ordinary people came to be dominated by Shahzad's personal and professional life. Though born in Pakistan, Shahzad was a naturalized U.S. citizen who had lived in the United States for more than a decade. He had earned an M.B.A., gained employment as a financial analyst, married, and bought a house. To all appearances, his life seemed not only mundane but also completely middle class. In other words, for many Americans, he seemed utterly and thoroughly *American*, an image not dispelled—and perhaps encouraged—by the photograph of him most frequently displayed and circulated by the media. The photo, which Shahzad appears to have taken of himself while driving, performs a carefully constructed and rather familiar identity. With his stylish jacket, mirror lens designer sunglasses, sharply trimmed beard, gel-combed hair, and Bluetooth headset, Shahzad embodies to no small degree the image of youth, affluence, and urbanity that so dominates American popular culture depictions of the ideal(ized) male.

Not long after the photo of Shahzad was released, Stephen Colbert quipped during his nightly American television show, "[M]y worst suspicions were confirmed when I saw this photo. Now, I don't want to stereotype, folks, but he's not just from Connecticut; he's a Connecticut douchebag." The photograph was shown on screen with the Bluetooth device highlighted. A little more than a week later, comedian Seth Meyers remarked during the Weekend Update segment of the sketch comedy program *Saturday Night Live* that Shahzad's terrorist nickname is Muhammad Al Corey Feldman, a reference to Shahzad's resemblance to the American actor and former child film star. Additionally, countless comments and discussions about Shahzad's supposed American-ness, most neither satirical nor humorous, appeared online in chat rooms, message boards, and blogs.

For many Americans, the idea that Shahzad could hate America—or more specifically, American culture—was simply and quite literally incomprehensible. And yet, despite having seemingly "bought into" American culture and ideology, Shahzad *had* become radicalized. Over and over, people expressed vexed perplexity and voiced in a variety of ways the same essential question: *How? How, when he had lived here for so long?*

Less than two months later, reports of sinister foreign plots against the United States appeared once again when a Russian spy ring was suddenly uncovered and ten alleged spies were arrested (and later deported). In direct contrast to the Times Square bomb scare, popular sentiment shifted from an initial uneasy bewilderment to bemused self-satisfaction. News reports repeatedly emphasized, with almost a sense of relief, the degree to which the spies had become *genuinely* Americanized during their long-term, deep-cover operation. While Shahzad's failure to complete his mission had been attributed to lack of knowledge, skill, and training,[1] the Russians' incompetence as spies was commonly framed as stemming from a lack of motivation following their total immersion in American culture. They'd gone native, as it were. The usual tropes of idealized Americana were deployed, as evidenced by the following *Los Angeles Times* report:

> Richard and Cynthia Murphy grew lettuce in a backyard garden, walked their daughters to the school bus each morning, and swapped Christmas cards with neighbors who had moved to Texas.
>
> Their modest three-bedroom house sported maroon shutters and a wrap-around porch, and sat on a winding street in a well-heeled suburb across from Manhattan. They drove a green Honda Civic.
>
> To all appearances, the Murphys were a typical, child-obsessed American family—not deep-cover Russian spies straight from a Cold War novel.
>
> *(Drogin & Baum, 2010, para. 1–3)*

The careful attention to the specifics of setting and location, to the lived environment, in the above passage works to engage the intended audience by providing a simulacrum of "ordinary" American life that is sentimentally familiar, thereby encouraging readers to locate themselves, physically, metaphorically, and emotionally, within the story.

The focus on place also functions to construct the "American-ness" of the Murphys. America as conceptual ideal and imagined geography is spatialized, so that only certain people (or certain *kinds* of people)—here, the Murphys—can dwell (or be imagined as dwelling) within its constructed borders. Thusly situated, its citizens not only inhabit but also embody the nation-state, their bodies marked by their experiences in, with, and through the environment. In contrast with depictions of Shahzad, whose American identity was viewed as superficial, as mere appearance, even though he was a legal citizen of the United States, the Russian spies, who were not legal citizens, were portrayed as having been thoroughly Americanized, a status evinced more by actions than appearances:

> If their cover jobs were ordinary, their secret lives had a humdrum side that sometimes seems more like Woody Allen than John LeCarre.
>   One suspect, Anna Chapman, bought a Verizon cellphone in Brooklyn, N.Y., with a patently false address: 99 Fake Street. She also posted sultry photos of herself on Facebook and videos on YouTube.
>   *(Drogin & Baum, 2010, para. 7–8)*

If the Murphys are June and Ward Cleaver, Chapman is Paris Hilton. Having the spies embody well-established identity constructs has the effect of rendering them more "American" than the average American. Indeed, the juxtaposition of two seemingly dichotomous versions of *American* strengthens rather than weakens the Russians' positionality. As Williams (2009) pointed out, irony and sentimentality are frequently juxtaposed in popular culture (p. 155). The effect of placing/place-ing the Russian spies firmly within the United States, then, is only intensified.

   As distinct as these two examples of (inter)national terror, politics, and ideologies are, both illustrate the importance of space and place, the material-metaphorical locations in which experiences occur and lives take place, in constructions and perceptions of identity and difference, in how subjectivities, as texts, are written and read. In this, they highlight the interconnected, rhetorical basis of self and environment. Informed by a postmodern perspective, scholars across disciplines have long viewed identity as a social construct rooted in language. Of course, to identify subjectivity as a text does not mean that the physicality of Shahzad and the Russian spies, their being-in-the-material-world, was not relevant or important. As many feminists have pointed out, recognition of the self as discursive construc-tion does not mean the body should (or can) be jettisoned. For Hélène Cixous, "writing the body" can be an empowering discursive practice for women. Other writers and scholars, many influenced by Cixous, have also sought to re-emphasize, re-establish, and/or re-insert the physical, literal body against the postmodern tendency to dismiss or erase the corporeal (Bordo, 1993; McLaren, 1988; Orner, Miller, & Ellsworth, 1995; Smith, 1993; Thomas, 1996). Advocates and scholars working in disability studies have also contributed much to our understanding of the discursive, embodied self by revealing the socio-rhetorical construction of bodily difference and privilege (Lewiecki-Wilson & Brueggemann, 2008; Lindblom & Dunn, 2003; Linton, 1998). The interconnectedness of discourse, identity, and the body has led many working in composition and literacy studies to theorize about such notions as "embodied writing" (Banks, 2003), "embodied rhetorics" (Hindman, 2001), "embodied practice" (Haas, 1996), and "embodied voice" (Ronald & Roskelly, 2002). Going further, others have argued for the materiality of language itself (Bleich, 2001) and explored the "ways in which we use language as a means of *enacting* our material being" (Iwanicki, 2003; emphasis in original) in the "physical, emotional, social, and discursive spaces" of daily life (Cain, 2003, p. 477), what Marback (1998) termed "material rhetoric." These spaces are the contexts or "scenes," to use Brodkey's (1996) term, of writing as embodied action and, as such, are themselves material-discursive social constructs. In short, identities are constructed as bodies move through sociospatial environments and interact with other bodies through language. In the process, these environments are themselves constructed even as they construct.

Viewed this way, reactions to Shahzad and the Russian spies within the U.S. not only demonstrate the importance of the sociospatial environment in the construction of identity. Those reactions also foreground the powerful influence of the nation-state as constructed—and constitutive—space/place. Undoubtedly, the sociospatial inscribed itself on Shahzad and the Russian spies (if in differing ways and to varying degrees) even as they affected the world in which they moved. More interesting to me, however, are the ways in which Shahzad and the Russian spies were read and used as popular culture texts and what those ways might suggest about literacy and place in an era of globalization and rapid technological advances. Clearly, knowledge of their having lived for an extended period of time on American soil (their temporal-spatiality) affected how the public construed and read them. Additionally, the available frames for interpreting these "foreigners" were to a great extent limited and conditioned by pre-existing sociospatial meanings. One could go a step further to suggest that in constructing these individuals in spatialized terms, writers were simultaneously (re)producing the borders of that space as (a particular) place—America.

Despite their physicality, Shahzad, the Murphys, and Chapman were constructed, consumed, and circulated within American popular culture as "disembodied" texts of a particular and familiar place. Crucially, it's not only physical bodies (or bodies-as-texts) that are moving across national borders with increasing ease and regularity. New technologies and the participatory popular culture of contemporary "convergence culture" (Jenkins, 2006) enabled and facilitated by these technologies, are bringing unprecedented numbers of people from all over the globe into contact with one another. New communities are forming in newly created spaces. As these digital inhabitants utilize the affordances of Web 2.0 technologies to not only consume but also produce popular culture texts, their literacy practices are ever more frequently crossing national borders. Almost certainly, such movement through space is affecting how these individuals interpret and negotiate difference. Members of transnational online communities must confront and grapple with the embodied materiality of texts that speak back from different and often unfamiliar sociospatial lifeworlds. Cross-cultural interactions in these online spaces are impacting literacy practices and conceptions of self in ways we are only beginning to explore. The present collection represents an important and significant move toward a deeper understanding of these online communities and literacies.

In seeking to contribute to this effort, I take as my starting point the assumption that writing is a geographical practice. As we examine how online literacy practices intersect with online popular culture in international contexts, we must not forget that language use is a material act even as it constructs—and reconstructs itself in terms of—the symbolic. More specifically, I contend that we must ground our investigations and analyses in an understanding of identity and literacy as embodied practices situated in the material world, in spaces and places that are both physical and metaphorical. We don't always notice the material spatiality of literacy practices, of course. Similar to other social practices, they frequently become so habitualized and taken-for-granted as to not only erase their own histories but also render transparent the processes and forces that continually construct and reconstruct them. Such rendered transparency is especially true of online literacy practices, in which the concept of cyberspace, as metaphorical construct, can so easily elide its materiality and position in actual physical space (and spaces).

The spatiality of writing and/in cyberspace can more easily remain unnoticed (or be consciously denied) when online writers and digital texts occupy—which is to say, regularly dwell within and move through—the same socially constructed space. But what about when they occupy different spaces or places? That is the question I wish to address here. Drawing upon Reynolds's (2004) notion of geographic rhetorics and the concept of place-identity developed by social psychologists and cultural geographers, I examine how the material spatiality of texts complicates writing and reading across borders. Specifically, I argue that popular culture texts, including those online, are both culturally and geographically situated, constructed, and "placed" within the material-metaphoric territory of the nation-state. Such place-ment suggests that national borders are perhaps more easily crossed than transcended. I begin by examining how space and place intersect with national identity and popular culture. Next, I consider the geography of online places. I then explore how the material spatialization of popular culture influences literacy practices by presenting a case study of an Albanian woman living and working in the United States.

Space, Place, and the Nation-State

LeFebvre's *The Production of Space* (1991) was influential in reconceptualizing space in non-mathematical terms, as something other than an empty area. Working from a Marxist perspective and utilizing the language of the social sciences, LeFebvre insisted that space is neither abstract nor material but both, a complex social construct, what he termed "social space," constituted by and constitutive of the physical, mental, and social. In this regard, space is both produced and, importantly, productive. The notion of social space has been taken up and expanded upon by scholars in a number of disciplines, including human and cultural geography, environmental psychology, philosophy, and social psychology. Scholars working in these fields have generally focused on the production, reproduction, and use of place, particularly in connection to the production of self and other social categories, such as community.

The social production of space as place is never more evident than when a site is contested. Such conflicts arise most frequently as the result of competing constructions of place in the same physical space. We typically associate contested spaces with conflicts between nation-states over territory, and such conflicts do of course occur. However, spaces are much more likely to be contested at the smaller scales of everyday life, as was evident during recent debates over a proposed plan to construct an Islamic community center (the so-called "Ground Zero Mosque") in lower Manhattan close to where the World Trade Center once stood. Groups can disagree about the significance of a particular totemic site, such as historic places or landmarks (Devine-Wright & Lyons, 1997); contest how an area is to be used (Wallwork & Dixon, 2004); or, more subtly but commonly, interpret—which is to say, construct—a certain location in oppositional ways, such as whether a neighborhood is "good" or "bad" (Reynolds, 2004, pp. 93–109).

An examination of contested spaces can serve to highlight not only the social nature of place but also—and this is crucial—the particular practices by which specific places are actively constructed. Increasingly, scholars across disciplines are recognizing the extent to which those practices are language-based and rhetorical. Drawing from rhetorical theory and discourse studies, scholars emphasize the discursive nature of place and place-identity. A conception of space/place as process and practice is much illuminated by Reynolds's (2004) notion of geographic rhetorics. Following LeFebvre, Reynolds conceptualized space as simultaneously material and metaphorical. What is more, spatial metaphors, far from simply reflecting reality, actually construct reality (p. 43). Accordingly, space is socially produced, geography is rhetorical, and identity and culture are sociospatial constructs. For writers, then, "location is an act of inhabiting one's words; location is a struggle as well as a place, an act of coming into being" (p. 11). In this sense, geography is a "lived event" (p. 10), for we compose our environments even as they are inscribed upon us. From this, Reynolds re-imagined writing as "a set of spatial practices informed by everyday negotiations of space" (p. 6). Despite the vital importance of the metaphorical to her ideas about writing and identity, Reynolds repeatedly stressed the need to begin with/from recognition of the material. In fact, metaphor and the material are interconnected/interrelated, working in tandem to produce space and spatial practices. As we move through and dwell in spaces (the stuff of material reality), we employ spatial metaphors and other spatial practices (such as writing) to shape and reshape space, the social lifeworlds in which we live.

In essence, space is an abstract metaphor (though the spatial metaphors used to construct a particular space are frequently concrete) and imagined geography; a social construct formed through purposeful (inter)actions with/in the materially real by means of spatial practices; and a "realm of practices" (p. 181) that structures our ways of knowing, seeing, and even being-in-the-world, for actions, identities, and emotions always take place *somewhere*.

While Reynolds chose to focus on the habitual pathways and contested places of the everyday, other scholars have been more interested in nation-states and the discursive construction of national identities (Blackledge, 2002; de Cillia, Reisigl, & Wodak, 1999; Wallwork & Dixon, 2004). The nation-state is a rich area of study for a multiplicity of reasons. According to Wallwork and Dixon (2004), "Nations are, *par excellence*, discursively *located* categories; indeed, the very term 'nation' straddles an ambiguity between the social and the spatial" (p. 23; emphasis in original). They asserted that the rhetoric of nationalism is so effective because "nations" are imagined "not only as social categories" but also as "entities possessing a geographic and historical 'reality' that somehow exceeds their human membership" (p. 22). In other words, nations and by extension national identities are essentialized, a strategy that elides their production through sociospatial rhetorical practices. Places are, by definition, more rigidly conceived—and thus experienced—than spaces, and the nation-state is arguably the most influential of places. Within the imagined borders of the nation, everyday spaces are, of course, still encountered and negotiated through spatialized practices. As Reynolds persuasively argued, these practices are what constitute reality. However, practices that activate the nation *as place* (i.e., spatialized practices that act upon rather than within the nation-place and thereby call forth or disclose the nation as construct) will likely be either ignored altogether or met with confusion or resistance. Put another way, place trumps space, especially when the place has a flag.

In this regard, one could view the "imagined community" (Anderson, 1991) of the nation-state as a mechanism—a kind of grand narrative or master genre—for achieving stability as well as unity through the construction of a monolithic social space, a common sense of place and thus of self. In their study of the Austrian nation and identity, de Cillia, Reisigl, and Wodak (1999) identified five semantic macro-areas:

1.   the idea of a "homo austriacus" and a "homo externus"
2.   the narrative of a collective political history
3.   the discursive construction of a common culture
4.   the discursive construction of a collective present and future
5.   the discursive construction of a "national body" (p. 158)

Their thick description of each area reveals that medium and content are concomitant with discourse, a fact that comes as no surprise. More revealing, however, is the wide variety of texts and artifacts brought to bear in the service of constructing a collective yet coherent national identity, from past governmental treaties to clothing, from landscapes to top athletes. Additionally, connections made between and among texts, including seemingly disparate ones, in which some texts framed or informed others, suggests the importance of intertextuality to the enterprise of national construction. What is more, while many texts were related to official discourse (e.g., Austria's accession to the EU, statements made by politicians, important architecture), many were decidedly more connected to everyday culture, such as cooking and travel. Indeed, the researchers discovered that the majority of the discussion participants and interviewees in their study relied more heavily on elements of common culture than on political or institutional concepts to define themselves as Austrian. While the elements identified did include such traditional cultural touchstones as language and religion, mundane and "popular" phenomena (e.g., sports, fashion, and the arts) were also prominent. To me, this suggests the growing importance of popular culture, at least in the contemporary world, in creating and sustaining the geography of common culture perceived to be the nation-state. That this should be the case is not surprising given the power and reach of mass media, a topic discussed by thinkers as diverse as Stuart Hall and Henry Jenkins. Cultural and postcolonial critics have long connected popular culture with power and ideology in ways that implicate the nation-state. It is on such grounds that global capitalism and the "cultural imperialism" of the West, and the U.S. in particular, have been criticized and resisted (Giroux, 1999; Ritzer, 2011).

Of the Virtual and the Material: Cyberspace as Cyberplaces

Given the power of place to define and delimit the geography of self, to fix it in space, it is not surprising that many have enthusiastically embraced a view of cyberspace as an alternate reality, an immaterial universe where time and distance cease to matter and disembodied minds are free to (re)fashion their identities at will. As John Perry Barlow (1996) famously proclaimed in his "A Declaration of the Independence of Cyberspace":

> Governments of the Industrial World, you weary giants of flesh and steel, I come from Cyberspace, the new home of Mind. On behalf of the future, I ask you of the past to leave us alone. You are not welcome among us. ... I declare the global social space we are building to be naturally independent of the tyrannies you seek to impose on us. ... Cyberspace does not lie within your borders.
>
> *(para. 1–3)*

Barlow's vision may now seem rather utopian, but his evocation of "social space" is quite apt. Even before the time of Barlow's declaration, scholars were analyzing the geography of cyberspace. A large and growing body of research and scholarship has since come to share the same general conclusion that, far from being spaceless, electronic or virtual space is indeed social space and, as such, can foster the creation of sociospatial communities. Wellman (2001) asserted that these communities "have transformed cyber*space* into cyber*places*, as people connect online with kindred spirits, engage in supportive and sociable relationships with them, and imbue their activity online with meaning, belonging, and identity" (p. 229; emphasis in original). Wellman's description of cyberplace as a collective of kindred spirits is echoed by Gee's (2004, 2005) notion of "affinity spaces." Online affinity spaces are virtual places where people "relate to each other in terms of common interests, endeavors, goals, or practices" rather than primarily in the more traditional terms of "race, gender, age, disability, or social class" (2005, p. 225). The affordances of Web 2.0 technologies have encouraged and allowed affinity spaces to appear in virtual space in numbers far, far greater than would ever be possible in physical space. And as Gee and others have pointed out, these online affinity spaces most often coalesce and center around popular culture (Black, 2008; Jenkins, 2006; Williams, 2009).

Given the interrelationship of place and identity, and the socio-discursive nature of both, how then are we to locate the member-participants of these online communities? How are we to map participatory popular culture on a global scale? Finally, how are literacy practices developing in and responding to these spatial negotiations? The heady idealism expressed by Barlow and others no longer seems adequate to the task of addressing questions such as these. For one, cyberspace is certainly not "naturally independent" of regimes of power. The authority of governments to tax goods sold over the Internet problematizes any view of cyberspace as lacking borders. Secondly, while virtual space does lack physicality, can we by extension proclaim it immaterial? After all, software is run on hardware, on machines connected to cables in the physical world (and never mind the implications of Einstein's famous equation, $E = mc^2$). And even if we restrict ourselves to defining only the virtual, its discursive construction as social space instantiates the materiality inherent in language use. Along those same lines, can we say that the inhabitants of Cyberia are disembodied minds? While the body may be physically absent in digital environments, the writing that produces virtual space is embodied, as are the avatars frequently employed there, being "grounded in the *practice* of the body, and thus in the world" (Taylor, 2002, p. 42; emphasis in original). Indeed, the embodied nature of online literacy practices can help deconstruct the mind/body split (Greenhill, 2002; McRae, 1996). Further, not only do attributes of the physical world find their way into the structure of virtual space (Adams, 1997), virtual experiences can sometimes intersect in consequential ways with physical space, as can occur with Internet dating and cyberstalking (Fletcher, 1998). Accordingly, Barlow's claim that cyberspace does not reside within the borders of any nation seems problematic, given the material spatiality of the virtual and the role of popular culture in constructing place-identity relationships.

While I certainly do not advocate a view that would attempt to situate cyberspace and/or popular culture within the imagined geography of a single nation-state, I do wish to argue against a view of space or place (or any particular space or place, including those that are virtual) as wholly deterritorialized or otherwise completely independent of the material-physical world.

Writing across Borders: A Brief Case Study

To illustrate the material spatiality of texts and identities, and how this material spatialization complicates writing across borders, I will briefly discuss some of the literacy practices of Eva, an Albanian national. The research presented here is part of a larger study, still in progress, investigating the online literacy practices of current and former international students living in the United States. She was selected for the focus of this study because she is not an American citizen but has lived in the United States for a significant amount of time. In addition, she possesses a native-like command of American English as well as an extensive knowledge of past and contemporary American popular culture. I present a short case study interpretively constructed from a series of interviews, field notes, informal communications, and a guided tour (DePew & Miller-Cochan, 2010; DeWitt, 1997) through her social networking page.

Eva had lived in the Albanian capital of Tirana before moving to the United States in 1999 to further her education. She had already earned a bachelor's degree in literature from the University of Tirana but felt a degree from the United States would be of more professional use. As she put it, "How many people read Albanian literature?" She subsequently earned a bachelor's degree in business administration and then a master's in public administration from a midsize, regional university. Upon graduation, she was hired as a human resources specialist by a local staffing agency, where she remains employed as an accounts supervisor. Her employment allows her to remain in the United States with an H-1B visa (an alien authorized to work in the U.S.). She is fluent in four languages: Albanian, English, Italian, and Spanish.

Eva actively maintains a Facebook page that she uses to connect with friends and family who live all over the world. She reported that most of her friends "back home" use two and sometimes even three different social networking sites. Eva, however, uses only Facebook, stating she doesn't have time to use more than one. Her communications via Facebook were heavily mediated through popular culture, especially popular music (in spite of her stated preference for "classical music" and Spanish guitar). Her site was clean and uncluttered, though her Wall was filled with posts from friends. Also clearly visible on her Wall was a self-posted music video of George Michael's "Father Figure." She laughed as she pointed it out and jokingly stated that she was almost too embarrassed for me to know that she had posted it. When I asked why, she laughed again and said she didn't want me to think she was someone "still hanging onto the 80s." She explained that while she had liked George Michael as a teenager, she hardly ever listened to his music now. She posted the video because many of her Albanian friends frequently post music videos from the 1980s and 1990s. To prove her point, she showed me several of her friends' pages. One friend, an Albanian now living in Spain, had filled her Wall with music videos from a variety of artists, almost all of them American, including Cher, Bon Jovi, R.E.M., Backstreet Boys, and Poison. "An American probably wouldn't do something like this," Eva told me. "It'd seem too silly." She explained that among her friends it's the ones who, like she, live abroad that tend to post references to older popular music. According to Eva, the reason they do so isn't because they only like popular music from that time. Instead, they do so because that music reminds them of Albania. "It's a nostalgia thing," she added.

This last statement led her to recount a childhood story involving the American singer Madonna. She recalled liking Madonna's "Papa Don't Preach" despite not knowing any English at the time. "We [she and her friends] were even trying to dress like Madonna," she told me, adding, "with emphasis on *trying*." One day, while watching the song's music video with others, a local girl who claimed to know a little English translated the song's title as "The Priest Doesn't Pray." Eva explained:

> Probably because the Albanian word for *Pope* is *Papa*. Of course that translation makes little sense in connection to the video—Madonna dancing around all provocatively and Danny Aiello being the angry but concerned father. But we [Albania] were still a communist state at the time, and religion was banned, so I think I just assumed Madonna was being subversive and making some sort of political statement. You know, about the reach of governmental control.

This discussion of Madonna led Eva to remark upon Lady Gaga: "I'm much too old to be a fan of hers, but I loved Christopher Walken's reading of 'Poker Face.'" She then showed me the YouTube video she had posted on the Wall of one her American friends. The video is a mashup of Lady Gaga's hit single "Poker Face" and actor Christopher Walken's satirically dramatic reading of the song's lyrics during a broadcast of the BBC's *Friday Night with Jonathan Ross*. When she indicated that she thought the video was rather humorous, I asked why she hadn't posted it to her own Facebook page. She said she doubted her non-American friends would find it funny, remarking, "I can already hear my cousin in Italy saying, 'The original [video for "Poker Face"] is bad enough; why post *this*?'" I then asked why she thought Americans, in contrast, would find the mashup comical. She quickly replied, "Well, Christopher Walken, of course. 'More cowbell' and all that. I heard that song[2] for the first time in years and years just the other day, don't ask where, and I swear, all I could hear was the cowbell!'"

Discussion

As with any case study, interpretations must be read as tentative and localized. Still, I believe Eva's comments, together with her online practices, suggest a transnational perspective strongly informed by an awareness of literacy as spatialized practices that are both material and geographic. Bicultural, biliterate, and multilingual, Eva has developed a hybrid identity that allows her to move confidently through and between multiple sociospatial worlds, including the imagined geographies of different nation-states. Studies of L2 writers frequently show the use of multiple social networking sites to interact with different audiences (DePew & Miller-Cochran, 2010; Yi, 2007; Yi & Hirvela, 2010). Eva's use of only one, Facebook, may stem from confidence in her own ability as a transnational to "move easily between different cultures" (Portes, 1997, p. 812). However, her hybridity and confidence is most clearly displayed in her use and reading of popular culture texts.

That a song should remind a person of the place where she or he first listened to it is not all that surprising, though it does indicate once again that experiences in the world are spatialized. More interesting to me from the perspective of the current study is Eva's decision to post only one music video related to her youth in Albania even though several of her friends had posted many. Together with her comments, this suggests that Eva believes that the same popular culture texts may have different meanings and be put to different uses in different countries. For Americans living within the U.S., an American pop song from the 1980s might evoke a particular *time*, with place, as transparent backdrop, ignored and unacknowledged. In a certain sense, the song *is* the place, functioning as it does in the ongoing process— or material-metaphorical spatialization—of constructing the nation as nation. Eva's remarks indicate that the same may be true for her Albanian friends, except that their having emigrated to other countries means that what is most emphatically evoked is the spatial rather than the temporal—specifically, the nation-state as place. Eva, then, seems to be deftly accommodating the rhetorical expectations of both audiences simultaneously. I am reminded of the rhetorical negotiation of "shuttling" between communities and languages discussed by Canagarajah (2006). We could say that she is negotiating the spaces of the everyday, spaces that aren't located solely within the imagined geography of cyberspace or the borderlands but also in two very real places on the globe.

Her use of and comments about the "Poker Face"-Walken mashup are even more revealing. As she explained later, her non-American friends and family members, such as her cousin in Italy, generally know who Christopher Walken is, broadly speaking: a famous American actor. However, her reference to "more cowbell" indicates that she believes a much wider, intertextual understanding of Walken and his place within popular culture is needed in order to appreciate the humor of the mashup. That she assumed I would fully understand both the cowbell allusion and the "that song" reference is also quite telling. "More cowbell" is a popular catchphrase that originated from a *Saturday Night Live* skit in 2000 in which Walken played a cowbell-obsessed music producer helping the band Blue Öyster Cult record its biggest hit, "(Don't Fear) The Reaper." The actual song does indeed feature a cowbell, if not as prominently as lampooned in the *SNL* skit. Eva assumed that I, as an American, would be able to trace these lines of inter-textual meanings. Additionally, by remarking that she can no longer hear the Blue Öyster Cult song without thinking about the Walken character in the *SNL* skit, Eva demonstrated that she too is an "insider." She "gets" the humor of the mashup.

A mashup of Lady Gaga's hit single "Poker Face" and actor Christopher Walken's dramatic reading of the song's lyrics does not require the viewer to know that Walken delivered the reading on the BBC's *Friday Night with Jonathan Ross*. (Or that Walken has performed similarly satirical readings throughout his career.) It does, however, require the viewer to know more than simply that Walken is an Oscar-winning actor. To fully "get" the mashup means to be familiar with not only Walken's eclectic career, including the kind of character he often portrays and his many television appearances, but also his complex status as a popular culture icon. He has developed a certain style and mystique, an identity construct the actor himself sometimes playfully exploits for comedic effect. But the Walken mystique exists more on the streets of everyday life than anywhere else. Even prior to the advent of the Internet, people in nightclubs, classrooms, and break rooms—not to mention on comedy club stages—were impersonating his distinctive manner of speaking (notably the very pregnant pause). Now, impersonations can be uploaded to YouTube or blogs. There's even a website, *Walken the Walk*, that hosts Christopher Walken impersonation contests, with notable entries circulating across the Internet. Recently, *Tosh.0*, a popular American television series that makes extensive use of new media technologies, aired a collection of these clips that only featured people of Asian descent. One of the featured Walken impersonators "wrote" back to Daniel Tosh, the program's host, by posting a response on YouTube (as Walken, of course). To "get" the intended humor[3] of a collection entitled "Asians Doing Christopher Walken" is to understand not only the Walken mystique but also how thoroughly *Tosh.0* mocks American popular culture, including itself. (The series also includes a recurring segment called "Is It Racist?"—yet another example of satirical effect depending upon knowledge contextualized "locally" in terms of the nation-state.) On the program's blog, someone had commented, "Is this Asia's way of getting back at Walken for *Balls of Fury*?" in reference to the 2007 comedy starring Walken that parodied Kung Fu movies.

In short, to fully understand the "meanings" and use of Christopher Walken in these contexts requires a certain intertextual *grounding*, in the sense of both a basic working knowledge of the subject(s) at hand *and* a familiarity with the complex circulation of particular texts that work to produce and reproduce certain material-metaphoric spaces and places. In other words, one must be firmly grounded, figuratively and literally, in America. Clearly, Eva is so grounded and, importantly, recognizes the need to adjust her communications accordingly, depending on her audience.

Implications and Conclusion

Literacy researchers have argued persuasively that literacy is a social practice contextualized within particular groups, communities, or systems of activity (Barton & Hamilton, 2000; Gee, 1996; Street, 1995). Scholars are now beginning to explore literacy practices in the intersecting local and global contexts and communities increasingly enabled and sustained by new media technologies (Brandt & Clinton, 2002; Cope & Kalantzis, 2000). Much of the scholarly focus has been on migrant populations, particularly on second language learning and literacy development among immigrant and Generation 1.5 adolescents. These studies have demonstrated that new technologies and online communities that cross national borders are powerful resources that students use to explore and negotiate their complex, shifting, and frequently hybrid bicultural-biliterate identities in multiple contexts while establishing and strengthening ties with peer and social groups in both "host" and "home" or heritage countries. As Yi (2010) asserted, "online literacy involvement allows transnational students to stay locally, but act globally while forging their transnational and transcultural identity" (p. 318). At the same time, scholars are coming to recognize that media convergence on a global scale increasingly affects everyone's literacy development and practice (Lu & Horner, 2009).

My purpose in this essay has been to contribute to this work by foregrounding the importance of material-physical places as sociospatial constructs to literacy and identity work in both physical and virtual environments. Certainly, numerous scholars have acknowledged the importance of the material, physical, and local. As Lu and Horner (2009) argued, "Clearly, it is cogent to attend to the physicality of social-historical locations, relations, and actions: the reality of tangible borders separating nation-states, neighborhoods, or public and private properties, and mobility across them, is still a central stratifying mechanism in the current United States and around the world" (p. 127). However, they were quick to add that "given the increasing value of extra-territorial mobility in the present-day imaginary, we need to question whether attention to the physicality of social-historical locations, relations, and actions is by itself sufficient" (p. 127). I certainly agree. Digital media have become major tools and avenues for people around the world, particularly young people, to communicate and form relationships across national borders. My concern is that in embracing these online communities as important places for fostering transnational perspectives, cultures, and literacies, we may neglect to fully acknowledge the complex manner in which virtual space is tied to localized material-metaphor places, most notably the nation-state, and how this connection complicates transnational literacy practices and identities.

In "Limits of the Local: Expanding Perspectives on Literacy as Social Practice," Brandt and Clinton (2002) argued that an increased attention to the material aspects of literacy can highlight "literacy's transcontextualized and transcontextualizing potentials of literacy … particularly its ability to travel, integrate, and endure" (p. 338). Certainly, as Brandt and Clinton asserted, we must take care not to exaggerate "the power of local contexts to set or reveal the forms and meanings that literacy takes" (p. 338). Nevertheless, I maintain that attention to the material dimensions of literacy also highlights literacy's role in constructing sociospatial lifeworlds, such as the nation-state, that struggle to "limit" literacy to the "local." Indeed, as discursive constructs, geographical places, local or global, are in fact produced and reproduced by texts and literacy practices—and in ways often mediated through and by popular culture.

Consequently, it is more useful to conceive of the Internet and cyberspace as "a contradictory space … a site of struggle … a space of flows" that is "in no way separate from other social spaces" (Froehling, 1997, p. 293). Rather, the physical and the virtual are interrelated (Tanney, 1997). In this, Cicognani's (1998) conception of cyberspace as a "hybrid space" is illuminating. For Cicognani, hybrid space, as a "self-referential system … which is part of another but only refers to itself and its own variables," belongs "to the main system of space, and claim[s] independence from it at the same time" (pp. 19–20). In this way, cyberspace is indeed a "'legitimate' space, in which relationships and communities can develop," and yet is not "'detached' and independent from physical space" (p. 20). Cyberspace is not some unbounded, disembodied space, and people can't be digitized into it à la *Tron* (1982) and *Tron: Legacy* (2010). Similar to any other space or place, cyberspace is a sociospatial construction located in material-physical reality. My contention is that participatory popular culture should be similarly conceptualized.

Because writing is a set of spatialized practices, texts, while not spatially bound (i.e., they can circulate), are or come to be spatially specific. They are connected to and with a particular space or place in a manner that usually intersects with, or is otherwise structured by, the imagined geography of the nation-state as organizing principle. Texts that circulate globally across spatial boundaries and national borders are reproduced and refashioned in and for local contexts, thereby altering the texts' meaning. This process of localization also connects these texts to other texts within the community. Research on literacy development has stressed the importance of intertextuality (Beach, Appleman, & Dorsey, 1990; Cairney, 1990, 1992; Hartman, 1992; Pantaleo, 2006; Roache-Jameson, 2005). More recently, literacy scholars have explored intertextuality in relation to popular culture, particularly as a way to connect home- and school-based literacies and learning (Compton-Lilly, 2006; Dyson, 1997, 2003; Williams, 2002). Shegar and Weninger (2010) recently demonstrated that "intertextuality is a useful analytic lens through which to describe children's popular culture literacy" (p. 444). When popular culture texts travel, they are "placed" within different contexts, resulting in different intertextual fields of understanding. Normally, community members have more or less common access to these fields by virtue of sharing the same intertextual background. Such access and understanding is complicated in online communities. Cicognani's (1998) notion of cyberspace as hybrid is especially relevant here. Members of a particular online affinity space, such as a fan website devoted to Harry Potter, almost certainly share certain knowledge and information, including textual references, in common. At the same time, these member-participants also dwell in and move through different spaces and places in the material-physical world, each with its own intertextual frame. How, for instance, is Harry Potter read in Japan? For a Japanese member of a Harry Potter website, any culture-specific readings would be separate from and yet connected to the collective meaning-making accomplished within and by means of the website's affinity space. What is more, meanings woven into the intertextual fabric of a physical place cannot be easily "linked" to that of a virtual place. Recalling that intertextuality is a social construction (Bloom & Egan-Robertson, 1993), what we are left with are fields of intertextuality that, like—and *as*—national borders, can include as well as exclude, but can also be crossed, redrawn, and reimagined.

Most people who engage with popular culture in digital environments will not have Eva's level of expertise as a bicultural, multilingual, and biliterate transnational. While online communities centered around popular culture can undoubtedly serve as valuable sources of and spaces for "collective intelligence" (Jenkins, 2006) that involve knowledge making with people, texts, and literacies that cross national borders, such communities and spaces are, at the same time, not completely unproblematic avenues for increased learning or understanding, given the material spatialization of both identity and literacy practices. In coming to recognize the complex, contested nature of cyberspace, I have found Queen's (2008) focus on circulation to be illuminating. In her examination of transnational feminist rhetorics, Queen introduced what she termed "rhetorical genealogy":

> [A] process of examining digital texts not as artifacts of rhetorical productions, but, rather, as continually evolving rhetorical actions that are materially bound, actions whose transformation can be traced through the links embedded within multiple fields of circulation. Rhetorical genealogy is rhetorical analysis that examines multiple processes of structuring representations rather than seeks to identify the original intentions or final effects of structured (and thus already stabilized) representations.
>
> *(p. 476)*

Central to Queen's notion of rhetorical genealogy as a methodology, it's "fundamental promise," is its ability to reconceptualize "and make visible the multiple interactions between electronic texts and the material realities from which they emerge and through which they circulate to produce alternative fields for encountering each other in the moment of rhetorical action" (p. 476). While Queen's focus lay with transnational feminist activism and scholarship (certainly an important and critical area of study), I believe rhetorical genealogy's utility as a methodology and critical lens can be extended to include a multiplicity of digital texts, literacies, and "global fields of rhetorical action" (p. 474). Focusing on circulation and interaction through space can help highlight the fields of intertextuality that influence how popular culture texts are read, produced, and used within spaces of hybridity, from online communities to nation-states.

Notes

1. And sometimes to a lack of intelligence as well. For instance, one *New York Times* article (Elliott, Tavernise, & Barnard, 2010) reported that he had been a "mediocre student" who had earned a D in high school composition (para. 20).
2. Blue Öyster Cult's "(Don't Fear) The Reaper." "More cowbell" is a popular catchphrase that originated in a *Saturday Night Live* skit featuring Walken in which "(Don't Fear) The Reaper" was parodied.
3. Of course, one could certainly argue that the bit was offensively racist rather than satirical.

References

Adams, P. C. (1997). Cyberspace and virtual places. *Geographical Review, 87*(2), 155–172.
Anderson, B. (1991). *Imagined communities*. London: Verso.

Banks, W. (2003). Written through the body: Disruptions and "personal" writing. *College English*, *66*(1), 21–40.

Barlow, J. P. (1996). A declaration of the independence of cyberspace. Retrieved 20 December 2010, from https://projects.eff.org/~barlow/Declaration-Final.html

Barton, D. & Hamilton, M. (2000). Literacy practices. In D. Barton, M. Hamilton, & R. Ivanic (Eds.), *Situated literacies: Reading and writing in context* (pp. 7–15). London: Routledge.

Beach, R., Appleman, D., & Dorsey, S. (1990). Adolescents' use of intertextual links to understand literature. In R. Beach & S. Hynds (Eds.), *Developing discourse practices in adolescence and adulthood* (pp. 224–245). Norwood, NJ: Albex Publishing Corporation.

Black, R. (2008). *Adolescents and fan fiction*. London: Peter Lang.

Blackledge, A. (2002). The discursive construction of national identity in multilingual Britain. *Journal of Language, Identity, and Education*, *1*(1), 67–87.

Bleich, D. (2001). The materiality of language and the pedagogy of exchange. *Pedagogy*, *1*, 117–142.

Bloom, D. & Egan-Robertson, A. (1993). The social construction of intertextuality in classroom reading and writing lessons. *Reading Research Quarterly*, *28*(4), 304–333.

Bordo, S. (1993). *Unbearable weight: Feminism, Western culture, and the body*. Berkeley, CA: University of California Press.

Brandt, D. & Clinton, K. (2002). Limits of the local: Expanding perspectives on literacy as social practice. *Journal of Literacy Research*, *34*(3), 337–357.

Brodkey, L. (1996). *Writing permitted in designated areas only*. Minneapolis, MN: University of Minnesota Press.

Cain, M. A. (2003). Listening to language. *College English*, *65*(5), 476–493.

Cairney, T. (1990). Intertextuality: Infectious echoes from the past. *The Reading Teacher*, *43*(7), 478–484.

Cairney, T. (1992). Fostering and building students' intertextual histories. *Language Arts*, *69*(7), 502–507.

Canagarajah, A. S. (2006). Toward a writing pedagogy of shuttling between languages: Learning from multilingual writers. *College English*, *68*(6), 589–604.

Cicognani, A. (1998). On the linguistic nature of cyberspace and virtual communities. *Virtual Reality*, *3*, 16–24.

Compton-Lilly, C. (2006). Identity, childhood culture, and literacy learning: A case study. *Journal of Early Childhood Literacy*, *6*, 57–76.

Cope, B. & Kalantzis, M. (Eds.) (2000). *Multiliteracies: Literacy learning and the design of social futures*. London: Routledge.

De Cillia, R., Reisigl, M., & Wodak, R. (1999). The discursive construction of national identities. *Discourse & Society*, *10*(2), 149–168.

DePew, K. E. & Miller-Cochran, S. (2010). Social networking in a second language: Engaging multiple literate practices through identity composition. In M. Cox, J. Jordan, C. Ortmeier-Hooper, & G. G. Schwartz (Eds.), *Reinventing identities in second language writing* (pp. 273–295). Urbana, IL: National Council of Teachers of English.

DeWitt, S. L. (1997). Out there on the web: Pedagogy and identity in face of opposition. *Computers and Composition*, *14*, 229–244.

Devine-Wright, P. & Lyons, E. (1997). Remembering pasts and representing places: The construction of national identities in Ireland. *Journal of Environmental Psychology*, *17*, 33–45.

Drogin, B. & Baum, G. (2010, June 29). Alleged Russian spy ring members led typical American lives. *The Los Angeles Times*. Retrieved 20 December 2010, from http://articles.latimes.com

Dyson, A. H. (1997). *Writing superheroes: Contemporary childhood, popular culture, and classroom literacy*. New York: Teachers College Press.

Dyson, A. J. (2003). "Welcome to the Jam": Popular culture, school literacy, and the making of childhoods. *Harvard Educational Review, 73*, 328–361.

Elliott, A., Tavernise, S., & Barnard, A. (2010, May 15). For Times Sq. suspect, long roots of discontent. *The New York Times*. Retrieved 20 December 2010, from www.nytimes.com

Fletcher, G. (1998). All that is virtual bleeds into reality. *Spaceless.com: Life online*. Retrieved 20 December 2010, from http://web.archive.org/web/20041015213540/www.spaceless.com/papers/1.htm

Froehling, O. (1997). The cyberspace "war of ink and Internet" in Chiapas, Mexico. *Geographical Review, 87*(2), 291–308.

Gee, J. P. (1996). *Social linguistics and literacies: Ideology in discourses* (2nd ed.). London: Taylor & Francis.

Gee, J. P. (2004). *Situated language and learning: A critique of traditional schooling*. London: Routledge.

Gee, J. P. (2005). Semiotic social spaces and affinity spaces: From *The Age of Mythology* to today's schools. In D. Barton & K. Tusting (Eds.), *Beyond communities of practice: Language, power, and social context* (pp. 214–232). Cambridge: Cambridge University Press.

Giroux, H. (1999). *The mouse that roared: Disney and the end of innocence*. New York: Rowman & Littlefield.

Greenhill, A. (2002). Critiquing reality: The mind/body split in computer-mediated environments. *AMCIS 2002 proceedings*, paper 222. Retrieved 20 December 2010, from http://aisel.aisnet.org/amcis2002/222

Haas, C. (1996). *Writing technology: Studies on the materiality of literacy*. Mahwah, NJ: Erlbaum.

Hartman, D. K. (1992). Intertextuality and reading: The text, the reader, the author and the context. *Linguistics and Education, 4*, 295–311.

Hindman, J. (2001). Making writing matter: Using "the personal" to recover(y) an essential(ist) tension in academic discourse. *College English, 64*(1), 88–108.

Iwanicki, C. E. (2003). Living out loud within the body of the letter: Theoretical underpinnings of the materiality of language. *College English, 65*(5), 494–510.

Jenkins, H. (2006). *Convergence culture: Where old and new media collide*. New York: New York University Press.

LeFebvre, H. (1991). *The production of space* (D. Nicholson-Smith, Trans.). Malden, MA: Blackwell.

Lewiecki-Wilson, C. & Brueggemann, B. J. (2008). Introduction. In C. Lewiecki-Wilson & B. J. Brueggemann (Eds.), *Disability and the teaching of writing: A critical sourcebook* (pp. 1–9). Boston, MA: Bedford/St. Martin's.

Lindblom, K. & Dunn, P. A. (2003). The roles of rhetoric in constructions and reconstructions of disability. *Rhetoric Review, 22*(2), 167–174.

Linton, S. (1998). *Claiming disability: Knowledge and identity*. New York: New York University Press.

Lu, M. & Horner, B. (2009). Composing in a global-local context. *College English, 72*(2), 113–133.

Marback, R. (1998). Detroit and the closed fist: Toward a theory of material rhetoric. *Rhetoric Review, 17*(1), 74–90.

McRae, S. (1996). Coming apart at the seams: Sex, text, and the virtual body. In L. Cherny & E. R. Weise (Eds.), *Wired women: Gender and new realities in cyberspace* (pp. 242–264). Seattle, WA: Seal Press.

McLaren, P. (1988). Schooling the postmodern body: Critical pedagogy and the politics of enfleshment. *Journal of Education, 170*(3), 53–83.

Orner, M., Miller, J., & Ellsworth, E. (1995). Excessive moments and educational discourses that try to contain them. *Educational Theory, 45,* 71–91.

Pantaleo, S. (2006). Readers and writers as intertexts: Exploring the intertextualities in student writing. *Australian Journal of Language and Literacy, 29*(2), 163–181.

Portes, A. (1997). Immigration theory for a new century: Some problems and possibilities. *The International Migration Review, 31,* 799–825.

Queen, M. (2008). Transnational feminist rhetorics in a digital world. *College English, 70*(5), 471–489.

Reynolds, N. (2004). *Geographies of writing: Inhabiting places and encountering difference.* Carbondale, IL: Southern Illinois University Press.

Ritzer, G. (2011). *The McDonalization of society* (6th ed.). Thousand Oaks, CA: Pine Forge Press.

Roache-Jameson, S. (2005). Kindergarten connections: A study of intertextuality and its links with literacy in the kindergarten classroom. *Australian Journal of Language and Literacy, 28*(1), 48–66.

Ronald, K. & Roskelly, H. (2002). Embodied voice: Peter Elbow's physical rhetoric. In P. Belanoff, M. Dickson, S. I. Fontaine, & C. Moran (Eds.), *Writing with Elbow* (pp. 210–222). Logan, UT: Utah State University Press.

Shegar, C. & Weninger, C. (2010). Intertextuality in preschoolers' engagement with popular culture: Implications for literacy development. *Language and Education, 24*(5), 431–447.

Smith, S. (1993). *Subjectivity, identity, and the body: Women's autobiographical practices in the twentieth century.* Bloomington, IN: Indiana University Press.

Street, B. (1995). *Social literacies: Critical approaches to literacy development, ethnography, and education.* Reading, MA: Addison-Wesley.

Tanney, S. (1997). *Evidence of place in electronic space.* Retrieved 20 December 2010, from www.hitl.washington.edu/people/susan/musings/e-place3.html

Taylor, T. L. (2002). Living digitally: Embodiment in virtual worlds. In R. Schroeder (Ed.), *The social life of avatars: Presence and interaction in shared virtual environments* (pp. 40–62). London: Springer-Verlag.

Thomas, C. (1996). *Male matters: Masculinity, anxiety, and the male body on the line.* Urbana, IL: University of Illinois Press.

Wallwork, J. & Dixon, J. A. (2004). Foxes, green fields, and Britishness: On the rhetorical construction of place and national identity. *British Journal of Social Psychology, 43,* 21–39.

Wellman, B. (2001). Physical place and cyberplace: The rise of personalized networking. *International Journal of Urban and Regional Research, 25*(2), 227–252.

Williams, B. (2002). *Tuned in: Television and the teaching of writing.* Portsmouth, NH: Boynton/Cook.

Williams, B. (2009). *Shimmering literacies: Popular culture & reading & writing online.* New York: Peter Lang.

Yi, Y. (2007). Engaging literacy: A biliterate student's composing practices beyond school. *Journal of Second Language Writing, 16,* 23–39.

Yi, Y. (2010). Identity matters: Theories that help explore adolescent multilingual writers and their identities. In M. Cox, J. Jordan, C. Ortmeier-Hooper, & G. G. Schwartz (Eds.), *Reinventing identities in second language writing* (pp. 303–323). Urbana, IL: National Council of Teachers of English.

Yi, Y. & Hirvela, A. (2010). Technology and "self-sponsored" writing: A case study of a Korean-American adolescent. *Computers and Composition, 27*(2), 94–111.

LIST OF CONTRIBUTORS

Sandra Schamroth Abrams, Ph.D., is an Assistant Professor in the Department of Curriculum and Instruction at St. John's University, New York. Her research, publications, and presentations address digital literacies, popular culture, and new media, with a focus on video game practices, dynamic learning structures, and adolescent education. Abrams examines virtual and place-based socio-cultural landscapes, contemporary modes of communication, and evolving power constructs, exploring new understandings of learning and implications for pedagogy and practice.

Arlene Archer is the coordinator of the Writing Centre at the University of Cape Town, South Africa. She teaches in Applied Language Studies, Higher Education Studies, Film and Media. Her research interests include drawing on popular culture and multimodal pedagogies to enable student access to Higher Education. She has published in journals such as *Language and Education*; *Teaching in Higher Education*; *English in Education*; *Social Dynamics*; and *Visual Communication*.

Melissa Burgess holds an Ed.D. in Reading with a focus on digital literacies. She is currently the Director of the Texas Virtual Learning Center (TVLC) at Region VI Education Service Center. Although varied, her specific research interests involve emerging technologies applied to teaching and learning, multi-user virtual environments, eLearning, and instructional design in all forms of distance education. Her research is heavily reliant upon theoretical frameworks/models including the Community of Inquiry (CoI), Bloom's Revised Taxonomy, and Optimal Experience. Her research in these areas has resulted in numerous publications, presentations, book chapters, and invitations to speak on these topics around the world.

Rick Carpenter is Associate Professor of English at Valdosta State University in Valdosta, Georgia, where he teaches undergraduate and graduate courses in writing, rhetorical theory, new media, and composition pedagogy. He has published in *M/C Journal: A Journal of Media and Culture*, *Computers and Composition*, and *Disability Studies Quarterly* and has a chapter in *Disrupting Pedagogies and Teaching the Knowledge Society: Countering Conservative Norms with Creative Approaches*. His research interests include genre theory, new media studies, disability studies, and identity construction.

Laurie Cubbison is the Director of Writing at Radford University in Radford, Virginia. Her scholarship focuses on the writing produced by fans of a variety of media genres, including film, television, comics, and animation, with particular attention to conflicts between fans and producers.

Hannah R. Gerber is an Assistant Professor of literacy at Sam Houston State University in Texas. She received her Ph.D. from The University of Alabama. Her current research interests lie in the study of adolescents' multiple uses of new literacies and popular culture, with a particular focus on the medium of video games. She conducts research on both the socio-cultural and cognitive aspects of gaming and literacy and is continuously searching for new ways to incorporate pedagogical tools inherent in new literacy learning into classroom instruction, as well as looking for practical applications for new literacy use within the curriculum.

Tüge T. Gülşen holds an MA in Learning and Teaching of English and Literacy (Institute of Education, University of London) and an MA in Cultural Studies (Istanbul Bilgi University). Her main areas of interest are academic literacies, critical discourse and genre analysis, and media literacy. She teaches academic skills courses with works on curriculum and materials design. She has also taught the MA course "Discourse Analysis in Language Teaching" in Bahçeşehir University in Istanbul. She is currently an instructor at Istanbul Bilgi University.

Karen Hellekson is an independent scholar based in Jay, Maine. She is a founding co-editor of the fan studies academic journal *Transformative Works and Cultures*.

Cheng-Wen Huang is a graduate of the University of Cape Town in South Africa with a Masters in English Language and Literature. She has taught English as a Foreign Language in numerous contexts, as well as courses in Film and Media. Her research interests include popular culture, social networking sites, social semiotics, visual literacy, multimodality, and multiliteracies.

Lynn C. Lewis is an Assistant Professor of English at Oklahoma State University. Her research focuses particularly on digital rhetorics and new literacy studies.

Mohanalakshmi Rajakumar is a writer and educator who has lived in Qatar since 2005. A scholar of literature, she has a Ph.D. from the University of Florida with a focus on gender and postcolonial theory. Her work has been published in *AudioFile Magazine*; *Explore Qatar*; *Woman Today*; *The Woman*; *Writers' and Artists' Yearbook*; *QatarClick*; and *Qatar Explorer*. Mohana has also published *Haram in the Harem* (Peter Lang, 2009) a literary analysis of the works of three Muslim women authors in India, Algeria, and Pakistan. She is the creator and co-editor of five books in the *Qatar Narratives* series as well as the *Qatari Voices* anthology, which features essays by Qataris on modern life in Doha (Bloomsbury Qatar Foundation Publishing, 2010).

Jessica Schreyer is an Assistant Professor of English and Writing Program Administrator at the University of Dubuque in Dubuque, Iowa, where she teaches a wide range of writing courses. She is also a Ph.D. Candidate in English (Composition and TESOL) at Indiana University of Pennsylvania. Her research interests include new media studies, basic writing, ecocomposition and sustainability, and writing program administration. Mimi, her online pet, enjoys fishing, dancing, and redecorating her palatial estate.

Bal Krishna Sharma is a doctoral student in Second Language Studies at the University of Hawaii at Manoa. His research interests include English as a global language, language ideology, popular culture and classroom interaction, and related discursive approaches to study these topics. He is actively involved, along with a group of scholars and researchers from Nepal, in promoting research and scholarship among English teachers in Nepal.

Ghanashyam Sharma is a doctoral fellow in English at the University of Louisville, Kentucky. His interests in research and scholarship include popular culture and literacy practices, the politics of language in academic discourse, writing in the disciplines, and multimodal composition. Along with Bal Krishna Sharma and a group of scholars from his home country Nepal, he supports the Nepal English Language Teachers' Association in its professional development initiative for its members across the country.

Mark Vicars is a Senior Lecturer in Literacy in the School of Education at Victoria University, Melbourne, Australia. He has worked as a literacy educator within the compulsory and post-compulsory sectors, in Japan, Korea, Thailand, Vietnam, Cambodia, England, and Australia. An overarching concern in his work is to understand the ways in which individuals make use of language and literacy in identity work. He is particularly interested in intercultural literacy and Mark has recently been funded by DFAT/Australia-Thailand institute to work on developing participatory programs for English language and literacy teacher development in Thailand. In 2010, Mark was awarded the Australian Learning and Teaching Council Citation for Outstanding Contributions to Student Learning.

Bronwyn T. Williams is a Professor of English at the University of Louisville. He writes and teaches about issues of literacy, popular culture, identity, digital media, and creative nonfiction. His books include *Shimmering Literacies: Popular Culture and Reading and Writing Online*; *Popular Culture and Representations of Literacy* (with Amy Zenger); *Identity Papers: Literacy and Power in Higher Education*; and *Tuned In: Television and the Teaching of Writing*.

Amy A. Zenger directs the Writing Center and Writing in the Majors initiative at the American University of Beirut, in Beirut, Lebanon. She teaches undergraduate and graduate level composition courses in the Department of English. Her research interests include relationships between visual and written texts, constructions of race in composition and rhetoric, and representations of literacy in popular culture.

INDEX